Environmental and Energy Policy and the Economy

T0344375

Environmental and Energy Policy and the Economy

Edited by
Matthew J. Kotchen, *Yale University and NBER,*
  United States of America
Tatyana Deryugina, *University of Illinois Urbana-Champaign
  and NBER,* United States of America
James H. Stock, *Harvard University and NBER,*
  United States of America

The University of Chicago Press
Chicago and London

NBER Environmental and Energy Policy and the Economy, Number 3, 2022

Published annually by The University of Chicago Press.
www.journals.uchicago.edu/EEPE/

Subscriptions: Individual subscription rates are $63 print + electronic and $30 e-only ($15 for students). Institutional print + electronic and e-only rates are tiered according to an institution's type and research output: $102 to $215 (print + electronic), $89 to $187 (e-only). For additional information, including back-issue sales, classroom use, rates for single copies, and prices for institutional full-run access, please visit www.journals.uchicago.edu /EEPE/. Free or deeply discounted access is available in most developing nations through the Chicago Emerging Nations Initiative (www.journals.uchicago.edu/ceni/).

Please direct subscription inquiries to Subscription Fulfillment, 1427 E. 60th Street, Chicago, IL 60637-2902. Telephone: (773) 753-3347 or toll free in the United States and Canada (877) 705-1878. Fax: (773) 753-0811 or toll-free (877) 705-1879. E-mail: subscriptions @press.uchicago.edu.

Standing orders: To place a standing order for this book series, please address your request to The University of Chicago Press, Chicago Distribution Center, Attn. Standing Orders/Customer Service, 11030 S. Langley Avenue, Chicago, IL 60628. Telephone toll free in the U.S. and Canada: 1-800-621-2736; or 1-773-702-7000. Fax toll free in the U.S. and Canada: 1-800-621-8476; or 1-773-702-7212.

Single-copy orders: In the U.S., Canada, and the rest of the world, order from your local bookseller or direct from The University of Chicago Press, Chicago Distribution Center, 11030 S. Langley Avenue, Chicago, IL 60628. Telephone toll free in the U.S. and Canada: 1-800-621-2736; or 1-773-702-7000. Fax toll free in the U.S. and Canada: 1-800-621-8476; or 1-773-702-7212. In the U.K. and Europe, order from your local bookseller or direct from The University of Chicago Press, c/o John Wiley Ltd. Distribution Center, 1 Oldlands Way, Bognor Regis, West Sussex PO22 9SA, UK. Telephone 01243 779777 or Fax 01243 820250. E-mail: cs-books@wiley.co.uk.

The University of Chicago Press offers bulk discounts on individual titles to Corporate, Premium, and Gift accounts. For information, please write to Sales Department—Special Sales, The University of Chicago Press, 1427 E. 60th Street, Chicago, IL 60637 USA or telephone 1-773-702-7723.

This book was printed and bound in the United States of America.

ISSN: 2689-7857
E-ISSN: 2689-7865
ISBN-13: 978-0-226-82173-3 (pb.:alk.paper)
ISBN-13: 978-0-226-82174-0 (e-book)

Environmental and Energy Policy and the Economy

Relation of the Directors to the Work and Publications of the NBER

1. The object of the NBER is to ascertain and present to the economics profession, and to the public more generally, important economic facts and their interpretation in a scientific manner without policy recommendations. The Board of Directors is charged with the responsibility of ensuring that the work of the NBER is carried on in strict conformity with this object.

2. The President shall establish an internal review process to ensure that book manuscripts proposed for publication DO NOT contain policy recommendations. This shall apply both to the proceedings of conferences and to manuscripts by a single author or by one or more coauthors but shall not apply to authors of comments at NBER conferences who are not NBER affiliates.

3. No book manuscript reporting research shall be published by the NBER until the President has sent to each member of the Board a notice that a manuscript is recommended for publication and that in the President's opinion it is suitable for publication in accordance with the above principles of the NBER. Such notification will include a table of contents and an abstract or summary of the manuscript's content, a list of contributors if applicable, and a response form for use by Directors who desire a copy of the manuscript for review. Each manuscript shall contain a summary drawing attention to the nature and treatment of the problem studied and the main conclusions reached.

4. No volume shall be published until forty-five days have elapsed from the above notification of intention to publish it. During this period a copy shall be sent to any Director requesting it, and if any Director objects to publication on the grounds that the manuscript contains policy recommendations, the objection will be presented to the author(s) or editor(s). In case of dispute, all members of the Board shall be notified,

and the President shall appoint an ad hoc committee of the Board to decide the matter; thirty days additional shall be granted for this purpose.

5. The President shall present annually to the Board a report describing the internal manuscript review process, any objections made by Directors before publication or by anyone after publication, any disputes about such matters, and how they were handled.

6. Publications of the NBER issued for informational purposes concerning the work of the Bureau, or issued to inform the public of the activities at the Bureau, including but not limited to the NBER Digest and Reporter, shall be consistent with the object stated in paragraph 1. They shall contain a specific disclaimer noting that they have not passed through the review procedures required in this resolution. The Executive Committee of the Board is charged with the review of all such publications from time to time.

7. NBER working papers and manuscripts distributed on the Bureau's web site are not deemed to be publications for the purpose of this resolution, but they shall be consistent with the object stated in paragraph 1. Working papers shall contain a specific disclaimer noting that they have not passed through the review procedures required in this resolution. The NBER's web site shall contain a similar disclaimer. The President shall establish an internal review process to ensure that the working papers and the web site do not contain policy recommendations, and shall report annually to the Board on this process and any concerns raised in connection with it.

8. Unless otherwise determined by the Board or exempted by the terms of paragraphs 6 and 7, a copy of this resolution shall be printed in each NBER publication as described in paragraph 2 above.

Contents

Contents

Introduction

Matthew J. Kotchen, *Yale University and NBER,* United States of America

Tatyana Deryugina, *University of Illinois Urbana-Champaign and NBER,* United States of America

James H. Stock, *Harvard University and NBER,* United States of America

Welcome to the third volume of *Environmental and Energy Policy and the Economy (EEPE).* The six papers published here were first presented and discussed in May 2021 via an online conference hosted by the National Bureau of Economic Research (NBER), with participants from academia, government, and nongovernmental organizations. The papers contribute original research consistent with the broad aim of the *EEPE* initiative: to spur policy-relevant research and professional interactions in the areas of environmental and energy economics and policy. Although conference participants missed out on the opportunity for in-person interaction for the second year in a row, we made up for it again with a larger-than-expected number of participants. The agenda also included a featured presentation by Heather Boushey, a member of the White House Council of Economic Advisors.

In the first paper, Rebecca Davis, Scott Holladay, and Charles Sims provide insight on recent trends and forecasts about coal-fired power plant retirements in the United States, with and without future climate policy. In particular, they summarize retirements over the past decade and develop a real options approach to predict when currently operating plants will retire. Their model projects a wave of coal plant retirements through the mid-2020s, but then a persistent tail of plants that will remain in operation for 2 decades, even if a carbon tax is in place.

Severin Borenstein and James Bushnell examine the extent to which inefficient pricing—that is, when market prices do not reflect the full social costs—of electricity, natural gas, and gasoline exists in the United States. Providing geographically refined estimates, they find that existing price

Environmental and Energy Policy and the Economy, volume 3, 2022.

distortions are much greater for electricity than for natural gas or gasoline. They then consider the implications in California of eliminating these price distortions, concluding that a move to efficient pricing would significantly increase Californians' incentives to switch to electricity for fundamental energy services, such as space heating, water heating, and transportation.

More generally, given decarbonization goals in the transportation sector, what future pathways of electric vehicle (EV) adoption might we expect in the United States? That is the question taken up in the paper by James Archsmith, Erich Muehlegger, and David Rapson. They consider how future EV growth is likely to depend on intrinsic demand, cost declines, and government subsidies. Many of the scenarios they consider are directly relevant to ongoing policy proposals, and a key insight of their analysis is that preferences for light trucks—for which there have been no EV alternatives on the market—will play a crucial role in the transition from internal combustion engines to EVs.

Also focused on EVs, Ken Gillingham's paper analyzes the question of how increased EV adoption might affect the way regulators design vehicle fuel economy standards. He shows that current practices intended to incentivize EV supply and demand have the unintended effect of weakening fuel economy standards and, under some conditions, even reduce the market share of EVs. Beyond identifying this perverse effect, the paper outlines some policy alternatives that could help address the trade-off, with consequences that depend on the amount of future innovation in the EV market.

Frank Wolak contributes a paper focused on long-term resource adequacy in wholesale electricity markets with significant intermittent renewables. The importance of the topic was highlighted recently with significant and consequential supply shortfalls in both California and Texas. The paper provides a "postmortem" analysis of both events, drawing conclusions about the underlying causes. The paper also develops an alternative approach for determining long-term resource adequacy with properties intended to avoid such crises in the future.

In the last paper, Barbara Annicchiarico, Stefano Carattini, Carolyn Fischer, and Garth Heutel summarize the literature that considers the relationship between business cycles and environmental policy. They translate key insights from the literature related to real business cycle models, New Keynesian extensions, open-economy variations, and topics related to monetary policy and fiscal regulation. In addition to summarizing the policy-relevant conclusions of these literatures, the authors discuss areas where future research is needed.

Finally, we make some important acknowledgments. We are grateful to all of the authors for their time and effort in helping to make the third year of *EEPE* a success. We are grateful to Jim Poterba, president and CEO of the NBER, for continuing to support the initiative, and to the NBER's conference staff, especially Rob Shannon, for making the organizing a pleasure. Helena Fitz-Patrick's help with the publication is also invaluable and greatly appreciated. We also thank Catherine Wolfram for her direct involvement in the first two volumes as a coeditor and hope the experience is now contributing to her success as deputy assistant secretary for Climate and Energy Economics at the US Department of the Treasury. Last, and most important, we would like to thank Evan Michelson and the Alfred P. Sloan Foundation for the financial support that has made the *EEPE* initiative possible.

Endnote

For acknowledgments, sources of research support, and disclosure of the authors' material financial relationships, if any, please see https://www.nber.org/books-and-chapters/environmental-and-energy-policy-and-economy-volume-3/introduction-environmental-and-energy-policy-and-economy-volume-3.

Coal-Fired Power Plant Retirements in the United States

Rebecca J. Davis, *Stephen F. Austin State University,* United States of America

J. Scott Holladay, *University of Tennessee,* United States of America

Charles Sims, *University of Tennessee,* United States of America

Executive Summary

We summarize the history of US coal-fired plant retirements over the past decade, describe planned future retirements, and forecast the remaining operating life for every operating coal-fired generator at each plant. Nearly one-third of the coal fleet retired during the 2010s and a quarter of the remaining capacity has announced plans to retire. We summarize the technology and location trends that are correlated with the observed retirements. We then describe a theoretical model of the retirement decision coal generator owners face. We use retirements from the past decade to quantify the relationships in the model for retired generators. Our model predicts that three-quarters of coal generation capacity will retire in the next 20 years, with most of that retirement concentrated in the next 5 years. Policy has limited ability to affect retirement times. A $20 per megawatt-hour electricity subsidy extends the average life of a generator by 6 years. A $51 per ton carbon tax brings forward retirement dates by about 2 years. In all scenarios, a handful of electricity generators remain on the grid beyond our forecast horizon.

JEL Codes: Q4, L1, L5, H4

Keywords: energy, market structure, barriers to exit, optimal stopping, uncertainty, irreversibility

I. Introduction

In 2010, coal-fired generation accounted for more than half of electricity produced in the United States. A decade later, that had fallen to around a quarter of total generation. This shift has been driven primarily by the

Environmental and Energy Policy and the Economy, volume 3, 2022.

retirement of existing coal-fired generators and has already had wide-reaching effects. Regions of the country that produce coal are likely to struggle economically as consumption falls. Coal generators are one of the largest sources of carbon dioxide in the country and their exit could lead to significant reductions in US carbon emissions. Carbon pricing policies are expected to perpetuate this shift away from coal generators (Cullen and Mansur 2017). Subsidies to keep coal generation on the grid have also been proposed for reliability reasons. When and where such policies will alter the trajectory of coal generator retirements remains an unanswered question.

Instead of a postmortem analysis of the drivers of retirement, we consider the effect of policies that may exacerbate or alleviate future coal-fired power plant retirements in the United States.[1] We predict the retirement time for every coal-fired generator in the country and then evaluate how environmental regulation and efforts to enhance grid reliability would affect those retirement dates. This generator-level analysis gives us a unique perspective on the relative influence of market forces and policy on the composition of the generating fleet. In our no-policy baseline, we find that nearly three-quarters of coal-fired generation capacity retires by 2040, the end of our simulation. Retirements are concentrated in the upper Midwest, the Ohio Valley, and the southeastern United States. A $20 per megawatt-hour (MWh) of electricity generated production credit, more than half the cost of delivered fuel on average, extends the median retirement date by 6 years. A carbon tax set to recent estimates of the social cost of carbon, $51 per ton, pulls the median retirement forward by about 2 years.[2]

A significant fraction of the remaining coal generating capacity is forecast to retire in the next 6 years in the no-policy baseline. Because so much capacity is forecast to retire soon, the ability of carbon taxes to speed up retirements is limited in much of the United States. There is more scope for reliability subsidies to extend the operations of generators than for carbon taxes to drive retirements. However, the magnitude of the subsidies required to maintain a large coal fleet is enormous. There are likely less expensive ways to ensure reliability.

In this paper, we do not explore entry of new coal plants. Given the electricity and coal prices we observe over our sample period, our model finds that entry of new coal plants is not economic. This is borne out by the data. The US Energy Information Administration (EIA) *2021 Energy Outlook* estimates the levelized cost of energy (LCE), the all-in cost of generating from a particular fuel type, as $73 per MW of coal-fired capacity. That is more than double the LCE of solar and wind capacity and nearly double the

LCE of combined-cycle natural gas. As of 2019, EIA reports 135,000 MW of proposed capacity additions across all fuel types. Of those additions, only 17 MW are coal-fired.[3] Building new coal plants would require new technological developments or energy-policy changes that are hard to foresee at the present time.

We start by briefly summarizing the history of recent retirements of coal-fired generators. Using publicly available data on electric generators and power plants, we show that retirements have increased and that those retirements are coming from smaller, older generators. We also identify differences in retirements across regions of the United States.

Next, we describe a new data set collecting all information on scheduled and planned retirements for every active coal generator on the grid. We collect scheduled retirement dates from the EIA and supplement that with media and financial database searches to identify announced retirements that have not yet been formally published in official sources.

Finally, we describe a novel three-step technique to back out the unobserved retirement costs implied by retired generators and map those costs onto active generators first proposed in Davis, Holladay, and Sims (2021). In step 1, we develop a real options model of power plant retirement decisions. The real options approach (Dixit and Pindyck 1994) treats retirement as an investment option and captures the uncertainty and irreversibility in the retirement decision. We model the evolution of fuel and electricity prices for every coal-fired generator in the United States that was active in 2009. Looking at actual retirement dates for generators that retired between 2009 and 2017, we back out the retirement costs consistent with the observed electricity and fuel prices. Whereas several papers use real options to model entry and exit of electric power plants, we use real options to impute unobservable retirements costs from observable retirement decisions.

In step 2, we impute retirement costs for active coal-fired generators based on the estimated retirement costs from the real options model using a machine learning (ML) approach. We take the estimated retirement costs from the real options model for the plants that have retired during our sample period as well as a wealth of data on the generators and use LASSO and Regression Forest algorithms to model the retirement costs at our sample of retired plants. Our models explain about 90% of the variation in retirement costs. We then take the model fit to retired plants and use it to predict the retirement costs at currently active plants. We find that these imputed retirement costs are correlated with plant characteristics in ways that are consistent with intuition.

In step 3, we use the real options model and the mapped retirement costs to predict the retirement date for every coal generator in the United States that was active in 2017. To test the validity of our approach, we check our predictions out of sample. We correctly predict 48 of the 69 (70%) generators that retired in 2018 and 2019.

Those retirement costs allow us to model retirement decisions for active generators based on the behavior of generators that have retired during our sample period. We then use this technique to determine the effect of two policies (carbon tax and coal fuel subsidy) on the timing of retirement. We find that a carbon tax of $51 per ton of carbon dioxide brings forward the average retirement age by just 2 years and that a fuel cost subsidy would have to cover more than half the cost of delivered fuel to extend the average life of a coal generator by 6 years. These results illustrate the relative importance of market versus regulatory drivers of coal-fired generator retirements and add to the broader literature on the role of environmental regulation on plant entry and exit (e.g., Ryan 2012; Suzuki 2013; Shapiro and Walker 2018). Few papers have attempted to estimate the impact of environmental regulation and market forces on coal-fired power plant retirements. Linn and McCormack (2019) find that slow demand growth and displacement by natural gas generation had reduced coal plant profits. Our analysis supports the findings of Linn and McCormack (2019) and suggests that there is little scope for policy to change the retirement dates of coal-fired power plants.

Our ability to generate counterfactual retirement dates across different electricity and fuel price levels allows us to model a variety of policy scenarios of interest to policy makers and the energy industry. We can identify specific retirement times for each existing coal plant in the country. The procedure could allow us to identify reliability issues and local environmental or economic impacts of plant retirements as well.

II. Coal-Fired Generator Retirements

Power plants typically include multiple separate generators, each of which can be fueled separately. The average coal plant active on the grid in 2010 had more than five generators of which three were coal-fired, and the others, typically much smaller in capacity, were oil- or gas-fired. The smaller units are mostly used to help start the coal-fired generators and manage small fluctuations in production or demand. Because each generator at a power plant can use different fuels and can be retired separately, we use electric generators as the unit of analysis in this study. Of the retirements we observe over the past decade, around 60% retire all coal units at a plant at the same time.

Coal-generating capacity has fallen steadily since its peak in 2011. Since that time, environmental regulations have increased, renewable generation capacity has expanded, and natural-gas prices have fallen, driving peak electricity prices lower. Given these headwinds, it is not surprising that coal generating capacity has shrunk. Figure 1 displays the location of the coal-fired generators that have retired between 2010 and 2019. They represent 473 generators with a nameplate capacity of nearly 80,000 MW. At the end of 2019, 632 coal-fired generators with a cumulative nameplate capacity of 244,000 MW remained active on the grid.[4]

Retiring generators were smaller and older than those that remained operating at the end of the decade. Generators that retired between 2010 and 2019 had a median capacity of 115 MW compared with 350 MW for surviving generators. The capacity-weighted average operating date for retired coal-fired generators was 1965, whereas active generators have a capacity-weighted average operating date of 1978.[5] Retired generators were much more likely to use diesel oil, rather than natural gas, as their start-up

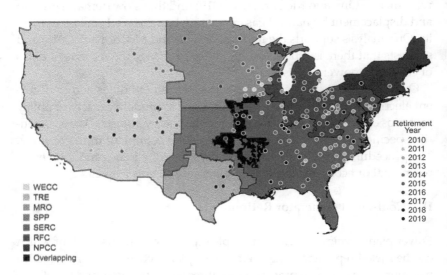

Fig. 1. Coal-fired generator retirements 2010–2020. Color version available as an online enhancement.

Notes: The location of the 473 coal-fired generators that have retired between 2010 and 2019. The color of the circle represents the year the generator retired. A small amount of jitter is added so that multiple generators at the same plant are all visible.

Source: Authors' mapping of US Energy Information Administration Form 860 data for 2019.

fuel source and less likely to have supercritical technology, which is more expensive to install but allows for more efficient generation.[6]

The North American Electric Reliability Corporation (NERC) breaks the country into six reliability regions. These regions represent well-connected portions of the grid where electricity can flow from generators to load with a minimum of congested choke points. The NERC's goal is to ensure generation capacity can meet demand within and across these regions.[7] In absolute terms, most of the retirements were in RFC (Midwest) and SERC (Southeast) with around 30,000 MW of coal-fired generating capacity retiring over the past decade. Relative to coal capacity, nearly one-third of coal generators in NPCC (New England) retired. In MRO (upper Midwest down to Oklahoma), only around 10% of coal-fired generating capacity retired.

III.   Announced Retirements

The wave of retirements we have witnessed over the past decade is likely just the beginning. Many operating coal generators have announced their intention to retire. In this section, we use EIA data on announced retirements to describe the coming wave of retirements. We supplement that data with hand-collected media reports to identify coal-fired generators that have publicly announced planned retirement dates but have not yet reported that information to the EIA.[8] To our knowledge, this data set represents the most complete list of planned coal generator retirements at this time.

We performed a series of Google and Lexis-Nexis searches for the names of power plants with active coal-fired generators. We found press releases, media stories, and official filings that mentioned these plants and looked for any mention of retirement plans. In some cases, we found specific retirement dates. More common were announcements of plans to retire a generator before a specific date (e.g., "by 2025" or "later this decade").[9]

Table 1 reports the planned coal-fired generator retirements by year. Planned retirements are front loaded with many of the planned retirements occurring in the next 3 years. The EIA 860 questionnaire asks respondents to report the date of planned retirements for each generator.[10] More than 10% of coal generating capacity plans to retire in the next 3 years. Including all announced retirements with a specific date, there are 50,000 MW of capacity planning to retire, more than a quarter of the total. Of course, additional capacity may retire before 2030. Over the past decade, the median time between announcement and actual retirement has been 3 years.

Table 1
Planned Coal Generator Retirements

Year	MW Scheduled to Retire	Generator Count
2020	9,709	35
2021	3,626	14
2022	8,437	23
2023	5,985	17
2024	2,697	7
2025	2,847	8
2026	621	1
2027	1,895	3
2028	2,286	3
2029	905	2
2030	3,875	6
2030+	9,046	16
Total	51,929	135

Note: Planned retirements reported in US Energy Information Administration Form 860 data in 2019. The form asks generators to report any retirement planned in the next 5 years. Some generators report retirements beyond that date by choice. The total row reports the sum of all retirements reported in the Form 860 across each year. The Form 860 data reports 463 active generators with a capacity of 192,000 MW in 2019.

Generators that may retire in the second half of the 2020s have not yet made that decision. For that reason, the 25,000 MW of planned retirements beyond 2024 should be considered a lower bound on the actual capacity retired.

Table 2 reports planned retirements by NERC region. Most of the announced retirements are in RFC (mid-Atlantic through the Midwest) and

Table 2
Planned Coal Generator Retirements by NERC Region

NERC Region	Num. Gen.	Total Cap. (MW)	Median Planned Retirement Year
MRO	21	7,438	2022
NPCC	2	1,055	2020.5
RFC	49	16,376	2022
SERC	28	9,008	2021.5
TRE	9	6,239	2030
WECC	28	12,747	2025

Note: Planned retirements reported in US Energy Information Administration Form 860 data in 2019. The form asks generators to report any retirement planned in the next 5 years. Some generators report retirements beyond that date by choice. The Form 860 data reports 463 active generators with a capacity of 192,000 MW in 2019. NERC = North American Electric Reliability Corporation.

WECC (West). Conditional on reporting a retirement date, the planned retirements in RFC are much sooner, with a median retirement date of 2022. The median retirement date for the 28 generators in WECC with an announced retirement date is 2025. NPCC (New England) has only 12 active generators and 2 of those are scheduled to retire in the near future.

After this wave of planned retirements, coal generation will become largely a regional phenomenon. RFC (mid-Atlantic through the Midwest) and SERC (Southeast) will have around three-quarters of national coal generating capacity. MRO (upper Midwest) will have less than 20%, and the Northeast (NPCC), Texas (TRE), and western United States (WECC) will have less than 5% total.

Figure 2 displays the coal-fired generators that have not yet reported a retirement date. These coal generators are expected to be online for at least 5 years and potentially much longer. These generators are concentrated in the eastern half of the United States, with Florida and Georgia in the Southeast retaining a cluster of generators. The generators are (mostly) exposed to higher electricity prices helping them maintain a profit as other coal-fired generators are squeezed out. Another swath of large generators

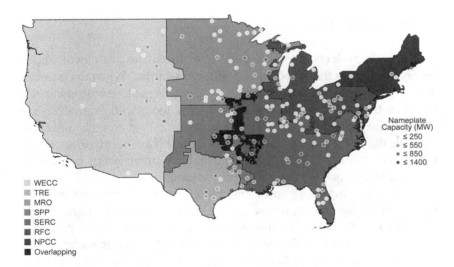

Fig. 2. Active coal-fired generators with no announced retirement date. Color version available as an online enhancement.

Notes: The location of the approximately 300 coal-fired generators that are currently operating that have not announced a retirement date. The color indicates the nameplate capacity of the generator.

Source: Authors' mapping of US Energy Information Administration Form 860 data for 2019.

runs from Appalachian coal country in West Virginia and Kentucky through Ohio over to Indiana. These generators have access to relatively inexpensive coal, which keeps them competitive even in the face of lower electricity prices that cause generators elsewhere to choose to exit.

IV.   Model of Coal Generator Retirement

The details of the model are described in Davis et al. (2021). Here we briefly describe the process, but focus on discussing future coal plant retirements and the implications of the retirements we are predicting. To predict future retirements of coal-fired power plants, we need a model of power plant owner's retirement decision process. Because retiring a power plant is irreversible and subject to uncertainty, we choose a real options model. We then use a ML algorithm to map characteristics of generators that retired over the past 10 years to the conditions that caused those generators to retire. We can use that mapping to predict future retirements of the remaining active generators on the grid. This section briefly describes each of those two steps.

A.   Real Options Model

Dixit and Pindyck (1994) define an investment as "the act of incurring an immediate cost in the expectation of future rewards." When these future rewards are uncertain and the immediate cost is sunk, investment rules based on traditional methods such as discounted cash flow analysis are biased. When an investment decision can be postponed and this delay will alleviate the uncertainty in future returns, there is an incentive, an option value, to delay this decision. The delay avoids the irreversibility of the sunk cost and allows one to respond to new information.

By incorporating the option value created by uncertainty and irreversibility, real options theory focuses on the optimal timing of an irreversible investment decision by accounting for the value of being able to postpone an uncertain investment. Traditionally, investment decisions ask "if" an investment should be made. In the presence of uncertainty and irreversibility and the option value they create, the investment decision becomes "when" the investment should be made.

Coal-fired power plant retirements face similar incentives. Retiring coal-fired generating units incurs sunk costs in the form of scrapping machinery, decommissioning sites, and selling suitable land. These sunk retirement costs (K) are typically not disclosed by utilities but are a key unobservable variable in modeling retirement decisions because they act as a barrier to exit (Caves and Porter 1976; Siegfried and Evans 1994). There are also significant uncertainties associated with future fuel costs, electricity demand, and regulations. The combination of sunk costs of retirement and uncertain future profits from coal-fired generation create an incentive for firms to delay retiring these units.

Our approach treats the decision to retire a coal-fired generating unit as a divestment option. If you own a coal-fired generator, you can remain online and earn profits based on local electricity and coal prices or you have the option of retiring the unit. If you exercise the option of retiring the unit, you incur a sunk retirement cost but forego all future losses that the unit might incur. If you choose to keep the unit online, you defer the retirement cost and the possibility of future profits remains open.

For each retired coal-fired generator, we observe coal prices, electricity prices, and the date of retirement. We use that data to create a threshold of electricity and coal prices that would induce the utility to pay a retirement cost and retire the generator. We identify the threshold by examining each possible electricity price and coal price combination and calculate whether the plant would be profitable at those prices. The firm receives a flow payoff:

$$\pi(P_E, P_C) = (P_E(t)q_E(t) - P_C(t)q_C(t) - VC(q_E(t)) - FC) \tag{1}$$

where $P_E(t)$ is the wholesale electricity price, $P_C(t)$ is the price of coal, $VC(q_E)$ is the variable operating and maintenance costs for the generator, and FC is the fixed levelized capital cost of the generator.[11] The term $q_E = f(P_E)$ represents the quantity of electricity supplied by the generator at price P_E, and the term $q_C = g(q_E)$ represents the quantity of coal used to generate q_E. As the price of electricity goes up, the quantity of electricity produced and coal consumed goes up as well. The relationship between q_C and q_E captures the generation technology of a specific generating unit with newer and more fuel efficient units requiring less fuel to generate an additional unit of electricity.

At points with very low electricity prices and high coal prices, the plant loses money and would choose to exit. At points with high electricity prices and low coal prices, the plant will make money and choose to operate. The real options model identifies the combinations of electricity and coal prices where the generator just breaks even and is indifferent between staying on the grid and generating or retiring. The set of pairs of electricity and coal prices where the generator breaks even is the threshold. That threshold also depends on the size of the retirement costs faced by these generators. A generator that is expensive to decommission faces a high barrier to exit; thus, there would be fewer combinations of electricity and coal prices where it would be profitable to retire the generator than to keep it online. However, there are also generators that require little in the way of retirement costs. Those generators would have a lower barrier to exit, meaning there would be more combinations of electricity and coal prices where it would be profitable to retire the generator.

To illustrate our approach, figure 3 shows the retirement thresholds for two coal-fired generators in Illinois. On the left is ST1 at the Vermilion Power Station in Vermilion, Illinois, with 75 MW nameplate capacity that came online in 1955. On the right is generator 7 at Crawford Generation Station in Cook County, Illinois. It had a 293 MW nameplate capacity and came online in 1958. For price combinations below the threshold, retiring the unit maximizes the discounted profits generated by the unit. Both thresholds slope upward, indicating that higher coal prices necessitate higher electricity prices to justify keeping the generator online. The threshold for the Vermilion generator is much flatter, suggesting it is less sensitive to fuel prices than the Crawford generator.

The three thresholds on each graph illustrate how the level of retirement cost (K) affects the electricity and coal price pairs for which retirement is optimal. Larger retirement costs shift the retirement threshold down, indicating that retirement is desirable over a smaller set of prices. We do not observe the retirement cost paid by each retired coal-fired generator. To

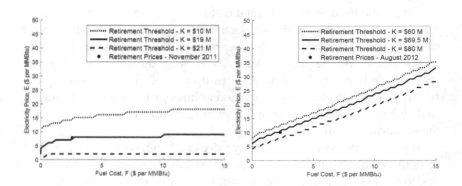

Fig. 3. Estimating implied retirement costs

Notes: The coal price and electricity price combinations that will result in retirements for two coal generators: ST1 at Vermilion Power Station (left) and generator 7 at Crawford Generating Station (right), both in Illinois. Electricity and coal price combinations above the diagonal line(s) keep the generator online. Pairs below the diagonal(s) induce retirement. Each threshold represents a different retirement cost level. The dot represents the observed prices on the date of retirement.

determine the costs associated with retiring each generator, we find the retirement cost that causes the retirement threshold to intercept the point represented by the coal and electricity prices observed at the time of retirement.[12] Higher retirement costs would imply the unit should have remained active after it was retired, whereas lower retirement costs would imply the unit should have been retired far sooner than it was actually retired.

Based on that information, we can back out what retirement costs must have been at those plants: the implied retirement cost. Specifically, we can find the retirement cost that places the electricity and coal price combination observed at the time of retirement on the retirement threshold. For reference, figure 3 displays retirement thresholds with retirement costs above and below the implied retirement costs. The retirement thresholds that intersect the electricity and coal price pairs at the time of retirement are represented by the solid lines in figure 3. The level of retirement costs that correspond with that retirement threshold become the implied retirement costs. For Vermilion ST1, that works out to be $19 million. For Crawford-7, the implied retirement cost is $69.5 million. The higher retirement cost for Crawford-7 is driven by the larger capacity.

We repeat this process for each of the 267 coal-fired generators that have retired since 2009 and use the implied retirement costs in the next step to train our ML algorithm to predict retirement costs for active coal-fired generators.

B. Predicting Electricity Prices, Retirement Costs, and Fuel Costs

In this section, we describe our ML model for predicting retirement costs for active generators. In this paper, we briefly summarize the data, the algorithm, and our results. Davis et al. (2021) describe the ML algorithms' implementation in much more detail and present detailed analysis of the predictions and prediction error for each algorithm as well as some empirical tests that show the predictions from the algorithms are reasonable.

We take retirement costs for each retired generator and collect data on the generator and plant characteristics for all active and retired generators. We train an ML model on the relationship between the characteristics of the generators and plants as well as characteristics of the county where the generator is located. We use a total of 99 features in the model including nameplate capacity of the generator and plant, whether the plant has access to a natural-gas pipeline, whether the plant has an ash impoundment, and sociodemographics such as education level and unemployment rates in the generator's county.[13] Because we observe fewer than 300 retirements and have nearly 100 features, ML is a good choice for prediction. We then use the algorithm trained on retired generator data to predict retirement costs at active coal-fired generators.

For each generator that has retired over the past decade, we know the implied retirement costs from our real options model. We use that as our target variable for the ML model. We collect the generator's nameplate generating capacity, operating date, pollution emissions, location, regulatory status, and information about the pollution abatement technology at the plant. We also compile the NERC region and utility owner for each generator.

We split the sample of retired generators into two groups. We train the ML algorithms on 80% of the sample. This portion of the sample is used to nonparametrically estimate the relationship between the generator's characteristics and the imputed retirement costs. We then use the relationship identified in the training data set to predict the retirement costs for the remaining 20% of the sample. We evaluate those predictions against the imputed retirement costs from the real options model for three different ML algorithms: LASSO, Regression Forest, and XGBoost. Regression Forest performs the best, with a prediction error of around 10% of a standard deviation.[14]

We use the Regression Forest parameters estimated on the retired generators to predict the retirement costs for all active generators. This process implicitly assumes that the relationship between retirement costs and plant characteristics is the same in the set of retired and active generators. Unfortunately, there is no way to directly test this assumption, but we find that running the ML algorithm on subsets of the retired generators does not materially affect the prediction accuracy, so we are optimistic that this assumption will hold. We use those predicted retirement costs in the retirement simulations to predict the retirement date of active generators.

Analysis of Retirement Costs

In this section, we describe a simple analysis, first reported by Davis et al. (2021), on the retirement costs we estimate from the real options model and predict from the ML algorithm. Because the ML procedure for forecasting retirement costs at active generators is new to the literature, we examine the relationship between predicted retirement cost and observed retirement decision. This analysis provides evidence that the predicted retirement costs are reasonable and generators respond to them in a way consistent with economic theory.

We estimate the probability of retirement for each generator in the sample as a function of imputed retirement costs and generator and local area characteristics. The estimating equation is

$$\text{Logit}[\text{Prob}(\text{Retire}_{ist} = 1)] = \alpha \text{RetireCost}_i + \beta \text{GenChar}_{it}$$
$$+ \gamma \text{Census}_i + \theta \text{Gas}_t + \delta_s + \zeta_m + \eta_y + e_{ist}. \tag{2}$$

The dependent variable is an indicator for whether a specific generator (i) is retired in time period t. RetireCost$_i$ is the imputed retirement cost described above, and the parameter α measures how changes in retirement cost affect the probability of retirement, all else equal. GenChar is a matrix of generator characteristics including the efficiency of the generator and the nameplate capacity. The GenChar matrix also includes separate indicators for whether the generator is in a regulated wholesale electricity market, has an ash impoundment, has mercury controls, and is in a county that is in nonattainment for any pollution criteria for any year during the sample period. Local sociodemographic conditions may play a role in an operator's decision to retire a generator. For that reason, we also included a matrix of variables from the US Census measured at the county level. The variables include median income, population density, unemployment rate, and the percentage of males and females with bachelor's degrees or higher. We also included lagged natural-gas prices to measure competition from other fuel types. Last, we included state (δ_s), month of year (ζ_m), and year of sample (η_y) fixed effects.[15]

The results of this estimation are presented in table 3. Column 1 reports a univariate regression of our imputed retirement costs on the probability of retirement. We found that increases in retirement cost are associated with a reduced probability of retirement, which is evidence that the imputed retirement costs are good proxies for actual retirement costs. In column 2, state, month, and year fixed effects add to the specification to control for unobserved spatial, seasonal, and time confounds. The estimated impact of retirement costs on the probability of retirement does not change. Column 3 adds generator characteristics; larger generators with ash impoundments are less likely to be retired. Including these generator characteristics moderates the relationship between the imputed retirement cost measure and the probability of retiring somewhat. Column 4 adds county-level sociodemographics to the estimation. We found no strong relationship between county characteristics and the probability of generator retirement. Finally, column 5 adds natural-gas prices lagged 6 months to the estimation. The coefficient is negative, statistically significant, and large in

Table 3

Estimates of the Probability of Retirement

	1	2	3	4	5
Retirement Costs	−.02***	−.02***	−.01**	−.01**	−.01**
	(0)	(0)	(0)	(0)	(0)
Efficiency (100%)			16.60	13.05	13.11
			(13.57)	(14.92)	(14.94)
Nameplate Cap. (MW)			−.01***	−.01***	−.01***
			(0)	(0)	(0)
Regulated			−.59	−.76	−.76
			(.61)	(.61)	(.61)
Ash Impoundment			−2.41***	−1.89***	−1.89***
			(.58)	(.55)	(.55)
Nonattainment			.29	−.05	−.05
			(.43)	(.47)	(.47)
Mercury Control			.42	.78*	.78*
			(.47)	(.47)	(.47)
Median Income				0	0
				(0)	(0)
Population Density				−142.13	−139.82
				(877.47)	(878.27)
Unemployment Rate				17.18	17.12
				(46.43)	(46.45)
Male Higher Ed.				0	0
				(0)	(0)
Female Higher Ed.				−0	−0
				(0)	(0)
Lagged Gas Price					−.15**
					(.06)
Constant	−1.12***	−.93	−11.55	−10.62	−9.76
	(.19)	(.85)	(11.73)	(12.70)	(12.68)
Month FE	No	Yes	Yes	Yes	Yes
Year FE	No	Yes	Yes	Yes	Yes
State FE	No	Yes	Yes	Yes	Yes
Pseudo R^2	.086	.342	.462	.470	.471
Observations	43,056	43,056	43,056	43,056	43,056

Note: The dependent variable in each regression is an indicator equal to 1 if the coal-fired generator was retired in that month. Retirement costs were imputed from a real options model as described in the paper. Nameplate capacity through mercury control is generator characteristics collected from US Energy Information Administration (EIA) Form 860 data. Median income through female higher education is for the generator's county collected from the 2000 US Census. Lagged gas prices are monthly national average electric power prices for natural gas as reported by EIA lagged by 1 year. Standard errors, clustered at the plant level, are reported in parentheses below the coefficients. FE = fixed effects.
*$p < .10$.
**$p < .05$.
***$p < .01$.

magnitude, suggesting that low natural-gas prices increase the probability of retirement.

The impact of estimated retirement costs on the probability of retirement are consistently negative and statistically significant, which holds true even after including a number of the controls used in the estimation of the retirement costs at active generators. This suggests that the estimated retirement costs are a good proxy for the actual retirement costs faced by the owners of coal-fired generators. Including logit coefficients means the marginal effects of changes in retirement costs are not obvious. The marginal effects of increases in retirement costs are negative across the distribution, but less precisely estimated at low levels of retirement costs. There is a small reduction in the magnitude of the marginal effect of increases in retirement costs on the probability of retirement, but any single $10 million increase is not significantly different from the previous. The mean retirement cost across the sample is $71.6 million and the standard deviation is $45 million. A one standard deviation increase in retirement cost from the mean is associated with an increase in retirement probability of 0.2%.

Forecasting Coal and Electricity Prices

Next, we estimate a statistical model to predict the fuel price and electricity prices at each generator. We collect a decade worth of data on fuel prices and electricity prices from publicly available data sources. We collect electricity prices at the balancing authority level from Federal Energy Regulatory Commission (FERC) Form 714.[16] Balancing authorities represent the smallest unit of the electric grid for which we can get electricity prices nationwide. We map each generator to its balancing authority and assign it an hourly marginal price for each MWh of generation.[17] We collect coal prices from EIA 923 data. That data includes plant-level coal prices for plants in regulated regions and state-level for plants in deregulated markets. Coal is delivered to plants, not generators, so we aggregate all coal deliveries to a plant in a month and assign the weighted average price of that coal to that generator for the month.[18]

We follow Pachamanova and Fabozzi (2011), who use a geometric mean reversion process to predict electricity and coal prices. In this model, prices hover around their long-run mean. Transitory shocks occur at random intervals that move the price above or below its mean for a period of time. As the shock fades, the price returns toward its mean.

Davis et al. (2021) show that electricity and coal prices have behaved in a manner consistent with geometric mean reversion over the past decade.

Their paper estimates the means, the timing, and the size of the shocks that move prices from their mean and the process by which prices return to their mean. All those parameters are the inputs to the electricity and coal price simulations used in the next section. In the simulations, prices evolve following the parameters of the mean reversion process and do not vary with the amount of coal-fired generation on the grid.[19]

V. Forecasting Coal Generator Retirements

In our baseline simulations, we project retirement dates for every coal-fired generator on the grid. We assume that energy policy, electricity prices, and coal costs evolve as they have over the past decade with no major changes. In the next section, we will explore the impact of potential policy changes on retirement dates.

In our business-as-usual baseline, we take the predicted retirement costs from the ML algorithm described above and generate retirement thresholds for each active generator using our real options model. We then simulate electricity and coal prices at each generator to find the expected time these prices cross the retirement threshold: the year that simulated future profits become small enough to justify paying the estimated retirement costs and taking the generator offline. This process requires simulating 20 years of monthly fuel and electricity prices at 492 surviving generators, making it extremely computationally intensive.

We find that under a business-as-usual scenario, 38 generators representing nearly 16,000 MW of capacity are predicted to retire in the first year. Another 118 generators representing more than 28,000 MW of capacity are predicted to survive beyond the end of our 20-year simulation. The remaining generators are predicted to retire at some point over the next 20 years, with retirements starting at a high level and dropping off as the coal fleet shrinks.

The generators that are predicted to retire do so quickly. The bulk of the exit happens in the first 5 years of the simulation, with nearly 150,000 MW of the approximately 200,000 MW of active capacity gone by 2025. Most of this exit happens in the first 2 years of the simulation with nearly a quarter of coal generators retiring in each of those years. Our model believes that a big portion of the coal fleet is at risk of retirement in the very near future. This is consistent with the planned retirements reported in table 1.

The implication of these predictions is that the coal fleet will shrink by 85% over the next 20 years, but there are a handful of generators that are likely to remain on the grid for the foreseeable future. Table 4 reports the

Table 4
Predicted Retirements in the Baseline Scenario

	Fraction Capacity Retiring (%)	Median Retirement Time (in months)	Mean Retirement Time (in months)	Generator Retirements (count)	Active Capacity (MW)	Active Generators (count)
MRO	76	18	23	78	47,338	231
NPCC	17	14	15	4	3,896	35
RFC	62	19	28	123	109,737	424
SERC	57	24	36	132	119,266	405
TRE	12	28	43	6	27,374	43
WECC	26	32	33	21	39,164	137

Note: Predicted generator retirements in our business-as-usual baseline scenario. Each row represents a North American Electric Reliability Corporation region's results in the simulation. The first column reports the fraction of coal-fired generating capacity predicted to retire during by the end of the simulation period. The second column is the median retirement time in months, conditional on retiring, and the third column is the mean retirement time in months, again conditional on retiring. The last two columns report the active coal-fired generating capacity and number of generators at the beginning of the simulation.

distribution of simulated retirement times across the active generators by NERC region. In three regions, more than half of all coal-fired generating capacity is expected to retire over the next 20 years. The largest share of retirements comes in the upper Midwest (MRO) region, with around three-quarters of coal-fired capacity expected to retire. Conditional on retiring, the mean retirement time is about 2 years. Our model predicts a large amount of coal retirement in MRO and expects it to happen relatively soon. This is generally consistent with our announced retirement data that finds 7,500 MW of announced coal generating capacity retirements in MRO with a median planned retirement year of 2022.

Generators that expected to remain operating through the end of the simulation are clustered in SERC (southeastern states) and are slightly smaller on average than the generators that are predicted to retire. The operating dates of survivors are also comparable to those that retire in the simulation. These plants are in locations that earn slightly higher electricity prices, which induces them to stay online for longer and endure occasional periods of financial losses to retain the possibility of future profits.

These predictions are contingent on the current policy landscape. We assume that the underlying process that leads to changes in prices of electricity and coal remains unchanged over the next 20 years. Obviously, this assumption is unlikely to hold in reality. In practice, environmental regulations have been mostly increasing and some generators may have chosen to retire taking that upward drift in regulation into account. Renewable energy penetration is increasing, but the rate of increase varies by region. For all of these reasons, we interpret the baseline as a tool to understand the implications of our model, not as a prediction of actual retirements as the policy landscape changes. In the next section, we explore some counterfactual simulations that allow us to forecast retirement times under different policy scenarios.

A. Out-of-Sample Validation

We take two approaches to provide out-of-sample validation for the predictions of our model. First we take data through the end of 2018 and use the model to predict observed coal generator retirements in 2019 and 2020. We find that our model predicts more retirements than we observe during that time period.

Our model correctly predicts 48 of the 69 coal generator retirements observed in 2018–2019. Of the remaining 21, 13 have announced retirement dates before 2024. Six have announced retirement dates after 2025. Two generators we predict to retire remain active and have not announced a retirement date. We take this as evidence that our model does a good job of predicting which coal-fired generators are likely to retire.

In addition to those 48 units we correctly predicted to retire in the first 2 years of the simulation, we predict 32 other units will retire that remain active. Our model produces many more false-positive retirement predictions than false negatives. Of those 34 false-negative predictions, 19 have announced retirement dates prior to 2025, 2 have announced retirement dates after 2025, and the remaining 13 have not announced any retirement plans. The generators we predict to retire that have not announced any retirement plans are smaller, more efficient, and more likely to be in the upper Midwest (MRO) than the generators whose retirements we correctly predict.

There are a number of reasons why we may be overestimating retirements in the first few years of the simulation. Our model identifies the date at which observed prices make it worthwhile to pay the retirement cost and exit the market. Once generators reach that point, it may take some time to formally announce retirement and have it appear in EIA records or media reports. It is also possible that unobserved characteristics of these generators may make retiring them more difficult than our model predicts. For example, if retirement would cause reliability issues, owners may wait until other generation or transmission becomes available before retiring the units. Some owners may be operating outside the real options framework, keeping coal-fired generators operating for political reasons rather than economic. All of these are realistic possibilities, but our model cannot incorporate these issues. We continue to refine the model to understand the source of the false positives to better understand the drivers of the generators' retirement decisions.

Second, we compare the predictions from our model to the National Energy Modeling System (NEMS).[20] NEMS does not report the retirement decisions for individual generators, but it does forecast coal generation capacity.[21] Figure 4 indexes observed capacity at the start of the simulation to 100 and compares aggregate capacity forecast in our model to the forecast from the base case of the NEMS. Our model predicts more retirement overall through 2035. Both models predict a large drop in capacity in the next 5 years, but our model predicts a large drop happening sooner.

We take these results with a grain of salt. We are predicting more retirement than the NEMS, but since the fracking boom NEMS has consistently overpredicted coal generation. Forecasts produced in 2009 for coal consumption in 2019 were too high by 50%. Even forecasts produced in 2018

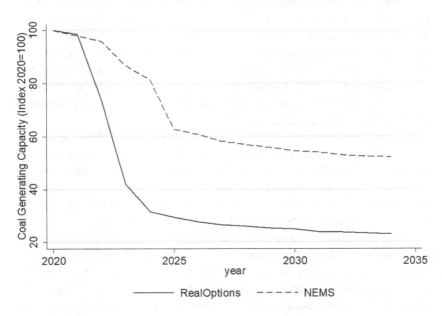

Fig. 4. Comparison of coal generating capacity from real options and NEMS models. Color version available as an online enhancement.

Notes: The forecast coal generation capacity from the US Energy Information Administration's National Energy Modeling System (NEMS) and our real options model. Coal capacity is indexed to 100 in 2020. Our model forecasts more retirement and that most of the retirements in the next decade will happen sooner than in the NEMS forecast.

for 2019 coal consumption were 10% too high. It is possible the systematic error in coal forecasts in the NEMS has been corrected and the most recent forecast will be more accurate, but our model suggests that this may not be the case.

Like our model, NEMS forecasts no coal-capacity additions in the base case. Given that NEMS has overpredicted coal consumption for more than a decade, if their model predicts no entry we can be reasonably confident that our model's no-entry prediction is consistent with the consensus.

VI. Policy Simulations

The previous section describes predicted retirements of coal generators under a business-as-usual scenario, but policy changes are likely to have a big impact on retirement decisions. In this section, we describe how two policy changes might affect which generators retire and when they choose to go offline.

Some policy makers have suggested that coal-fired generation provides important reliability benefits not rewarded by the market. Coal plants store a considerable amount of fuel on-site, meaning that they are not subject to pipeline interruptions or intermittency that can affect natural gas and renewable generators, respectively. Some policy makers have argued that electricity markets do not provide enough incentive to provide this type of reliability and that coal generators should be subsidized to ensure a steady supply of fuel-secure generators.

In 2018, US Secretary of Energy Rick Perry asked FERC to "ensure financial returns" for any plant that could store at least 90 days worth of fuel on-site.[22] In 2019, the state of Ohio enacted a bill to subsidize nuclear and coal-fired generators that had been scheduled for retirement. The subsidies included $60 million in payments through 2030 for two Midwestern coal plants owned by the Ohio Valley Electric Corporation.[23]

The rationale for proposed coal subsidies was that they would slow the retirements of coal-fired generators, but it is not clear how large a subsidy would be needed or how long a given subsidy would delay retirement. We can use our model to understand how subsidizing coal-fired generators will affect their retirement decisions. There are many ways that policy makers could choose to implement a coal generator subsidy, but we model a simple output subsidy of $20 per MWh. In this simulation, each coal-fired generator receives payment for the electricity they generate and an additional credit of $20 per MWh, equivalent to around 100% of the revenue from electricity sales.

We rerun the baseline simulation above including the subsidy to coal-fired generators and identify the retirement times based on revenue from electricity sales, subsidies, and costs for coal using our estimated retirement costs. The results suggest that large production credits can move the average retirement times by a few years, but are unlikely to keep coal-fired generators online far into the future.

Figure 5 reports the change in simulated retirement date from the no-policy baseline to the coal subsidy. The median retirement age increases by 6 years. A number of retirements remain unchanged, either because the subsidy was not enough to prevent the plant from retiring at the beginning of the simulation or because the plant was not predicted to retire in next 20 years in the no-policy baseline. The total subsidy cost in 2018 would be around $20 billion, but as coal-fired generators retire the cost would fall.[24]

In our second policy counterfactual, we examine the impact of environmental regulation on coal plant retirements. The Biden administration has recently released guidance suggesting that a social cost of carbon of

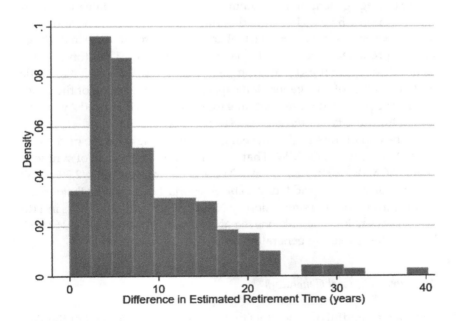

Fig. 5. Difference in retirement times under a $20 coal generation credit. Color version available as an online enhancement.

Notes: The distribution of changes in coal generator retirement times in the no-policy baseline and under a $20 production credit. The vertical axis is the fraction of generators in a bin, and the horizontal axis is how much later the generator retires under the subsidy plan.

$51 per ton should be used in evaluating federal policy. We next simulate implementing that carbon tax and again find the predicted retirement date for each coal-fired generator. We weight each generator's coal usage by the average carbon content for that fuel and state based on EIA's published Carbon Dioxide Emission Factor.[25] The average carbon content across a million British thermal units (Btu) of coal is a little more than 200 pounds. We multiply total coal use (measured in millions of Btu) by the carbon tax rate of $51 per ton and add that to the production cost for each generator. This shifts the retirement thresholds illustrated in figure 3 up, increasing the combination of electricity and coal costs that would induce retirement.

We again simulate electricity and coal prices monthly more than 20 years. We identify whether those prices, inclusive of the carbon tax, induce the generator to pay the retirement cost and exit the market. The carbon tax adds around $6 to the average coal price of $2 per million Btu. This represents a major increase in environmental regulation, and our model predicts that it will lead to large changes in retirement behavior relative to the baseline scenario.

The average generator in our sample has its retirement date moved forward around 2.5 years by the carbon tax. The median is just more than 2 years. Seventy-seven generators that are not predicted to retire in the baseline are predicted to retire under a carbon tax set to $51 per ton of emissions. Those generators have an aggregate capacity of 21,000 MW, a little more than 10% of coal generation capacity at the beginning of the simulation. The predicted retirement time for those plants is around 2 years after the introduction of the carbon tax.

By the end of the simulation coal is an afterthought on the grid. Total capacity is under 1,500 MW. That is comparable to the level of synthetic gas (1,326 MW), waste heat (1,089 MW), and gas from landfills (2,508 MW) as fuel sources on the grid today. Table 5 reports the generators that remain online throughout the simulation by NERC region. All generators in TRE (Texas) have retired and only one remains in WECC (western United States). Most of the remaining generators are in SERC (Southeast).

A.   Surviving Coal Generators

There are a handful of generators that survive through the end of the simulation in the baseline and both policy counterfactuals. These generators have some combination of low retirement costs, high electricity prices, or low coal prices that induce them to stay online even in the face of significant environmental regulation.

Table 5
Predicted Retirements under a Carbon Tax Scenario

NERC Region	Capacity (MW)	Generators	Average Operating Date
MRO	381	7	1965
NPCC	500	3	1959
RFC	1,300	6	1965
SERC	4,796	19	1975
TRE	0	0	. . .
WECC	290	1	1985

Note: Predicted generator retirements under a $51 per ton carbon tax. Each row represents a North American Electric Reliability Corporation region's capacity surviving to the end of the 20-year simulation facing a carbon tax. The first column reports the predicted coal capacity in the NERC region. The second column reports the number of generators online at the end of the simulation. The third column reports the capacity-weighted average operating date for the generators that remain online through the end of the simulation.

Table A1 lists the generators our model predicts will remain in operating status for decades even in the face of significant environmental regulation. The list includes 22 generators with a combined capacity of around 4,200 MW compared to around 400 generators with just under 200,000 MW of generating capacity at the beginning of the simulation. Fifteen of those generators are in the SERC reliability region in the southeastern United States.

The remaining generators represent a tiny fraction of the coal generating capacity currently on the grid, but they will each produce large amounts of damaging local pollutants. These units typically have sulfur dioxide (SO_2), nitrogen oxides (NOx), and particulate matter controls, but a handful of units do not report any abatement equipment for one or more pollutants. Even the units with abatement technology emit hundreds, and in some cases thousands, of tons of SO_2 and NOx per year.[26]

Even a socially efficient carbon tax of $51 per ton of carbon emissions is not expected to force these generators into retirement for decades. These units will also collectively generate tens of millions of tons of carbon dioxide (CO_2) per year until their retirement. Units like these represent a puzzle for policy makers concerned with reducing pollution exposure in communities around power plants and looking for ways to further reduce US CO_2 emissions.

VII. Conclusion

Coal-fired generators have been retiring at an increasing rate over the past decade. These retirements have shifted the electricity generation portfolio across the country. In 2015, natural gas surpassed coal as the primary fuel source for electricity generation. Renewable generation will soon surpass coal-fired generation, if it has not already. This shift has consequences for regional economies, the environment, and the electric grid.

Given the importance of the coal sector to the economy, it is crucial to understand why coal generators have retired and which remaining generators are likely to retire. We have shown that coal generator retirements have increased over the decade and that smaller and older generators are the most likely to retire. Over the next 5 years nearly a quarter of the current coal generating capacity is planning to unplug from the grid. This exit will be concentrated in the Midwest and western United States. Managing these retirements will require additional generation capacity and energy efficiency to replace departing base-load generation. The reduction in coal demand will continue to accelerate, leading coal-producing regions into even deeper economic distress.

The exit of these coal-fired generators is just the tip of the iceberg. Our analysis shows that entry is currently uneconomic for new coal-fired generators. The remaining coal-fired generators will continue to exit the market. To help predict future changes in coal generation capacity beyond announced retirements, we describe a model of coal generator retirement introduced by Davis et al. (2021). That model uses a real options framework to identify the optimal retirement time for an electric generator given electricity prices, coal prices, and retirement costs. Using the observed retirement decisions of coal generators over the past decade, we estimate the unobserved retirement costs for each retired generator.

We then use a ML algorithm to map the retirement costs from the real options model on to generator characteristics. We take this mapping to the remaining active coal-fired generators to predict their retirement costs. We simulate electricity and coal prices for each generator over the next 20 years. For each surviving generator, we identify whether and when it makes sense for them to retire given simulated prices and their estimated retirement costs. This creates a set of predicted retirement times for each generator currently on the grid. Around 85% of coal capacity is estimated to retire in the next 20 years. Those retirements are front loaded with nearly a quarter happening in the next 3 years. This is broadly consistent with the announced retirements, but our model predicts around 10,000 MW more retirement than has been announced. It remains to be seen whether our model is overly pessimistic about coal-fired generation prospects or whether more retirements are likely to be announced.

We use the model to estimate to policy counterfactuals. First, we estimate the impact of a production credit for coal-fired generators. State and federal governments have considered subsidizing coal plants to maintain fuel-secure base-load generation and for political reasons. Our analysis suggests that for these subsidies to have a significant impact on coal-fired generation retirement decisions, they must be very large. A $20 per MWh production credit extends the life of the median generator in our sample by around 6 years. The cost of such a policy would be around 5% of total electricity expenditure.

Finally, we estimate the impact of a carbon tax on retirement dates. We estimate the carbon content of fuel for each generator on the grid and apply a $51 per ton carbon tax. That tax rate is the current preferred estimate for the social cost of carbon, the total cost of society-wide damage from emitting a ton of carbon. Introducing that policy brings forward the median retirement time by only 2 years. Our model predicts that a substantial portion of the nation's coal-fired generating capacity will retire in the near future, leaving little room for policy to pull forward retirements. The carbon tax policy does have an impact on the amount of the coal-fired generation on the grid at the end of our simulation. We find that only around 1,500 MW of coal capacity remain online after 20 years under a carbon tax, less than 1% of operating capacity today.

Owners of coal-fired generation have experienced increasing environmental regulation for the past 2 decades. They likely expect increases in environmental regulation to continue. This background has influenced not only the level of retirements we observe but also retirement simulations in the future. Our baseline scenario assumes no change in policy. In fact, coal-fired generator owners might reasonably expect regulation to increase over the next 20 years. In that case, our baseline might overpredict retirement; or more subtly, generators might retire expecting environmental regulation and then regret that decision when no regulation happens. The difference hinges on whether owners know that no environmental policy changes will happen for 20 years. Some versions of the carbon tax policy counterfactual might more accurately represent reality in a world where environmental regulation continues to ratchet up in the United States.

Coal-fired generation retirements have reshaped the grid over the past decade. That process is likely to continue. Our model identifies which generators are at risk of immediate retirement and which generators are likely to remain online for the foreseeable future. We also show that there is limited scope for policy to affect retirement dates. Large subsidies extend the life of generators by a handful of years. Stringent environmental policy brings retirements forward by a couple of years. Our model suggests that no matter the policy landscape, electric grid operators, environmentalists, and policy makers should expect the retirement of coal-fired generators to continue until coal essentially disappears from the grid.

Appendix

This appendix includes a list of generators that survived through the end of the 20-year simulation in all the baseline and both counterfactuals, maps describing the relevant regions that ensure reliability and balance electricity supply with demand, and a list of all variables with the data sources used in the analysis.

A handful of generators do not retire in any of the three simulations we describe in the main text. This table lists each of those generators. Our model suggests these are likely to be the most persistent generators least likely to be driven to retirement by market conditions or policy changes. This list will be useful to a variety of market participants. The communities that host these plants should plan to deal with local pollution emissions and enjoy any tax revenue for the foreseeable future. Environmental advocates might focus on which local policy is most likely to affect these generators. Coal suppliers for these generators are best positioned to make long-term investments in capacity. Grid planners are more likely to get base-load generation from these generators, helping ensure reliability.

Figure A1 displays the six mainland US North American Electric Reliability Corporation (NERC) regions. NERC regions are a convenient way to summarize generating capacity geographically. NERC regional entities are charged with ensuring electrical service is efficient and reliable in their region. Electricity flows between WECC, TRE, and the other four NERC regions are trivial. Flows between the four eastern regions are small, but can help balance supply and demand for electricity at the margin. NERC regions monitor generation capacity retirements and entry to ensure that there is enough generation capacity to meet demand and a safety margin to maintain service if generators or transmission lines are out of service.

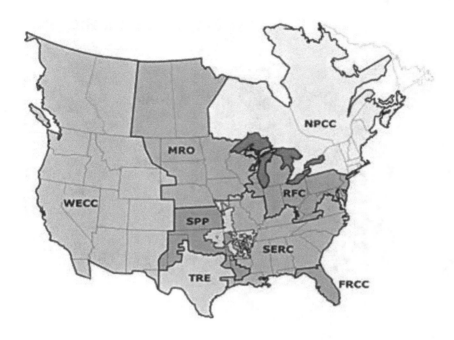

Fig. A1. NERC regions. Color version available as an online enhancement
Note: The six mainland US North American Electric Reliability Corporation (NERC) regions are internally well connected with transmission capacity to ensure that generation can serve load with a minimum of congestion.
Source: US Energy Information Administration.

Figure A2 shows the 66 balancing authorities in the United States. Balancing authorities are responsible for managing the balance of electricity supply and demand hour-by-hour to maintain grid in their geographic region. We collect electricity market price data for these regions because they represent the most disaggregated electricity prices for which we can collect data nationwide. Some generators are in wholesale markets where we can collect electricity prices at the generator level. Unfortunately, large sections of the country are not in electricity markets and this detailed data is not available. Differences between zonal and generator level-prices would typically only occur during times when the grid is congested.

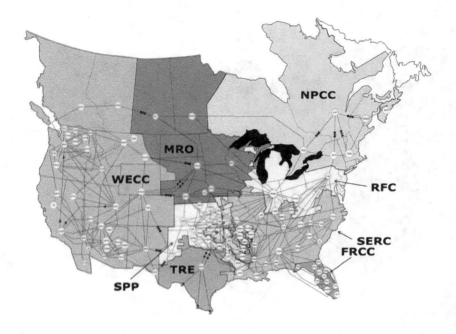

Fig. A2. Balancing authority map. Color version available as an online enhancement.
Note: The 66 balancing authorities in the United States.
Source: US Energy Information Administration.

Table A2 describes each of the variables used in the machine learning analysis mapping retirement costs from retired generators onto active generators.

Table A1
Surviving Generators in Every Simulation

Plant Name	Generator	County	State	Nameplate Capacity (MW)	Operating Year
Big Bend	ST4	Hillsborough	FL	486	1985
Indian River Generating Station	4	Sussex	DE	445.5	1980
Big Bend	ST3	Hillsborough	FL	445.5	1976
Winyah	2	Georgetown	SC	315	1977
Winyah	3	Georgetown	SC	315	1980
Winyah	4	Georgetown	SC	315	1981

Table A1
Continued

Plant Name	Generator	County	State	Nameplate Capacity (MW)	Operating Year
Northside Generating Station	1	Duval	FL	297.5	1966
Northside Generating Station	2	Duval	FL	297.5	1972
Birchwood Power	1	King George	VA	258.3	1996
Deerhaven Generating Station	2	Alachua	FL	250.7	1981
McIntosh	1	Effingham	GA	177.6	1979
B L England	2	Cape May	NJ	163.2	1964
Hammond	1	Floyd	GA	125	1954
Chesterfield	3	Chesterfield	VA	112.5	1952
Crist	4	Escambia	FL	93.7	1959
Mecklenburg Power Station	GEN1	Mecklenburg	VA	69.9	1992
Mecklenburg Power Station	GEN2	Mecklenburg	VA	69.9	1992
Schiller	4	Rockingham	NH	50	1952
Schiller	6	Rockingham	NH	50	1957
Muscatine Plant #1	7	Muscatine	IA	25	1958
Lon Wright	7	Dodge	NE	22	1963
Lon Wright	6	Dodge	NE	16.5	1957

Note: These generators do not retire any of our policy simulations. Our model predicts these will be the final generators to retire and that they are unlikely to retire in the next 10 years even if significant environmental policies are implemented.

Table A2
Data Sources

Variable	Source
Median Income	US Census (2010)
Population Density	US Census (2010)
Unemployment Rate	US Census (2010)
Male Higher Education	US Census (2010)
Female Higher Education	US Census (2010)
Utility	EIA 830 Data
Nameplate Capacity (MW)	EIA 830 Data
Operating Year	EIA 830 Data
Natural Gas Pipeline Access	EIA 830 Data
Total Plant Generating Capacity	EIA 830 Data
Fraction Plant Coal Capacity	EIA 830 Data
Ash Impoundment	EIA 830 Data
Ash Impoundment Lined	EIA 830 Data

Table A2
Continued

Variable	Source
Ash Impoundment Status	EIA 830 Data
NOx Rate	Shawhan et al. (2014)
SO$_2$ Rate	Shawhan et al. (2014)
Heat Rate (Efficiency)	Shawhan et al. (2014)
Dollars of Environmental Damage per MWh	Shawhan et al. (2014)
State	EIA 830 Data
Sector	EIA 830 Data
Energy Source (Coal Type)	EIA 830 Data
NERC Region	EIA 830 Data
Regulatory Status	EIA 830 Data
Ownership (Single/Joint)	EIA 830 Data
Mean Fuel Price	Authors' Calculations from EIA 923 Data
Variance Fuel Price	Authors' Calculations from EIA 923 Data
Mean Electricity Price	Authors' Calculations from EIA 923 Data
Variance Electricity Price	Authors' Calculations from EIA 923 Data

Note: This table reports the data used in the machine learning algorithm that maps retirement costs for retired generators to active generators. After creating categorical variables, there are 99 features for 720 active and retired generators.

Endnotes

Author email addresses: Davis (davisrj4@sfasu.edu), Holladay (jhollad3@utk.edu), Sims (cbsims@utk.edu). Thanks to Jim Stock and Tatyana Deryugina for helpful feedback. Kate Martella provided outstanding research assistance. This research was funded in part by the Alfred P. Sloan Foundation grant no. G-2015-14101, "Pre-Doctoral Fellowship Program on Energy Economics," awarded to the National Bureau of Economic Research. Holladay and Sims also gratefully acknowledge funding from the Alfred P. Sloan Foundation grant no. G-2019-11399 and the Tennessee Valley Authority. For acknowledgments, sources of research support, and disclosure of the authors' material financial relationships, if any, please see https://www.nber.org/books-and-chapters/environmental-and-energy-policy-and-economy-volume-3/coal-fired-power-plant-retirements-us.

1. A coal-fired power plant typically has multiple separate generators that can be built, operated, and retired separately from each other. We use the term *plant* in the title and introduction to be consistent with the policy discussion.

2. Our model does not produce standard errors or other traditional measures of uncertainty. Simulation of coal and electricity prices, as well as forecasting retirement costs, could produce an analog of sampling variation. In Davis et al. (2021), we examine those individual sources of variation.

3. The University of Alaska Fairbanks has proposed replacing its existing coal-fired combined heat and power system with a new coal-fired system: https://www.uaf.edu/heatandpower/background.php.

4. An additional 32 generators with 3,200 MW in capacity were on standby, a likely precursor to retirement. Those generators are not included in this analysis.

5. The industry refers to the date that a unit first produced electricity for the grid as its operating date. Each generator at a plant can have a different operating date.

6. Less than 10% of retired generators reported supercritical generation ability, but nearly 90% of active generators have that technology. Supercritical boilers heat steam

to such high temperatures that it exhibits properties of both liquid and gas phases, allowing it to spin generators more efficiently.

7. The six regions are the northeastern states (NPCC), the southeastern states (SERC), the Midwest and mid-Atlantic states (RFC), the middle of the country from the upper Midwest down to Oklahoma (MRO), Texas (TRE), and the entire western part of the country from New Mexico to Washington state (WECC). See figure A1 for a map of NERC regions.

8. The EIA requires that any generator with a planned retirement date in the next 5 years to report this information. In practice, a number of generators with later retirement dates report that information as well.

9. Because these unofficial retirement announcements are nonbinding, we do not use them in the summary statistics that follow.

10. Specifically, the latest version of the EIA 860 survey on line 8 reads, "If this generator will be retired in the next ten years, what is its estimated retirement date?" Previous version of the survey only asked for retirement dates in the next 5 years. Respondents can enter a month, but are told to enter June if they are uncertain which month. We choose not to use the month portion of the response because most generators report planned retirements of June or December, whereas actual retirements typically occur during the lower demand spring or fall.

11. Following Baumol and Willig (1981), we define "sunk costs" as costs that cannot be eliminated even by total cessation of production. In contrast, "fixed costs" are costs that are not reduced by decreases in output so long as production is not discontinued altogether. Thus, not all sunk costs are fixed and not all fixed costs are sunk.

12. Ideally we would identify the electricity and coal prices at the time the owners made the decision to retire the unit. Unfortunately, the decision date is not consistently reported so we use retirement date. This generates some measurement error when assigning retirements to observed prices. Owners have the option of ignoring the announced retirement and extending the life of the generator up until the actual retirement date, so we think the assumption that electricity and coal prices on that date drove retirement is a reasonable one.

13. The full list is provided in table A2.

14. The other algorithms performed similarly. The prediction error for XGBoost was around 13% of a standard error and LASSO was just more than 15%. The correlation coefficient among prediction for the three different algorithms was more than 0.8, so the choice of algorithm for learning the relationship between generator characteristics and retirement costs is unlikely to materially affect our retirement prediction results.

15. We did not include the same variables used in the propensity score matching procedure due to multicollinearity issues. For example, the total cost of existing abatement technology and the indicator for having an ash impoundment measure a generator's level of abatement and are highly correlated.

16. See figure A2 for a map of the balancing authorities.

17. The FERC 714 data include system lambda which is the zonal locational marginal price for deregulated markets and the incremental cost of providing more electricity from thermal units in regions with no market prices.

18. Coal plants can store several months of fuel on-site. We choose to assign coal consumed in a month the weighted average price of coal deliveries because we consider that the opportunity cost of burning coal that month. See Chu, Holladay, and LaRiviere (2017) for more discussion of the trade-offs in this decision.

19. This implicitly assumes that coal-fired generator retirements do not affect electricity prices or coal prices. For small numbers of retirements, this is likely to hold. Grid managers are likely to ensure that retirements are matched with entry of other generators or transmission to ensure no large electricity price effects. Retirements of large numbers of coal generators will affect demand for coal and potentially reduce prices, though exports may make up for some of the difference.

20. We collect NEMS results from the 2021 *Annual Energy Outlook* published by EIA (2021). These results are reported in table 54, Electric Power Projections by Electricity Market Module Region, for the reference case.

21. NEMS also reports capacity by "model regions." Unfortunately, those regions do not line up well with NERC regions making it difficult to compare regional results across the two models.

22. FERC considered this request and eventually chose not to act.

23. The Federal Bureau of Investigation is currently investigating the former speaker of the Ohio House of Representatives as well as other legislators for corruption related to this subsidy. It is not certain whether the plants will accept the payments or remain online.

24. Coal generated 1.15 billion MWh in 2018.

25. We collected the data on the carbon content of fuels from EIA's *Annual Energy Outlook 2019*, table A8 (Electricity Supply, Disposition, Prices, and Emissions), available at https://www.eia.gov/outlooks/aeo.

26. Northside Generating Station 2 in Duval County Florida emitted more than 1,600 tons of SO_2 and 774 tons of NOx in 2019, for example.

References

Baumol, W. J., and R. D. Willig. 1981. "Fixed Costs, Sunk Costs, Entry Barriers, and Sustainability of Monopoly." *Quarterly Journal of Economics* 96:405–31.

Caves, R. E., and M. E. Porter. 1976. "Barriers to Exit." In *Essays on Industrial Organization in Honor of Joe S. Bain*, ed. J. S. Bain, R. T. Masson, and P. D. Qualles, 36–69. Cambridge, MA: Ballinger.

Chu, Y., J. S. Holladay, and J. LaRiviere. 2017. "Opportunity Cost Pass-Through from Fossil Fuel Market Prices to Procurement Costs of the US Power Producers." *Journal of Industrial Economics* 65:842–71.

Cullen, J. A., and E. T. Mansur. 2017. "Inferring Carbon Abatement Costs in Electricity Markets: A Revealed Preference Approach Using the Shale Revolution." *American Economic Journal: Economic Policy* 9:106–33.

Davis, R. J., J. S. Holladay, and C. Sims. 2021. "Drivers of Coal Generator Retirements and their Impact on the Shifting Electricity Generation Portfolio in the US." Working paper, University of Tennessee.

Dixit, A. K., and R. S. Pindyck. 1994. *Investment Under Uncertainty*. Princeton, NJ: Princeton University Press.

EIA (US Energy Information Administration). 2021. *Annual Energy Outlook 2021: With Projections to 2050*. Washington, DC: Government Printing Office.

Linn, J., and K. McCormack. 2019. "The Roles of Energy Markets and Environmental Regulation in Reducing Coal-Fired Plant Profits and Electricity Sector Emissions." *RAND Journal of Economics* 50:733–67.

Pachamanova, D. A., and F. J. Fabozzi. 2011. "Modeling Asset Price Dynamics." In *The Theory and Practice of Investment Management: Asset Allocation, Valuation, Portfolio Construction, and Strategies*, 2nd ed., ed. F. J. Fabozzi and H. M. Markowitz, 125–58. Hoboken, NJ: Wiley.

Ryan, S. P. 2012. "The Costs of Environmental Regulation in a Concentrated Industry." *Econometrica* 80:1019–61.

Shapiro, J. S., and R. Walker. 2018. "Why Is Pollution from US Manufacturing Declining? The Roles of Environmental Regulation, Productivity, and Trade." *American Economic Review* 108:3814–54.

Shawhan, D. L., J. T. Taber, D. Shi, R. D. Zimmerman, J. Yan, C. M. Marquet, Y. Qi, et al. 2014. "Does a Detailed Model of the Electricity Grid Matter? Estimating the Impacts of the Regional Greenhouse Gas Initiative." *Resource and Energy Economics* 36:191–207.

Siegfried, J. J., and L. B. Evans. 1994. "Empirical Studies of Entry and Exit: A Survey of the Evidence." *Review of Industrial Organization* 9:121–55.

Suzuki, J. 2013. "Land Use Regulation as a Barrier to Entry: Evidence from the Texas Lodging Industry." *International Economic Review* 54:495–523.

Headwinds and Tailwinds: Implications of Inefficient Retail Energy Pricing for Energy Substitution

Severin Borenstein, *University of California, Berkeley and NBER,* United States of America

James B. Bushnell, *University of California, Davis and NBER,* United States of America

Executive Summary

Electrification of transportation and buildings to reduce greenhouse gas emissions requires massive switching from natural gas and refined petroleum products. All three end-use energy sources are mispriced due in part to the unpriced pollution they emit. Natural gas and electricity utilities also face the classic natural monopoly challenge of recovering fixed costs while maintaining efficient pricing. We study the magnitude of these distortions for electricity, natural gas, and gasoline purchased by residential customers across the continental United States. We find that the net distortion in pricing electricity is much greater than for natural gas or gasoline. Residential customers in much of the country face electricity prices that are well above social marginal cost (private marginal cost plus unpriced externalities), whereas in some areas with large shares of coal-fired generation, prices are below social marginal cost. Combining our estimates of marginal price and social marginal cost for each of the fuels with a large survey of California households' energy use, we calculate the distribution of annual fuel costs for space heating, water heating, and electric vehicles under actual pricing versus setting price at social marginal cost. We find that moving prices for all three fuels to equal their social marginal cost would significantly increase the incentive for Californians to switch to electricity for these energy services.

JEL Codes: Q41, L97, Q50

Keywords: energy prices, externality costs, electrification, decarbonization

Environmental and Energy Policy and the Economy, volume 3, 2022.

I. Introduction

Around the globe, strategies for mitigating the emissions of greenhouse gases (GHGs) are coalescing around a common blueprint that involves decarbonizing the electric sector and transitioning as many energy-using activities as possible away from fossil fuels and into electricity usage. This process is known as electrification. In the United States, the first phase of this strategy is much more advanced than the second. Although GHG emissions from the electricity sector have been declining steadily over the past 2 decades, emissions from the transportation and building sectors have continued to grow.[1]

The process of transitioning buildings and transportation away from their primary sources of energy—natural gas and petroleum, respectively—is at the forefront of climate plans, but it faces significant barriers. The capital stock of existing vehicles and appliances is enormous, and replacement is relatively slow under normal conditions. There are also potentially significant additional infrastructure investments needed to support the large-scale expansion of electrification, particularly of transportation. At the same time, an enormous amount of existing infrastructure and other capital could become "stranded" if the consumption of natural gas and petroleum declines as rapidly as called for by some climate policies. Fortunately, technological advancements have recently closed many of the quality gaps between conventional vehicles and household appliances—a term we use to mean all in-home energy-using devices, including furnaces and hot water heaters—and their electric-powered counterparts, though some differences remain.

One additional challenge to the process of electrification that is obvious to economists, but surprisingly less prominent in policy discussions, is overcoming relative retail price disparities between the three fuels. For many US residents, electricity can be the most expensive of the three energy sources on an energy-equivalent basis. Furthermore, the advancement of the two-pronged electrification strategy could enlarge this gap. Although low carbon electricity production sources have rapidly declined in costs, most analyses predict that "deep" decarbonization will require costly investments in battery storage, transmission, and more exotic (and expensive) technology solutions, such as hydrogen for long-duration storage. In addition, whereas electricity may become more expensive as it gets cleaner, the demand reductions produced by any success of electrification would almost certainly depress fossil fuel prices.

For economists, the logical solution to such a pricing gap would be carbon pricing either through a tax, cap and trade, or some other mechanism.

This solution is complicated by the fact that there are existing taxes and other pricing distortions that have already caused fuel prices to deviate from marginal costs. The strict application of a Pigouvian tax to account for the environmental externalities without accounting for preexisting distortions could exacerbate rather than correct some of these preexisting distortions.

In this paper, we examine the relative pricing distortions of the three primary energy sources most relevant to electrification policies: electricity, natural gas, and gasoline. For each of these fuels, we develop an estimate of the social marginal cost (SMC) of supplying the fuel to residential customers and compare it with the relevant retail price faced by individual residential customers. In each case, retail prices can be inefficiently inflated by regulatory pricing structures (in the case of electricity and natural gas) or market power and inefficiently depressed by a lack of accounting for environmental externalities. There are two aspects of pricing distortions in retail energy: the within-fuel gap between retail price and its SMC and the across-fuel "gap in gaps" that compares the relative signs and magnitudes of the mispricing between fuels. This latter pricing gap is particularly relevant for assessing the prospects for, and implications of, a large-scale strategy of substituting from end-use fossil fuel combustion to electricity.

The paper is divided into two main sections. The next section describes our calculations of marginal prices and SMC for the three fuels. In Borenstein and Bushnell (2021), we find that significant pricing distortions arise in electricity, where prices can be up to four times SMC in some states, and 25% or more below SMC in other states. In much of the United States, however, the distortions of regulatory rate design offset those of the omitted externality pricing, leaving prices fairly close to SMC on average. Residential natural gas prices, which include substantial margins designed to recover sunk infrastructure costs, are only modestly above SMC in much of the country due to unpriced negative environmental externalities that increase SMC. Gasoline, by contrast, is largely underpriced relative to SMC, a gap that is most extreme in dense urban areas most vulnerable to local air pollution.

The degree to which any pricing gaps would change behavior will depend in part upon the availability of a reasonable substitute for any given appliance or vehicle. The second half of this paper applies the pricing findings from the first half to specific electrification goals in California, a state that is pushing the electrification policy perhaps harder than any other. We examine the degree to which the pricing distortions we document influence the economics of the fuel costs for electrifying space heating and water heating—which combined account for about 86% of residential natural gas use in California. We show that, for both space heating and hot water heating, changing the volumetric prices of electricity and natural gas from their current levels to SMC would greatly alter the economics of the energy choice for these primary residential uses. In both cases, current energy prices tilt strongly in favor of natural gas, but pricing at SMC would effectively eliminate that difference. We also do a rough comparison of the pricing distortions in California between gasoline and electricity in the context of two examples of vehicle substitution. Lower fuel costs are supposed to be one of the big advantages of electric vehicles, but at current rates in California— where we find gasoline is priced below SMC in most locations and electricity is priced well above SMC—we find the fuel cost advantage of electric vehicles would increase by about $500 per year on average if each fuel were priced at SMC.

II. Estimation of Existing Pricing Distortions

In this section, we develop estimates of both marginal retail prices and SMC for the three main residential energy sources: electricity, natural gas, and gasoline. Each energy source presents some specific issues in developing such estimates. Electricity and natural gas are both distributed by regulated utilities, and the regulatory rate-making process plays an important role in setting prices for residential customers. As we describe below, infrastructure and other fixed costs comprise a significant share of retail prices (see Borenstein, Fowlie, and Sallee 2021). In some areas, these costs are at least partly recovered through a fixed monthly charge component of a two-part tariff, but in all cases variable prices of electricity and gas are designed to also recover some share of these fixed costs. Gasoline, which is distributed at commercial retail stations, is sold exclusively at a variable price in a fairly competitive market that is under little economic regulation and that likely reflects some degree of market power.

To develop externality costs for each fuel, we lean heavily on estimates developed by Nicholas Muller in the current version of his Air Pollution Emission Experiments and Policy model of air pollution damages, AP3.[2] These estimates account for damages from four criteria pollutants as well as CO_2. We do not account for externalities that are unlikely to differ significantly based on fuel type, such as the traffic congestion and accident externalities associated with driving, because they would not affect the net efficiency of fuel choice. We use Muller's parameters for the damage from criteria air pollutants, but we adjust the damage from CO_2 to be \$50 per metric ton.[3]

We do not include in our estimates the upstream emissions in the production or extraction of the energy sources or hardware for energy production. Emissions from extraction of fossil fuels are likely to be the largest of these factors and are almost certainly greater for gasoline and natural gas than for electricity, because a large share of electricity is produced from sources other than fossil fuels. Thus, inclusion of upstream emissions would likely raise the gap between price and SMC for electricity relative to gasoline or natural gas. Nonetheless, reliable estimates of the marginal impact of consuming any of the sources on upstream emissions are difficult to find, so we have omitted them at this point. Our estimates also do not account for tax breaks and subsidies for either fossil fuels or renewable energy. To the extent that these lower the wholesale prices of energy—which we use as an indicator of private marginal cost, as explained below—our estimates will understate the private marginal cost and therefore the SMC.[4]

A.   Previous Evaluation of Electricity Price versus SMC

In previous work, Borenstein and Bushnell (2021), we develop estimates of the marginal residential retail price and SMC of electricity. Our sample covered the years 2014–2016. For comparability, we use these years for analysis of all three fuels. We summarize our methodology and results from Borenstein and Bushnell (2021) here.

Retail Prices

To construct estimates of marginal residential retail electricity prices, we combine data from the Energy Information Administration (EIA) Form 861 and the Utility Rate Database (URDB). The EIA-861 reports total customers, sales, and revenues for each major electric utility by customer class, including residential. The average residential price can therefore be calculated by dividing total revenues by total sales. The URDB provides, among other things, information on the fixed component of a two-part tariff for utilities that apply them. We multiply the fixed charge by the number of customers to calculate the revenues derived from fixed charges. We then subtract this fixed charge revenue from total revenue, and then divide by total sales to calculate an average marginal price for residential customers. In some areas, this average will mask additional heterogeneity in marginal customer prices if the utility applies an increasing or declining block rate structure. However, the "step size" in these rate structures is relatively modest for all but utilities in California, and even California electricity rates have undergone a significant compression of the prices across tiers in recent years. See Borenstein and Bushnell (2021) for more details.

Using this process, we derive prices for about 2,100 utilities over 3 years serving virtually all residential customers in the United States. In areas with retail competition for energy provision, there are overlapping service areas, so we aggregate to the utility distribution provider—the companies that own and maintain the physical distribution infrastructure—which leaves 1,756 utility-state pair.

Private Marginal Costs

The private marginal costs (PMCs) of electricity are primarily derived from wholesale pricing data published by independent system operators (ISOs).[5] The ISOs operate wholesale electricity markets across the bulk of the US electric system and calculate locational marginal prices (LMPs) at least hourly. The LMPs are calculated as the shadow cost of meeting one more unit of demand in a given location including the bid-in marginal cost of generation as well as the shadow cost of transmission congestion and other operating constraints. In other words, ISOs calculate and apply a textbook definition of the marginal cost of supply that includes almost all relevant operating constraints.

We match each utility in our data set with the three nearest ISO pricing "hub" locations that capture the hourly marginal cost of electricity in a regional location. The primary component of the hourly marginal cost of electricity for each utility is the (inverse distance-weighted) average of these three prices.[6] These prices, however, are for delivery of electricity to the local interface between the high-voltage transmission network and the lower-voltage distribution networks. Moving the electricity from this interface to the residential customer creates additional costs, because some of the electricity is dissipated as heat. We account for these line losses to then determine the marginal cost of supplying electricity to the residential customer.

Externality Costs

Many sources of electricity generation produce some or all of the criteria pollutants covered in the AP3 model, as well as CO_2. Detailed emissions data from every major emitting power plant are collected by the US Environmental Protection Agency's (EPA) continuous emissions monitoring system (CEMS) and published quarterly. We adapt procedures developed in Holland et al. (2016) that map electricity demand at a given location to output from given power plants. The general procedure converts emissions from the CEMS to monetary damages using values taken from the AP3 model. We aggregate these hourly emissions damages by summing the damages from all plants in a region for a given hour. We then regress the hourly emissions damages from each region on the level of demand, or "load," in the region in which the plant is located as well as other neighboring grid-connected regions. In our case, we divide load within a region ("own region") and in neighboring regions ("other region") into terciles to generate a piecewise linear estimate of the relationship between load and the emissions located in a given region.

The damages associated with electricity consumption in a given region at a given time are derived by summing the coefficient values that attribute the share of a region's hourly emissions damage to load in a specific region. For example, roughly $12 of the $13 per marginal megawatt (MW) of the CO_2 damages from power plants in California is attributable to electricity consumption in California, and consumption in California is responsible for about $5 of the $30 per marginal MW of the CO_2 damages created by power plants in the non-California west.

Both private marginal cost and externality costs vary hour to hour in the electricity industry. For the purposes of this analysis, however, we aggregate these hourly marginal costs into quantity-weighted averages.

Results

The results of these calculations—averaged across 2014, 2015, and 2016—are presented in figure 1 and table 1. Figure 1 shows the wide range of differences between price and SMC across the country and the percentage of customers in each of the bins. For 15.3% of residential customers, including most of California and much of New England, the residential retail price exceeds average SMC by at least $0.08 per kWh. Nearly half of customers, however, face a retail price that is within $0.02 of SMC, the lightest colors on the map. There is also a swath of areas, mostly in the upper Midwest, where price is significantly below SMC, though only about 6% of customers face a price more than $0.03 below SMC.

Table 1 summarizes the variation of electricity prices and costs across the utilities in our sample. Electricity prices and costs vary substantially

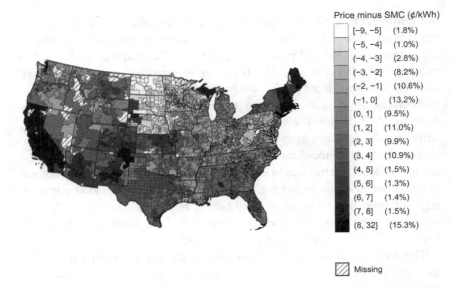

Price minus SMC (¢/kWh)

	[−9, −5]	(1.8%)
	(−5, −4]	(1.0%)
	(−4, −3]	(2.8%)
	(−3, −2]	(8.2%)
	(−2, −1]	(10.6%)
	(−1, 0]	(13.2%)
	(0, 1]	(9.5%)
	(1, 2]	(11.0%)
	(2, 3]	(9.9%)
	(3, 4]	(10.9%)
	(4, 5]	(1.5%)
	(5, 6]	(1.3%)
	(6, 7]	(1.4%)
	(7, 8]	(1.5%)
	(8, 32]	(15.3%)

Missing

Fig. 1.   Electricity marginal price minus social marginal cost (SMC) per kWh. Color version available as an online enhancement.

Note: Percentages in parentheses are share of residential electricity customers in each category.

more over space than do the other fuels studied in this paper. Electricity costs (and wholesale prices) are also uniquely volatile over time; variations of more than an order of magnitude can be experienced within a single day.[7] In this paper, we restrict our analysis to the difference between retail prices and longer-term average SMC, because our focus is on the customer choice of durable, energy-using appliances and vehicles.

Although figure 1 presents the geographic variation of the gap between price and SMC, it is harder to see the overall distribution and relationship

Table 1
Electricity Averages of Prices and Marginal Costs (2014–2016)

	Mean	SD	Min	P25	P75	Max
Retail variable price (P, ¢/kWh)	11.46	3.00	2.38	9.73	12.13	41.18
Private marginal cost (¢/kWh)	3.72	.70	2.43	3.18	4.10	6.26
External marginal cost (¢/kWh)	6.20	2.38	2.53	4.55	8.81	11.91
Social marginal cost (SMC, ¢/kWh)	9.92	2.50	6.06	8.05	12.39	15.42
P − SMC (¢/kWh)	1.54	4.04	−8.85	−1.02	3.14	31.86
(P − SMC)/P	.09	.29	−2.70	−.10	.28	.77

Note: Each observation is the average for one utility-state pair over 2014–2016. $N = 1,756$ (utility-state pair). Statistics are sales weighted.

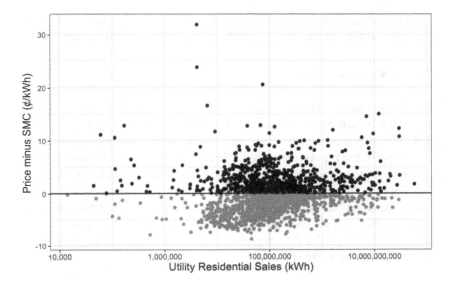

Fig. 2. Electricity price minus social marginal cost (SMC) versus average annual residential sales (by utility). Color version available as an online enhancement.

to usage. Figure 2 shows a scatterplot of the gap versus each utility's average annual residential sales (in log scale). The graph shows that there are many more utilities with prices well above SMC than well below, and some of those are among the largest utilities in the country.

B. Natural Gas Price versus SMC

Our analysis of residential natural gas pricing closely follows the approach we use for electricity.

Retail Prices

As with electricity, aggregate data on residential revenues, customers, and quantities are available by utility from the EIA (Form EIA-176), but further adjustment is needed to derive marginal price. Fixed monthly charges are also quite common in natural gas. Thus, as with electricity, we subtract estimated aggregate fixed charges from total residential revenues and divide by quantities to get an estimate of marginal retail price. To implement this approach, we started from the data on residential fixed charges collected by Catherine Hausman (2019). We then hand-collected data from additional gas utilities to get to the total data set we use, which covers 97%

of all residential customers with natural gas service. About half of all residential households in the United States have natural gas service.

Private Marginal Costs

The private marginal cost of natural gas delivered to the home is nearly entirely attributable to the marginal cost of acquiring gas for the utility's distribution system. Every state has one or more "city gate" locations at which gas in the pipeline is priced. We use city gate prices as the marginal cost of supplying natural gas. We make one adjustment to the city gate price, which reflects the gas that is lost or stolen in the distribution process, known as "lost and unaccounted for" gas (LAUF). Utilities report LAUF to the EPA for their entire distribution system. We adjust the marginal cost of supply for the proportion of gas that is lost in the distribution process, as reflected in the LAUF.

Externality Costs

The primary pollution externalities from residential combustion of natural gas are CO_2 and NO_x. In addition, some natural gas, which is nearly all methane, leaks out from the distribution pipes. There is significant disagreement about how well LAUF reflects leaks, as discussed in detail in Hausman and Muehlenbachs (2019). They argue that although LAUF is a noisy measure, it is correlated with actual leaks. We use LAUF for the proportion of gas that is leaked in the distribution system and assume a global warming potential (GWP) for these methane leaks of 34, that is, we assume that 1 pound of natural gas leaked into the atmosphere has a climate change cost that is 34 times greater than 1 pound of CO_2.[8] It is worth noting that residential distribution involves more miles of pipe per unit of energy delivered than distribution to commercial and industrial customers, so very likely the share of gas that leaks in residential distribution is higher than the overall utility average.

Using Muller's AP3 model, we estimate the monetary costs of these emissions, and then we add these externality costs to the estimated private marginal cost to create the SMC per MMBTU of natural gas.

Results

The results of these calculations are presented in figure 3 and table 2.[9] Figure 3 shows the differences in the standard units of natural gas, price per

Fig. 3. Natural gas marginal price minus social marginal cost (SMC) per MMBTU. Color version available as an online enhancement.

Note: Percentages in parentheses are share of residential natural gas customers in each category.

MMBTU. These are not the same units as for electricity, so these maps are not yet directly comparable. But figure 3 shows that the general pattern of deviations from SMC is similar to electricity, with higher prices relative to SMC on the coasts and lower in the middle of the country. To compare the results to electricity, below we convert energy units from MMBTU to kWh.

As with electricity, we also present the scatterplot of the gap between price and SMC across utilities of differing size. Figure 4 shows less tendency for the larger gaps to be among the largest utilities but again

Table 2
Natural Gas Averages of Prices and Marginal Costs (2014–2016)

	Mean	SD	Min	P25	P75	Max
Retail variable price (P, $/MMBtu)	8.36	2.05	4.53	6.90	9.28	17.18
Private marginal cost ($/MMBtu)	4.65	.52	3.17	4.43	4.91	8.61
External marginal cost ($/MMBtu)	3.55	.52	2.74	3.16	4.00	4.95
Social marginal cost (SMC, $/MMBtu)	8.19	.70	6.78	7.75	8.67	11.65
P – SMC ($/MMBtu)	.16	2.23	−3.80	−1.28	1.26	9.40
$(P - \text{SMC})/P$	−.04	.26	−.84	−.18	.14	.57

Note: Each observation is the average for one utility-state pair over 2014–2016. $N = 189$ (utility-state pair). Statistics are sales weighted.

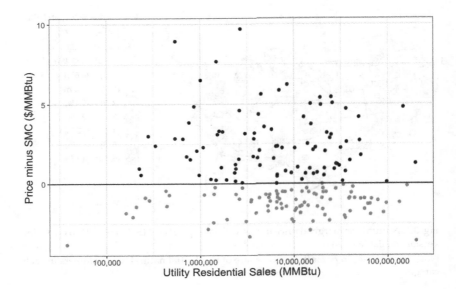

Fig. 4. Natural gas price minus social marginal cost (SMC) versus average annual residential sales (by utility). Color version available as an online enhancement.

illustrates that the gaps with price greater than SMC are much larger than the gaps with price less than SMC.

C.   Gasoline Price versus SMC

Unlike electricity or natural gas, gasoline is not sold in a market subject to direct economic regulation or exhibiting attributes of natural monopoly. Still, we can take a similar approach to establishing the relationship between price and SMC. The literature on optimal gasoline taxation generally assumes that the ex-tax retail price of gasoline is equal to its private marginal cost of supply (see, e.g., Parry and Small 2005; West and Williams 2007). This assumption potentially biases estimated PMC upward to the extent that refining or retailing of gasoline exhibits any market power, which seems especially likely in retailing due to spatial differentiation. Concerns about market power are particularly relevant to our analysis of technology choice in California, presented in the next section (see Borenstein 1991; Petroleum Market Advisory Committee 2017; Borenstein 2020). On the other hand, the standard assumption potentially biases estimated PMC downward to the extent that taxes are passed through to retail price less than 100%, that is, that suppliers bear some of the burden of gasoline taxes, though this seems less likely in the long run.[10]

Retail Prices

We take the state-level average retail price of regular grade gasoline as the benchmark for this analysis, because that is the most common type of gasoline sold in the United States.[11]

Private Marginal Costs

We assume that private marginal cost is equal to the state-level average wholesale (rack) price plus an adjustment for retailing costs. This adjustment we make is 2.5% of the retail price (to reflect credit card fees) plus $0.06 for the delivery cost from the wholesale rack to the gas station, plus $0.04 for marginal labor costs and other marginal costs of retailing.[12]

Externality Costs

We follow Holland et al. (2016) for calculation of the air pollution externalities due to burning gasoline in light-duty vehicles. The only change we make to their calculations is to assume a social cost of CO_2 emissions of $50/ton rather than $41/ton as they assume. Like Holland et al. (2016), we ignore externalities from congestion and accident risk, instead assuming that they are unchanged by whether the vehicle is powered by an electric or internal combustion engine. We do the calculation of price minus SMC first in the familiar units of dollars per gallon. In the next subsection, we translate them into cents per kWh for comparison across the fuels.

Results

The results of these calculations are presented in figure 5 and table 3. Figure 5 shows the differences in the standard gasoline units of price per gallon, which again is not directly comparable to the earlier maps, as well as the population falling in each bin. The only areas in which the price of gasoline is substantially above SMC are areas with very low population densities. Overall, approximately 14% of the population lives in areas where the price of gasoline is above SMC. The lighter shades that correspond to most of the major metropolitan areas reflect the fact that burning gasoline among high population density is particularly harmful and is not reflected in retail prices.

We again also present a scatterplot of the gap between price and SMC, but in this case by county rather than utility. Unfortunately, we do not

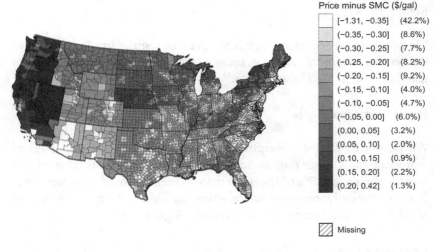

Fig. 5. Gasoline price minus social marginal cost (SMC) per gallon. Color version available as an online enhancement.

Note: Percentages in parentheses are share of population in each category.

have data on county-level sales, so we sort based on county population. Figure 6 shows clearly that the gaps of price below SMC are much larger than the gaps of price greater than SMC, and they occur in counties of much larger population.

D. Comparison of Price versus SMC across Energy Sources

Figure 7 presents the price versus SMC maps for the three fuels, but for ease of comparison all are now in cents per kWh with the same legend.[13] Besides converting the units, we make one further adjustment for gasoline, recognizing that internal combustion engines are only about 33%

Table 3
Gasoline Averages of Prices and Marginal Costs (2014–2016)

	Mean	SD	Min	P25	P75	Max
Retail variable price (P, $/gal)	2.68	.24	2.37	2.50	2.76	3.20
Private marginal cost ($/gal)	2.12	.09	1.98	2.04	2.14	2.29
External marginal cost ($/gal)	.86	.26	.50	.73	.93	1.82
Social marginal cost (SMC, $/gal)	2.98	.30	2.49	2.80	3.06	3.95
P – SMC ($/gal)	−.30	.25	−1.30	−.43	−.16	.41
$(P$ – SMC$)/P$	−.12	.09	−.52	−.17	−.06	.13

Note: Each observation is the average for one county over 2014–2016. N = 3,107 (counties). Statistics are population weighted.

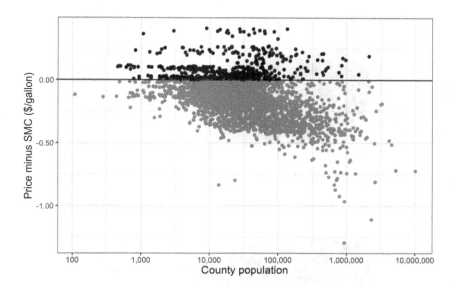

Fig. 6.   Gasoline price minus social marginal cost (SMC) versus county population. Color version available as an online enhancement.

efficient on average, which triples both the price and the SMC of delivering energy to the engine.[14] Thus, regardless of the sign, this adjustment triples the gap between price and SMC in cents per kWh.

It is immediately evident that electricity is mispriced to a much greater degree than gasoline or natural gas. Relative to SMC, electricity is overpriced to a greater extent in most of the country, but where it is underpriced, that underpricing is larger on average than where natural gas or gasoline are underpriced. The explanation for overpricing electricity is fairly straightforward: The utility is recovering fixed costs associated with the natural monopoly operation of the company, and in some cases, such as California, also recovering costs for a variety of public purpose programs. The areas of underpricing are associated with large amounts of unpriced externalities from coal-fired generation.

Although all three energy sources are underpriced or overpriced in different parts of the country, the customer/population share column next to the legend of each map suggests that overpricing is far more prevalent on a customer-weighted basis for electricity, whereas underpricing is far more prevalent for gasoline. The results are less clear-cut for natural gas.

In the appendix, we also present an alternative analysis of the gap between price and SMC, using the Lerner index, $(P - SMC)/P$, rather than

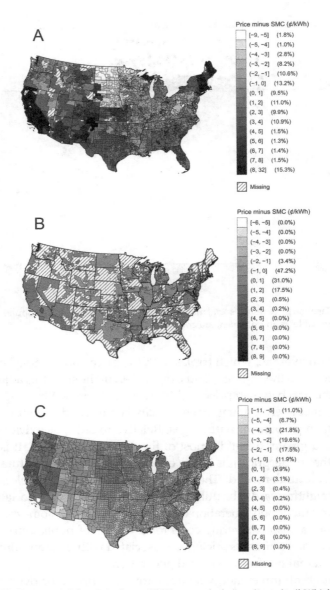

Fig. 7. Price minus social marginal cost (SMC) across fuels (in adjusted ¢/kWh) for electricity (*A*), natural gas (*B*), and gasoline (*C*). Color version available as an online enhancement.

levels. Though in some ways proportional markups for each of the fuels are more intuitive, we do not think they are as useful as the analysis in levels (with all fuels in the same energy units) when thinking about the implications of moving prices to SMC for fuel choices. As we show in the next section, the financial incentive impact on fuel switching when fuel prices change depends on the change in the relative level of costs of using each fuel and on the comparison of these cost differences to other costs and characteristics of the appliances or vehicles. Nonetheless, looking at the proportional distortions suggests the same conclusion, that distortions in electricity pricing are far larger than in natural gas or gasoline.

In the last year or two, there has been increasing discussion and research suggesting that the social cost of GHG emissions may be substantially higher than $50 per metric ton. In the appendix, we also present an analysis that is identical to our primary analysis except we use a $100 per metric ton cost of GHG emissions rather than $50. Of course, all of the maps turn a lighter shade with a higher cost of GHG emissions. An extra $50 per metric ton translates to an SMC increase of about $0.40/gallon of gasoline, which turns the entire gasoline map a light shade.[15] The natural gas map becomes mostly gray, with some darker gray still present in a few locations, but mispricing in both directions is relatively small. The electricity map shows substantial change in the Midwest and Plains states, as well as parts of the South, but changes fairly little in California or New England, where the grids are already relatively low carbon.

As discussed in the introduction, as opportunities for fuel switching increase, the differences in mispricing across the energy sources become more policy relevant. In the next section, we apply the results of this analysis to appliance and transportation choices for households in California.

III. Implications for Building and Transportation Electrification

In this section, we explicitly consider the implications of the mispricing of alternative energy sources by examining how those prices affect the relative costs of key household services that rely on energy inputs. We first consider the two largest in-home appliance energy uses: space heating and water heating. The EIA estimates that these services account for about 62% of all home energy use,[16] and the vast majority of residential natural gas consumption. In each case, electric power alternatives, based on heat pump technology, have emerged as viable substitutes for many households. We then consider the light-duty vehicle market by comparing the operating costs of electric vehicles to somewhat comparable gasoline-powered internal combustion engine (ICE) vehicles.

Extending these calculations to estimates of the welfare losses created by pricing inefficiencies would require estimates of consumer preferences over the attributes offered by appliances with different fuel sources, which is beyond the scope of this paper. However, we show that for these large residential energy uses, pricing inefficiencies can tip the economics of fuel costs from one source of energy to another and can have a significant impact on the overall economics of appliance choice.[17]

For each of the in-home appliances, we evaluate the energy requirements for providing specific services—furnace heat output or increase in tank water temperature—using electricity or natural gas as the energy source. We carry out this study for California, both because electrification is a major policy goal in the state and because the state's 2019 Residential Appliance Saturation Survey (RASS) allows us to infer estimated distributions of space heating and water heating service demand quantities across households. These quantity distributions imply distributions of the fuel cost difference from providing these services using electricity versus natural gas. All of the comparisons in this section are carried out based on 2016 price data.

To evaluate the range of impacts that electricity and natural gas pricing in California could have on energy costs for each appliance, we focus on the 27,583 single-family detached dwellings and townhouses in the RASS.[18] We exclude apartments, mobile homes, and other dwellings. For each household, the RASS reports every appliance in the home and an estimate of the appliance energy usage, based on a simulation that incorporates total household usage, appliance specifications, household demographics, and other survey responses. From these simulated energy usage quantities, we apply specific efficiency measures to infer the energy services produced.

The RASS surveys customers in the service territories of the five largest electricity distribution utilities in California: Pacific Gas & Electric, Southern California Edison, San Diego Gas & Electric, Los Angeles Department of Water and Power, and Sacramento Municipal Utility District. Together, these utilities serve about 92% of all residential customers in California. The survey covers virtually all residential natural gas customers. The survey includes the name of the utility that provides electricity or natural gas to the household. We use those identifiers to match each household to a marginal energy rate for each fuel from the analysis in Section II.

We then use the RASS to infer the household's quantity demanded from the appliance. Unfortunately, the data made available do not include direct estimates of the quantity of appliance usage, so we infer quantity from the estimated energy input combined with an assumed efficiency of the appliance. The RASS does not include the efficiency of the appliance, but it does include the age of the appliance, in multiyear categorical variables. For each age category, we take the efficiency to be a weighted average of the federal minimum efficiency standard and the federal Energy Star efficiency standard over the years of manufacture within that age category.[19] The efficiency standards are weighted by data on national sales proportion of Energy Star appliances over the manufacture years within the age category.

Once we have the quantity of services demanded from a particular appliance, we can convert to energy use for any particular energy source for that appliance using another efficiency assumption. We do this by assuming new appliances using electricity or natural gas and meeting the 2019 Energy Star standard for either. Thus, information from the RASS is used to establish a distribution of energy service quantity demanded from each appliance across the households in the survey, and then we compare the energy cost of providing that quantity of service from new appliances powered by, alternatively, electricity or natural gas. Implicitly, we are assuming no change in energy service quantity demanded with the change in energy price. Given marginal retail prices for electricity and natural gas, this yields a distribution of dollar savings or additional costs from using electricity rather than natural gas. We create these distributions if each fuel were sold at its actual marginal retail price and if each fuel were instead sold at its SMC.

For light-duty vehicles, we follow a similar logic, but we have a direct measure of services provided, vehicle miles traveled, from a survey carried out by the Federal Highway Administration. We discuss the light-duty vehicle analysis in more detail below.

Our analysis compares the cost of energy sources using total-demand-weighted average prices, not accounting for the ability of consumers to reallocate their consumption toward lower cost periods. It is worth noting that this omission almost certainly biases our analysis against electricity, because short-term price variation in electricity is much greater than in the other two (far more storable) energy sources. Thus, the option to shift demand to lower price time intervals would likely reduce the cost of using electricity by more than it would reduce the cost of using natural gas or gasoline.

A. Space Heating

The 2019 RASS suggests that 79% of California residences used on-site natural gas combustion as their primary heat source and 12% used electricity, with the remainder coming primarily from propane and wood. Electricity has long been considered an inefficient and expensive energy source for heating, but attractive to some households (and landlords) because of the low upfront capital investment required (see Davis 2021a). This view is based on the electric resistance heating technology that is in nearly all portable electric space heaters and electric baseboard heating.

In the last decade, however, heat pump space heating has made significant technological progress (see Energy+Environmental Economics 2019). A heat pump uses expansion and compression of a gas to move heat from one location to another. Refrigerators are heat pumps that use the principal to move heat out of the enclosure to the surrounding air. The same technology can be used to move heat from outside a home to inside, even when the outside temperature is substantially below the inside temperature. If it gets too cold outside, however, the heat pump is able to extract very little heat from the outside air and becomes much less efficient. With recent technological improvements, heat pumps can now operate more effectively even at low temperatures.

To maximize comparability, we ignore portable and room heaters and focus on whole house forced-air natural gas furnaces versus whole house forced-air air-source heat pump furnaces, both of which use a fan to push the air through ducts to the rooms of a house. In both cases, calculations include the electricity used to run the fan. The top panel of table 4 presents the underlying assumptions used to evaluate the two appliances that we compare for space heating. Note that the 0.401 in the "Units In/Out" column for heat pump space heating suggests that only 0.401 kWh of electricity in is required to create 1 kWh of heat out, due to the absorption of heat from outdoor air. This is considerably more efficient than an electric resistance heater, which has a ratio of about 1.0. The last two columns of the table suggest that at current retail prices heat pumps cost about twice as much as natural gas furnaces on average, but if prices were set to SMC, the cost would be about equal. Figure 8 shows the distribution of annual energy savings from using a heat pump furnace rather than a gas furnace, given our assumptions about efficiency and the distribution of usage. At current prices, in the areas of California covered by the RASS (which does not include most of the Sierra-Nevada mountain areas), the fuel cost of heat pump furnaces is greater than natural gas almost everywhere, implying negative fuel cost savings. On average, heating with natural gas is $157 less expensive per year. If both fuels were priced at SMC, however, there would be virtually no difference in the fuel costs of each.[20] For a rough

Table 4
Average Energy Price and Cost Assumptions for Appliances

Appliance	Efficiency Index	Efficiency	Units In	Price ($/..)	SMC ($/..)	Units Out	Units In/Out	Cost per Unit of Energy Service At P	At SMC
Space heating:									
Gas	AFUE	.90	therm	1.057	.682	kWh	.038	.046	.028
HP	HSPF	8.50	kWh	.180	.059	kWh	.401	.084	.027
Water heating:									
Gas	EF	.67	therm	1.057	.682	kWh	.051	.054	.035
HP	EF	2.00	kWh	.180	.059	kWh	.500	.090	.029

Note: AFUE = annual fuel utilization efficiency; EF = energy factor; HP = heat pump; HSPF = heating seasonal performance factor; P = actual retail price; SMC = social marginal cost.

comparison, homeadvisor.com estimates the total purchase and installation cost for an Energy Star gas furnace to be $3,400 and the total purchase and installation cost for an Energy Star heat pump central furnace to be $6,400. We found, however, that these estimates vary quite a bit

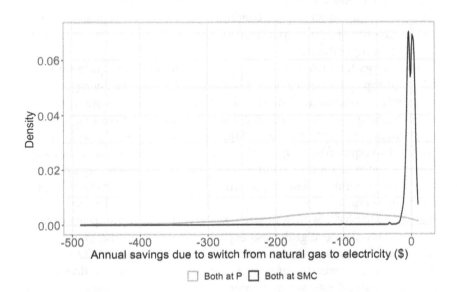

Fig. 8. Distribution of annual energy cost savings for space heat. Color version available as an online enhancement.

Note: P = actual retail price; SMC = social marginal cost.

across sources and depend very much on the need to upgrade electrical service or gas service. In addition, as discussed earlier, the two appliances deliver different service characteristics. Importantly, heat pumps are built to also run in the opposite direction as air conditioners, which potentially greatly increases their value. So a complete choice analysis would need to include many other factors. Still, given that furnaces typically last 20 or more years, the difference in annual energy costs for heating is likely to be a major factor in appliance choice.

B.   Hot Water Heating Energy Sources

Our analysis of water heaters follows along the same lines as space heating. We consider only tank water heaters. We compare an efficient (Energy Star) gas-fired water heater with a heat pump electric water heater. As of 2019, natural gas tank water heaters were present in 74% of surveyed California homes and electric tank water heaters were in 7%. Most of the remainder were tankless or were on propane. Heat pump electric tank water heaters were about 0.5%, but advocates of electrification generally argue they are the preferred technology to replace water heaters that use natural gas or propane. As with space heating, we derive the energy service units as the quantity of heat output (measured in kWh), in this case in the form of higher-temperature water.

The energy technology of a heat pump water heater is quite similar to a heat pump space heater, so it is not surprising that the energy cost differentials are also quite similar. Table 4 suggests the average cost differential again goes from nearly a 2:1 ratio at current prices to about parity, actually a slight cost advantage for heat pumps, if energy prices were set to equal SMC. Figure 9 incorporates the distribution of usage, showing once again that at current retail prices for electricity and natural gas, the operating cost of gas is much lower than for an electric appliance, an average savings with gas of $155 per year. But if both prices were reset to SMC, at current efficiency levels of heat pump water heaters, they would be slightly less expensive to operate than natural gas water heaters, an average savings with the heat pump of $22 per year. According to homeadvisor.com, full purchase and installation cost of a medium-sized gas water heater would be $1,300 compared with $2,300 for the heat pump water heater. The same caveats apply in this case as with the space heating comparison, but it is even more clear with water heating that the difference in annual energy costs, and how that

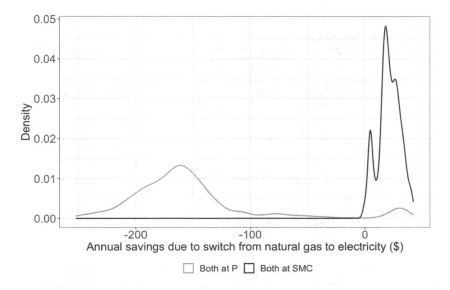

Fig. 9. Distribution of annual energy cost savings for water heating. Color version available as an online enhancement.

Note: P = actual retail price; SMC = social marginal cost.

would change if prices reflected SMC, would be very material to the appliance choice.

C. Implications for Electric Vehicles

Light-duty vehicles, to a much greater extent than home appliances, feature a wide range of amenities and disamenities that can be closely linked with the choice of an electric versus ICE vehicle. The most obvious is the trade-off of slower charging and potentially less driving range with the convenience of refueling at home. Others, for example Muehlegger and Rapson (2021), consider the full range of costs and conveniences associated with the choice of electric versus gasoline-powered transportation. In this paper, we limit ourselves to consideration of the impact of energy pricing on the operating costs of relatively comparable vehicles.

Table 5 summarizes the efficiencies and unit costs of a selection of battery electric (BEV), ICE, and plug-in hybrid electric (PHEV) vehicles. The two most directly comparable options are the battery electric Nissan Leaf and its ICE analog, the Nissan Versa, and electric versus gasoline operation of the Prius Prime PHEV. The Prius Prime presents the most

Table 5
Average Fuel Price and Cost Per Mile

Make	Model	Units	Units per 100 mi	P ($/unit)	SMC ($/unit)	MPGe	$/Mile P	$/Mile SMC
Nissan	Leaf S Plus	kWh	30.0	.176	.059	108	.053	.018
Nissan	Versa	gallons	2.9	2.677	2.861	34	.078	.083
BMW	740i	gallons	4.2	2.677	2.861	24	.112	.120
Tesla	Model S	kWh	30.0	.176	.059	111	.053	.018
Tesla	Model 3	kWh	24.0	.176	.059	135	.042	.014
Prius	Prime	kWh	25.0	.176	.059	133	.044	.015
Prius	Prime	gallons	1.9	2.677	2.861	54	.051	.054

Note: P = actual retail price; MPGe = miles per gallon for gasoline vehicles, miles per gallon equivalent for electric; SMC = social marginal cost.

direct opportunity for energy price arbitrage given its ability to run on either electricity (for 25 miles) or gasoline. Note that at recent average marginal prices in California, the costs per mile are almost equivalent for the Prius Prime. This result, based upon California average marginal electricity price, masks the substantial number of households that pay electricity prices above this average for whom powering a PHEV with gasoline would be less expensive than with electricity. At SMC, the comparison is not close: Powering vehicles with electricity is clearly substantially less expensive.

To gauge the magnitudes of the operating costs differential in terms of annual costs for typical consumers, we apply data from the 2017 National Household Travel Survey (NHTS). The NHTS is a periodically held comprehensive survey of household travel behavior collected by the Federal Highway Administration. There were roughly 47,000 California vehicles participating in the 2017 survey. Following Davis (2019), we divide the vehicle's odometer reading by the age of the vehicle to construct an annual average vehicle miles traveled (VMT). The distribution is then reweighted by the sample weights provided in the NHTS.

The survey results allow us to identify the usage and location of each household, and apply the energy price and marginal cost associated with that location. For example, we match the marginal electricity price based upon the utility service territory in which the household is located and apply the externality damages from combusting fuel within that household's county.[21] We then multiply the per mile cost of operating a specific vehicle by the number of miles driven for each household in the survey. The thought exercise is basically looking at the annual operating cost implications of choosing a gasoline- or electric-powered vehicle—setting aside any differences in convenience, amenities, and purchase costs. We then summarize the annual operating cost "savings" (or premium) of the electricity choice for all households in the survey.

We apply the operating cost differences from table 5 to the resulting distribution of 2017 California VMT to generate estimates of the distribution of annual operating savings under two choice options. The first compares the Nissan Leaf to the Nissan Versa, and the second compares the Tesla Model S to the BMW 740i. This calculation is summarized in figures 10A and 10B. Again, the light gray line illustrates the savings for the electricity choice at 2016 retail prices, and the black line summarizes the distribution of savings if the both energy sources were priced at SMC. In both cases, drivers save on operating costs even at retail price, but the savings are relatively modest (about $100 annually on average) for the Leaf comparison at current prices. That savings would be about five times larger on average if both fuels were priced at SMC. The Tesla, which is much more efficient than a BMW 740i, produces large savings under either scenario, but again those savings are substantially larger when both fuels are priced at SMC.

IV. Conclusion

Achieving real change in emissions of GHGs and local pollutants will require both achieving enormous technological progress in "green" energy and removing incentive and institutional barriers to the adoption of those new technologies. In California and some other parts of the United States, distorted electricity prices are likely to be among the most significant incentive barriers to reducing fossil fuel emissions through electrification, particularly as costs of electric appliances and vehicles decline.

We have shown that prices of all three major energy sources for homes and light-duty vehicles differ from their SMC, in some cases substantially, and there is quite a bit of geographical variation in these differences. Even the sign of the deviation varies regionally. We estimate that, in general, electricity in the continental United States is priced above its SMC, though there are regions—covering about 38% of customers—where it is priced below. Importantly, the largest deviations in electricity are due to overpricing and cover substantial shares of the entire US residential customer base. About 32% of US households face electricity prices at least $0.03 per kilowatt hour above SMC—a larger gap than we estimate more

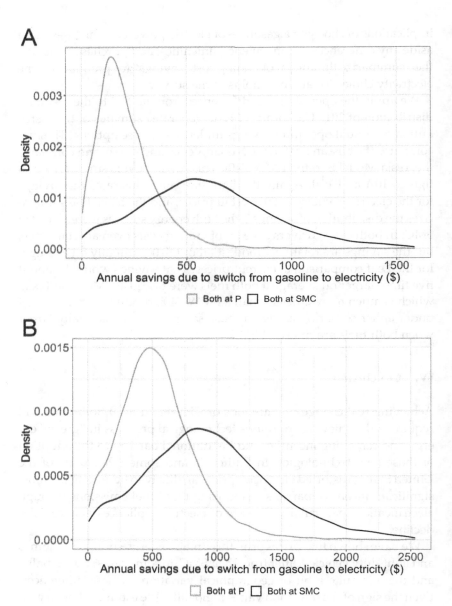

Fig. 10. Distribution of annual fuel savings for California drivers. *A*, Versa versus Leaf. *B*, Tesla S versus BMW 740i. Color version available as an online enhancement.

Note: *P* = actual retail price; SMC = social marginal cost.

than 99% of households face when buying gasoline or natural gas. For 15% of households, electricity prices are at least $0.08 above SMC.

If shifts toward electricity for home appliances and vehicles are expected to happen through customer choices, then distortions in energy prices could substantially deter those choices. If these shifts are mandated, then the high electricity prices create both potential hardship for low- and middle–income households and the potential for serious political resistance.

To date, the preferred policy intervention to promote electrification has been to subsidize the purchases of electric appliances and vehicles through tax credits, rebates, or share mandates. Our results demonstrate that the size of such implicit or explicit subsidies necessary to induce switching may be substantially increased by the inefficient pricing of the underlying fuels, particularly electricity. Beyond the direct burden of subsidies on pub-lic funds, there are other reasons why addressing retail fuel pricing distor-tions would be a more efficient solution and could at least complement sub-sidizing appliance and auto purchases. First, programs focused on the purchase of new appliances suffer from a variety of inefficiencies in the use and life extensions of the existing installed base, which in this case rely on fossil fuels (see Stavins 2006). Second, although purchase subsidies may correct for the extensive margin purchase of the new devices, reform of fuel prices is still necessary to address the intensive margin of their use.

This study also shows the importance of accounting for preexisting distortions in discussions of pricing GHG emissions. Even without California's low carbon price, its retail electricity prices greatly exceed SMC, so adding the impact of a carbon price will not necessarily increase efficiency. Luckily, policy makers do have alternatives to raising reve-nue through volumetric prices that are multiples of SMC, including fixed monthly connection charges, which can be income-based to im-prove equity, or shifting many of the programs paid for through electric-ity prices to state budgets.[22]

Appendix

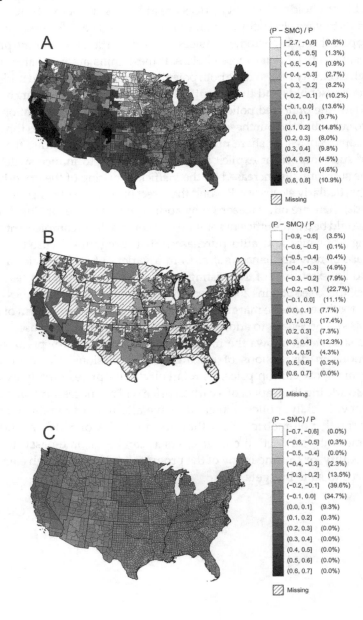

Fig. A1. $(P - \text{SMC})/P$ comparison across fuels for electricity (*A*), natural gas (*B*), and gasoline (*C*). Color version available as an online enhancement.

Note: P = actual retail price; SMC = social marginal cost.

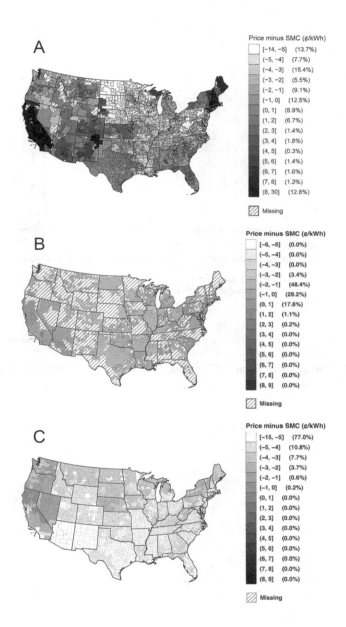

Fig. A2. Price minus social marginal cost (SMC) across fuels (in adjusted ¢/kWh) with social cost of carbon = $100/ton, for electricity (*A*), natural gas (*B*), and gasoline (*C*). Color version available as an online enhancement.

Note: Analysis of in-home appliance savings that includes efficiency assumptions from Energy+Environmental Economics study.

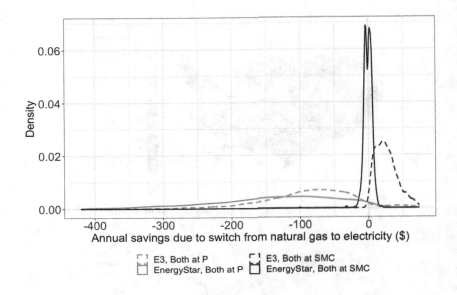

Fig. A3. Distribution of annual energy cost savings for space heat. Color version available as an online enhancement.

Note: E3 = Energy + Environmental Economics; P = actual retail price; SMC = social marginal cost.

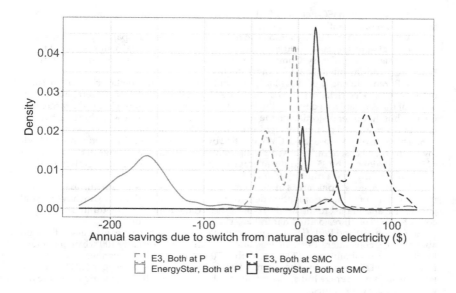

Fig. A4. Distribution of annual energy cost savings for water heat. Color version available as an online enhancement.

Note: E3 = Energy + Environmental Economics; P = actual retail price; SMC = social marginal cost.

Endnotes

Author email addresses: Borenstein (severinborenstein@berkeley.edu), Bushnell (jbbushnell@ucdavis.edu). For outstanding research assistance and very helpful comments, we thank Sara Johns, Jenya Kahn-Lang, and Dan Mazzone. For valuable comments and discussions, we thank Mohit Chhabra, Alejandra Meija Cunningham, Lucas Davis, Tatyana Deryugina, Ari Gold-Parker, Catherine Hausman, Matthew Kotchen, Matthew Lewis, Amber Mahone, Erin Mansur, Nicholas Muller, Allison Seel, James Stock, and participants in presentations at the Energy Institute at Haas, University of California, Berkeley, and the Third Annual National Bureau of Economic Research Conference on Environmental and Energy Policy and the Economy. We also thank Catherine Hausman and Matthew Lewis for sharing data. This research was supported in part by a grant from the California Public Utilities Commission to the Energy Institute at Haas. For acknowledgments, sources of research support, and disclosure of the authors' material financial relationships, if any, please see https://www.nber.org/books-and-chapters/environmental-and-energy-policy-and-economy-volume-3/headwinds-and-tailwinds-implications-inefficient-retail-energy-pricing-energy-substitution.

1. See https://cfpub.epa.gov/ghgdata/inventoryexplorer/index.html.

2. See https://public.tepper.cmu.edu/nmuller/APModel.aspx and Clay et al. (2018).

3. This is in line with the Biden administration's interim finding on the social cost of carbon. See https://www.whitehouse.gov/wp-content/uploads/2021/02/TechnicalSupportDocument _SocialCostofCarbonMethaneNitrousOxide.pdf.

4. Our estimates also do not incorporate the distortions that might replace the ones that we identify here to the extent that price is lowered to equal SMC and a revenue shortfall results.

5. We use the term ISO here to refer to both independent system operators and regional transmission organizations.

6. A small number of utility regions do not have ISOs, and transparent prices are therefore not available. For these utilities, we apply the "system lambda" value reported to the Federal Energy Regulatory Commission in the FERC Form 714. See the appendix of Borenstein and Bushnell (2021) for more details.

7. In Borenstein and Bushnell (2021), we contrast the relative inefficiencies of the static nature of retail electricity prices to those created by an inefficient *level* of average prices. In much of the central United States, the lack of time-varying retail pricing is the larger distortion, but the larger distortion on the West Coast and in the Northeast is due to extremely high prices relative to quantity-weighted average SMC over time.

8. This is also very close to the GWP implied by the Biden administration's interim finding on the social cost of carbon. At a 3% discount rate, it finds the average of the social cost of CO_2 emissions to be $51 and the average of the social cost of methane emissions to be $1,500 per metric ton, a multiplier of 29.4.

9. The large geographic areas of the country that show as missing are due in part to the fact that much of the low population density areas of the United States do not have natural gas service and in part to the need to collect these data manually. The utilities shown account for 97% of all residential natural gas customers in the country.

10. Chouinard and Perloff (2004) suggest that federal gasoline taxes are passed through about 50% to consumers, but state gasoline taxes are borne virtually 100% by consumers. Doyle and Samphantharak (2008) find that 70%–100% of tax adjustments are passed through to retail even in the short run, whereas Marion and Muehlegger (2011) find full pass-through on average but suggest that the short-run pass-through varies with the degree of supply constraints.

11. Retail gasoline price data are from AAA. For each state, we taken an unweighted average of the regular gasoline price in cities for which AAA posts prices.

12. For delivery costs, see https://www.thetruckersreport.com/truckingindustryforum /threads/how-much-does-it-cost-to-transport-a-gallon-of-fuel-to-a-retail-gas-station .223454/. The 2.5% credit card fee is the median of many websites we study on the cost of running a gas station. Marginal labor cost is based on $10/hour all-in labor cost, and an assumed 1 minute per transaction and an average transaction size of 8 gallons, resulting in marginal labor cost of about $0.02 per gallon. Still, adjustments to this margin up or down by $0.10 per gallon would not qualitatively change our findings.

13. Natural gas units are converted at a ratio of 293.07 kWh per MMBTU. Gasoline, with an adjustment for 10% ethanol, is converted at a ratio of 0.0305 kWh per gallon.

14. See https://www.fueleconomy.gov/feg/evtech.shtml.

15. It is important to recall that these calculations do not include congestion and accident externalities from driving. If one desired to internalize those externalities through gasoline pricing, then gasoline would be even further underpriced. Those externalities, however, are very imperfectly correlated with gasoline consumption, so other approaches to pricing them may be preferred.

16. See https://www.eia.gov/todayinenergy/detail.php?id=37433.

17. Although we calculate the impact of energy prices on operating cost, Davis (2021b) studies empirically how energy prices affect the home heating fuel choice.

18. The RASS data set includes sampling weights, which we use in constructing the summary statistics and fuel cost distributions.

19. For details on the standards, see https://www.energy.gov/eere/buildings/appliance -and-equipment-standards-program.

20. Some studies, such as Energy+Environmental Economics (2019), suggest that the heat pump efficiency level that we are using, matching the qualification level for the Energy Star program, is lower than some models that are now available. We are not aware, however, of data showing that such models have significant market share, perhaps due to their novelty, high price, or other attributes. To the extent that heat pumps are more efficient than we assume, this would shift both distributions to the right. Results using the assumptions for heat pump efficiency that are assumed in Energy+Environmental Economics (2019) are in the appendix.

21. Because we do not have gasoline price data for most locations, we carry out the analysis using the statewide average gasoline price. Externality costs, however, are matched to the location of the household.

22. See Borenstein et al. (2021) for more discussion of these options.

References

Borenstein, Severin. 1991. "Selling Costs and Switching Costs: Explaining Retail Gasoline Margins." *RAND Journal of Economics* 22 (3): 354–69.

———. 2020. "California's Mystery Gasoline Surcharge Strikes Back." Energy Institute at Haas Blog, February.

Borenstein, Severin, and James Bushnell. 2021. "Do Two Electricity Pricing Wrongs Make a Right? Cost Recovery, Externalities, and Efficiency." Working Paper no. 294R, Energy Institute at Haas, University of California, Berkeley.

Borenstein, Severin, Meredith Fowlie, and James Sallee. 2021. "Designing Electricity Rates for an Equitable Energy Transition." Working Paper no. 314, Energy Institute at Haas, University of California, Berkeley.

Chouinard, Hayley, and Jeffrey M. Perloff. 2004. "Incidence of Federal and State Gasoline Taxes." *Economics Letters* 83 (1): 55–60.

Clay, Karen, Akshaya Jha, Nicholas Z. Muller, and Randy Walsh. 2018. "The External Costs of Shipping Petroleum Products by Pipeline and Rail: Evidence of Shipments of Crude Oil from North Dakota." *Energy Journal* 40 (1): 55–72.

Davis, Lucas W. 2019. "How Much Are Electric Vehicles Driven?" *Applied Economics Letters* 26 (18): 1497–502.

———. 2021a. "Evidence of a Homeowner-Renter Gap for Electric Appliances." Working Paper no. 316, Energy Institute at Haas, University of California, Berkeley.

———. 2021b. "What Matters for Electrification? Evidence from 70 Years of U.S. Home Eating Choices." Working Paper no. 309R, Energy Institute at Haas, University of California, Berkeley.

Doyle, Joseph J., Jr., and Krislert Samphantharak. 2008. "$2.00 Gas! Studying the Effects of a Gas Tax Moratorium." *Journal of Public Economics* 92 (3–4): 869–84.

Energy+Environmental Economics. 2019. "Residential Building Electrification in California: Consumer Economics, Greenhouse Gases and Grid Impacts." Working paper, Energy+Environmental Economics, San Francisco, CA.

Hausman, Catherine. 2019. "Shock Value: Bill Smoothing and Energy Price Pass-Through." *Journal of Industrial Economics* 67 (2): 242–78.

Hausman, Catherine, and Lucija Muehlenbachs. 2019. "Price Regulation and Environmental Externalities: Evidence from Methane Leaks." *Journal of the Association of Environmental and Resource Economists* 6 (1): 73–109.

Holland, Stephen P., Erin T. Mansur, Nicholas Z. Muller, and Andrew J. Yates. 2016. "Are There Environmental Benefits from Driving Electric Vehicles? The Importance of Local Factors." *American Economic Review* 106 (12): 3700–3729.

Marion, Justin, and Erich Muehlegger. 2011. "Fuel Tax Incidence and Supply Conditions." *Journal of Public Economics* 95 (9–10): 1202–12.

Muehlegger, Erich, and David Rapson. 2021. "The Public and Private Economics of Electric Vehicles." Working paper, University of California at Davis.

Parry, Ian W. H., and Kenneth A. Small. 2005. "Does Britain or the United States Have the Right Gasoline Tax?" *American Economic Review* 95 (4): 1276–89.

Petroleum Market Advisory Committee. 2017. "Final Report." California Energy
    Commission, Sacramento, CA.
Stavins, Robert. 2006. "Vintage-Differentiated Environmental Regulation." *Stan-
    ford Environmental Law Journal* 25 (1): 29–63.
West, Sarah E., and Roberton C. Williams III. 2007. "Optimal Taxation and
    Cross-Price Effects on Labor Supply: Estimates of the Optimal Gas Tax." *Jour-
    nal of Public Economics* 91 (3–4): 593–617.

Future Paths of Electric Vehicle Adoption in the United States: Predictable Determinants, Obstacles, and Opportunities

James Archsmith, *University of Maryland,* United States of America

Erich Muehlegger, *University of California, Davis, and NBER,* United States of America

David S. Rapson, *University of California, Davis,* United States of America

Executive Summary

This paper identifies and quantifies major determinants of future electric vehicle demand to inform widely held aspirations for market growth. Our model compares three channels that will affect electric vehicle market share in the United States from 2020 to 2035: intrinsic (no-subsidy) electric vehicle demand growth, net-of-subsidy electric vehicle cost declines (e.g., batteries), and government subsidies. Geographic variation in preferences for sedans and light trucks highlights the importance of viable electric vehicle alternatives to conventional light trucks; belief in climate change is highly correlated with electric vehicle adoption patterns; and the first $500 billion in cumulative nationwide electric vehicle subsidies is associated a 7%–10% increase in electric vehicle market share in 2035, an effect that diminishes as subsidies increase. The rate of intrinsic demand growth dwarfs the impact of demand-side subsidies and battery cost declines, highlighting the importance of nonmonetary factors (e.g., charging infrastructure, product quality, and/or cultural acceptance) on electric vehicle demand.

JEL Codes: R4, Q47, Q48, Q55

Keywords: electric vehicles, demand growth, future adoption, transportation policy

I. Introduction

The rate of transportation electrification in the United States will be determined by three forces: intrinsic growth in demand for electric vehicles

Environmental and Energy Policy and the Economy, volume 3, 2022.

(EVs), production cost declines, and government stimulus of the industry. Many climate change mitigation plans incorporate rapid adoption of light-duty EVs as a central pillar of decarbonization efforts. The aspiration in many circles is to achieve 100% electric transportation, and several countries and states have declared their intention to ban gasoline car sales.[1] To ascertain the feasibility (and even the desirability) of these goals, a clearer understanding of the obstacles and opportunities to widespread EV adoption is needed.

This paper has three main goals. First, we seek to identify cross-sectional patterns in recent adoption of light-duty cars and trucks using a large, nationwide micro-level data set of car purchases from the market research firm MaritzCX ("Maritz"). These patterns reflect potential determinants of future EV adoption in the United States. Second, we demonstrate the important role that growth in intrinsic demand (as opposed to subsidy-induced demand) plays in achieving targets for future EV market share.[2] For our analysis, "intrinsic demand growth" includes such factors as increased widespread acceptance of EVs, the convenience of charging infrastructure, and the effect of EV quality improvements that will likely result from continued technological advancements in battery production. Third, we use a range of plausible EV demand elasticities to estimate the effect of EV purchase subsidies. This allows us to present the range of aggregate subsidy bills that will be required to meet different EV market share targets by 2035 under a given set of assumptions. The reader may then observe the subsidy bill associated with the reader's preferred assumptions about intrinsic EV demand growth, the demand elasticity of EVs, and the availability of viable substitutes for gasoline-powered light trucks.[3]

Methodologically, this exercise requires developing EV market share forecasts—the range of counterfactual levels of adoption that could be expected to occur without government subsidies. We use Maritz microdata to identify cross-sectional drivers of EV demand using a probit model. This model can be projected forward to include factors such as population and income growth, which are allowed to vary at the state level. We then adjust these forecasts upward to account for a range of intrinsic growth rates in EV demand. Policy nudges and changing tastes for EVs will have heterogeneous impacts across the population. Through our modeling approach, price effects and intrinsic demand influence future market shares in ways that make intuitive sense; consumers close to the margin for purchasing an EV are much more responsive to changes in prices or intrinsic demand than consumers far from the margin. This leads to substantial spatial heterogeneity in the impact of subsidies on future EV market shares.

The results of these scenario forecasts reveal several key insights into the future trajectory of EV market shares. First, demographic and geographic differences in vehicle preferences are large and important. EV demand is strongly correlated with higher levels of income and education, and EV adoption is highest among car buyers 35–45 years old. More liberal and coastal states tend to have higher demand for sedans and EVs, which, to date, are primarily available as sedans. On the other hand, car buyers in interior states have substantially higher demand for light trucks and lower demand for EVs. These patterns speak to the importance of a portfolio of EV light trucks in achieving adoption targets. Because light trucks comprise more than half the new cars sold in the United States and have not been widely available in EV power trains, it is difficult to rely on revealed preference approaches to estimate future demand in this crucial market segment. If (or when) a robust slate of EV light trucks is available, the difference between the demographics of EV buyers and those of buyers of conventional light trucks suggests an uphill climb for EV adoption in the interior of the country. These demographic patterns mirror stated environmental preferences—EV demand exhibits a strong, positive correlation with stated preference for environmental cleanliness, and regions with high light truck market share report low rates of concern about climate change.

Second, the rate of growth in intrinsic demand for EVs is the most important determinant of future EV market share. It reflects the extent to which, in the absence of government subsidies, buyers prefer EVs to gasoline-powered cars. Our "high-," "medium-," and "low-" growth scenarios intend to capture the wide range of potential outcomes in the market. Beliefs about the intrinsic growth rate going forward are likely to differ from reader to reader. In the absence of government subsidies, and assuming that EV light trucks have emerged as viable substitutes in that segment, the low-growth scenario leads to a nationwide EV market share of 10% in 2035. The medium and high-growth scenarios lead to EV market shares of 17% and 42%, respectively. These nationwide market shares obscure substantial geographic heterogeneity. In the medium-growth scenario, EVs have a 2035 market share of 26% in California and New Jersey and 14%–16% in states like Mississippi, Arkansas, and Louisiana.

Third, government subsidies can be an effective tool for stimulating EV demand, but the aggregate subsidy bill grows dramatically as the size of the EV market increases. Assuming an EV demand elasticity of 2.0, the first $500 billion in cumulative EV subsidies over the period 2020–35 increases EV market share by roughly 7–10 percentage points in each of the (low/medium/high) intrinsic growth scenarios. If the reader prefers a higher demand elasticity (3.0) or lower (1.0), the first $500 billion in subsidies has a slightly larger (10–12 percentage points) or smaller (5–6 percentage points) increase, respectively. However, there are diminishing returns. Under the 2.0 elasticity assumption, each subsequent $500 billion increases EV market share by closer to 5–8 percentage points.

These findings offer several considerations for policy makers. Geographic heterogeneity in the demand for EVs reinforces the efficiency of policies that differ across time and space.[4] The growth rate in EV market share should be monitored by authorities and may inform optimal adjustments in EV targets. This is particularly true when considering the optimal level of consumer purchase subsidies for EVs. The subsidy bill required to achieve even moderate EV market share could likely measure in the hundreds of billions of dollars, and possibly trillions, and the effect of these subsidies is dwarfed by other factors that influence the intrinsic demand for electrified transportation services.

Section II describes the data sets that we use; Section III discusses recent trends and correlations in EV adoption; Section IV describes the probit model and methodology underlying the intrinsic growth rate scenarios; and Section V presents the main results and implications for EV adoption in the United States. Section VI concludes.

II. Data

This section describes our three data sources. The primary data source is a large-scale, nationwide survey of vehicle purchase decisions, which we use to investigate cross-sectional patterns in demand. The forecasting scenarios also require data on state-level EV incentives and demographic forecasts.

A. Vehicle Choice Survey

The primary data underlying our analysis are a survey of US new vehicle purchasers conducted by Maritz. The survey is sent to a random sample of households who purchased a new vehicle in the past year. More than 200,000 individuals respond each year. The survey includes questions about vehicle attributes, intended uses, personal attitudes that may affect vehicle choice, preferences over hypothetical vehicle attributes, financing and purchase details, household composition, demographic information, and vehicle holdings, and forward-looking questions about future vehicle purchases.

Maritz additionally incorporates information such as the home zip code of the buyer and portions of the vehicle identification number (VIN) that are known at the time of vehicle purchase. We match supplied components of the VIN with a VIN decoder from DataONE to determine detailed vehicle attributes such as the power train type and—in the case of EVs—the battery capacity and all-electric range.

We rely on data for vehicles purchased in the 2017 and 2018 calendar years, which are the most recent years available at the time of this writing. This is a rich source of information on EV purchases. Of the 474,274 survey responses during this period, 6,196 were purchases of BEVs and a further 9,280 were PHEVs, covering the full range of BEV and PHEV models available at the time.

Although surveys are sent to a random sample of new vehicle purchasers, responses are a nonrandom subset. In all analyses, we reweight the responses using nationally representative sampling weights provided by Maritz. These weights balance the composition of vehicle make-model pairs in survey responses with the true national distribution.

B.   Incentives

To calculate the subsidy available to the buyer, we focus on large-scale, statewide incentive programs that provide monetary subsidies for EV purchases, either through rebates or tax credits, as well as the federal tax credit. We do not account for corporate incentive programs, such as those provided locally by utility companies, local government subsidies, or charging infrastructure incentives. We compile data on the amount of subsidy, the qualification requirements, and eligible purchase dates for each program primarily from the database of laws and incentives from the Alternative Fuels Data Center (AFDC) at the US Department of Energy.[5] The AFDC database is updated at the closure of each state's legislative season and contains information on current and expired subsidy programs. Supplementary information is sourced from state-specific program websites, state departments of revenue websites, automotive industry websites, and contemporary news articles for expired programs. For the years of the sample, 2017–18, 16 states operated incentive programs. Table 1 details the programs, dates, and maximum subsidy offered by each state. As we observe purchase date, income, and vehicle characteristics, we are able to accurately attribute potential subsidy amounts, which vary along these dimensions in most states. However, we do not observe actual subsidy take-up at the individual level. Conditional on qualifying for a state-level subsidy, the average subsidy amount is $2,164, with 46% of nationwide EV sales qualifying for a state-level subsidy.

Table 1
State-Level Plug-in Electric Vehicle Incentives

	State-Level Electric Vehicle Policies		
State	Policy	Max. Subsidy	Notes
Arkansas	Alternative Fuels Vehicle and Rebate Program	$2,500	Rebate for the cost difference between an EV and similar ICE. Ran out of funds in 4/2018
California	Clean Vehicle Rebate Project	$2,500	Means-tested rebate program for EV purchases
Colorado	Innovative Motor Vehicle Credit	$5,000	Tax credit of $5,000 for EVs
Connecticut	Connecticut Hydrogen and Electric Automobile Purchase Rebate	$3,000	Rebate that varies by the electric range of the vehicle
Delaware	Delaware Clean Vehicle Rebate Program	$3,500	Varies by price and electric engine type
District of Columbia	Excise Tax Credit for Plug-in Vehicles	6%	Vehicle excise tax waiver that can reach up to 6% of the purchase price
Louisiana	Alternative Fuel Vehicle Tax Credit	$3,000	Tax credit available for BEV purchases only
Maryland	Excise Tax Credit for Plug-in Electric Vehicles	$3,000	Tax credit starting in July 2017 that varies by battery size
Massachusetts	Massachusetts Offers Rebate for Electric Vehicles	$2,500	Rebate that varies by the purchase price of the vehicle and electric engine type
New Jersey	Sales Tax Exemption	6.87%	Sales tax exemption that applies to only BEV purchases
New York	Drive Clean Rebate	$2,000	Varies by purchase price and electric range of vehicle
Oregon	Clean Vehicle Rebate Program	$2,500	Begins in 2018 for BEVs only. Varies by battery size and purchase price
Pennsylvania	Alternative Fuel Vehicle Rebate	$2,000	Rebate varies by battery size and purchase price
Rhode Island	Driving Rhode Island to Vehicle Electrification Rebate Program	$2,500	Rebate varies by battery size and ends in July 2017
Texas	Alternative Fuel Vehicle Rebate	$2,500	Rebate starts in September 2018. Does not apply to Tesla vehicles
Washington	Alternative Fuels Tax Credit	6.50%	Ends in July 2017 and varies by battery size

Note: BEV = battery electric vehicle; EV = electric vehicle; ICE = internal combustion engine.

C. Demographic Forecasts

Demographic forecasts account for changes in population by age group and race across states. We collect forecast data from the Demographics Research Group at the University of Virginia's Weldon Cooper Center. Population estimates are published for 2020, 2030, and 2040, broken out by state, race, and age group cells. The model is built upon data from the past three decennial national censuses from the US Census Bureau as well as the July 2017 population estimate update from the bureau. The 2020 state population totals are projected from 2010 and 2017 state levels, assuming an exponential growth pattern. The 2030 and 2040 estimates use the Hamilton-Perry projection approach and account for birth rate, mortality, and migration patterns.[6]

III. Past Evidence on EV Adoption

The goal of this paper is to project EV market share to (1) understand the feasibility and costs associated with achieving ambitious fleet adoption targets and (2) compare the relative importance of various drivers of EV adoption. But before we discuss the projection of EV market share, we summarize historical trends in rates of adoption and the cross-sectional variation relevant to our analysis.

Early adoption of EVs, like early adoption of many other new technologies, has experienced dramatic growth in a short period of time. Figure 1 graphs the 3-year moving average year-on-year growth rate of EV sales from 2012 to the present for California and the United States more generally. In the first few years of EV sales, sales doubled every year or two. Yet, similar to many other new technologies, as annual sales increase, year-on-year growth rates decline, reflecting both the greater difficulty in achieving a high growth rate over a larger base of sales and the maturation of the technology. In the case of EVs, the year-on-year growth rate has fallen to roughly 30% for the United States (and slightly lower for California, where the market share of EVs is higher).

The growth rates illustrated in figure 1 represent adoption that, up to the present, has been selective in many ways. As an example, California's robust rates of EV adoption have been supported by aggressive state-level incentives, supplementary to those offered federally, with the goal of further closing the upfront cost gap between electric and conventional vehicles. In addition, the population of California might be predisposed to adopt EVs, even in the absence of a subsidy. The population is relatively

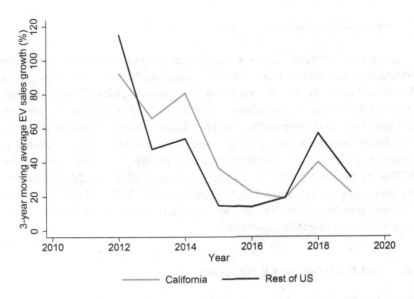

Fig. 1. Moving average electric vehicle (EV) sales growth. Color version available as an online enhancement.

Notes: Three-year moving average growth in EV sales for California and the remainder of the United States.

wealthy, liberal, and concerned about climate change. Drivers in the state have a relative preference for sedans, for which a suite of electric-powered options are available; this draws a distinction with light trucks, for which current EV options are limited. Rates of adoption have lagged in states with a higher rural population share, states that offer little in the way of supplementary EV incentives, or states with populations less engaged with environmental issues and more likely to purchase light trucks.

Regional purchase patterns in the Maritz data highlight the correlation between state-level EV adoption and preferences for different types of vehicles. Figure 2 maps the market shares of EVs, sedans, and SUVs and pickup trucks by state, as reported in the Maritz data. As panels A and B illustrate, states that have experienced relatively high EV adoption to date (panel A) were states that also had a relative preference for sedans. In contrast, many of the states with relatively low EV adoption to date are states whose drivers reveal a preference for vehicle classes currently lacking models with electric power trains. The central challenge in our paper is unpacking the various drivers of EV adoption so as to understand whether adoption rates in much of the country will catch up to those in California or whether adoption in many parts of the country will

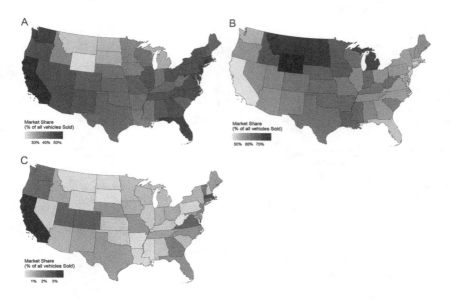

Fig. 2. Vehicle type market shares. Color version available as an online enhancement. Notes: Market share for sedans (*A*), trucks (*B*), and electric vehicles (*C*) from Maritz survey respondents in 2017 and 2018. Washington, DC, excluded from the scale.

continue to lag, even after EV prices fall closer to parity with conventional vehicles and automakers expand the suite of EV light trucks.

As a starting point for examining cross-sectional variation in adoption, we summarize the demographics of EV purchasers in the Maritz data to illustrate the selection into the decision to purchase an EV. The graphs in figure 3 report average EV adoption by income, age, education, and ethnicity. The relationship between early EV adoption and income aligns with previous academic evidence (e.g., Borenstein and Davis 2016), which finds that early tax credits accrue disproportionately to high-income households. From a policy perspective, the strong correlation between adoption and incomes motivates policy makers to means test EV incentives so as to better achieve distributional objectives (see, e.g., the Enhanced Fleet Modernization Program [EFMP] studied by Muehlegger and Rapson [2018] and adjustments to California's Clean Vehicle Rebate Program in and after 2016). Although our data cover a later time period than that covered by Borenstein and Davis (2016), we also observe that EV ownership and incomes are positively correlated, reflective of the high cost of upfront purchase and the continued relative scarcity of used EVs. Less well documented are the relationships between other sociodemographic variables and EV adoption. Educational attainment, like income, is strongly correlated with

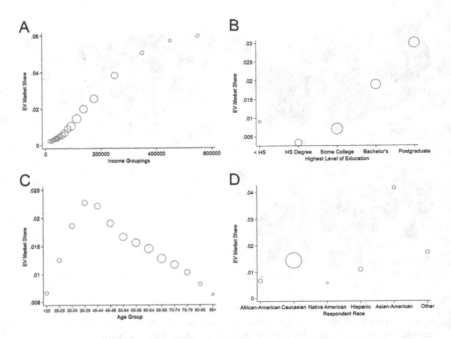

Fig. 3. Demographic characteristics and electric vehicle (EV) adoption. Color version available as an online enhancement.
Source: Maritz.

EV adoption. College graduates and those with postgraduate degrees are roughly three times as likely to own an EV as less educated drivers. In panels C and D, patterns of ownership emerge for age brackets and self-designated ethnicity: Middle-aged drivers (between ages 35 and 44) are the most likely to own EVs, as are Asian Americans.

Just as demographics vary for buyers of EVs and conventional light trucks, so do the environmental attitudes of areas preferring one or the other. In figure 4 we plot the fraction of the state population that affirmed a belief in climate change (Howe et al. 2015) against the EV share of the sedan market (panel A) and the light truck share of the overall market. Although we can only speculate as to how current buyers of light trucks might choose among electric and conventional options, panels A and B of the figure provide suggestive evidence that, even with a suite of EV light trucks, adoption may lag in states that have historically preferred light trucks to sedans. The data in panel A illustrate a strong positive relationship between environmental beliefs and EV share of the sedan market. Although some of the positive relationship is likely driven by the endogeneity of state-level incentives (such as the largest circle, representing California), state-level incentives

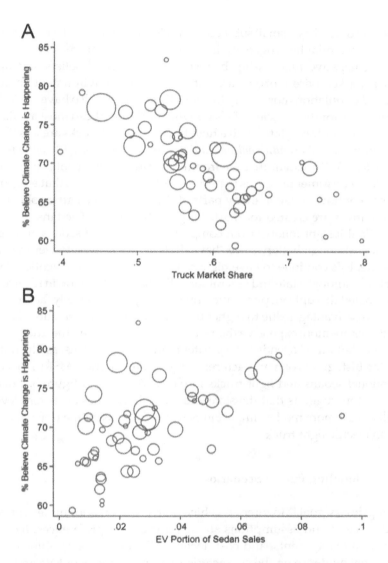

Fig. 4. Climate change beliefs and vehicle adoption. Color version available as an online enhancement.

Notes: The x-axis plots to the share of EVs as a fraction of total sedan sales (*A*) and the share of light trucks as a fraction of total vehicle sales (*B*). The y-axis plots the share of a state's population that answered affirmatively to the question "Do you believe that climate change is happening?" (Howe et al. 2015), available via the Yale Climate Opinion Map, https://climatecommunication.yale.edu/visualizations-data/ycom-us/. The size of the circles reflects 2020 population.

are only offered by a small subset of states. In contrast, panel B suggests not only substantial heterogeneity in preferences for light trucks but also a strong negative relationship between environmental beliefs and light truck market share. Not only are states with a more environmentally concerned population more likely to adopt EVs, but they also have a relative preference for the vehicle classes for which EVs have been most available to date. In contrast, states with a high fraction of light trucks are less likely to purchase EVs *conditional on buying a sedan for which EV options are available*. To the extent that environmental preferences continue to play a role in consumer decisions to purchase EVs, this suggests that adoption might continue to lag in many parts of the country even after robust EV alternatives are created for market segments outside of sedans.

A final insight follows from comparing the prices of sedans and light trucks. Although battery prices have declined substantially over the past decade, EVs continue to have higher upfront costs than conventional vehicles.[7] Although state and federal subsidies have reduced or, in rare cases, eliminated this upfront price differential, EV light trucks likely face greater price disadvantages due to higher battery capacity requirements.[8] Larger batteries are more expensive than smaller ones. Moreover, the underlying price of light trucks tends to be greater than those of sedans, as illustrated by the histograms of manufacturer suggested retail price (MSRP) for conventional sedans and light trucks in panels A and B of figure 5. Collectively, this suggests that the state and federal subsidies at current levels will have a more modest impact in percentage terms on the upfront price of an electric light truck.

IV. Modeling Future Scenarios

Our primary goal is to forecast vehicle purchase behavior under various estimates of and assumptions about vehicle class preferences, technological advancements, and cost declines. To do so, we combine cross-sectional evidence on the characteristics of past buyers of EVs and past buyers of sedans with a projection of the continued rate of growth in intrinsic demand for EVs.

A.   *Estimating Cross-Sectional Patterns in Adoption*

Using the individual-level Maritz survey data of recent new vehicle purchases, we model a discrete purchase choice of individual i, such as whether the vehicle is classified as a light truck or is an EV, as a function

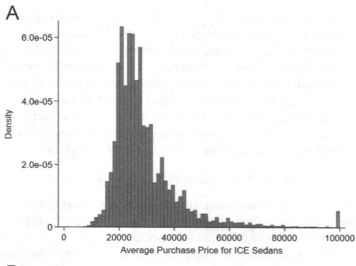

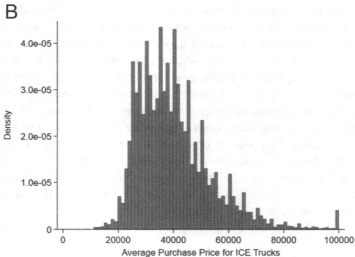

Fig. 5. Vehicle purchase price by vehicle class. Color version available as an online enhancement.

Notes: Figures plot the histograms of vehicle purchase price for conventional sedans (*A*) and light trucks/SUVs (*B*).

Source: Maritz.

of the purchased vehicle price (p_i), a vector of demographic information of the purchaser (X_i), and an unobserved error μ_i. We additionally include a term representing consumers' intrinsic preference for the attribute (δ_i), which can change over time. It is assumed to be zero during the period used to estimate model parameters but may change in the future as consumer preferences change. We assume the market share of choice y is the inverse normal with variance one of a linear combination of these factors. In this probit framework, the probability that consumer i chooses a vehicle with discrete attribute y, and hence the market share of y $(S(y))$, is

$$S(y) = Pr\,(Y_i = y) = \Phi(\alpha p_i + X_i\beta + \delta_i + \mu_i),$$

where $\Phi(\cdot)$ is the cumulative distribution function of the standard normal.

Paramount among these drivers of consumer choice is vehicle price. Rather than empirically estimate the impact of prices on purchase decisions, we rely on estimates of price responsiveness from the literature. We assume the price elasticity of new vehicle demand is –0.4. We additionally model substitution between conventional cars and EVs and assume, conditional on purchasing a vehicle of a given class, the elasticity of demand for EVs is –2.0. We have chosen –2.0 as an approximate midpoint of the range of existing estimates that are not focused exclusively on lower-income segments (which are likely to be more price elastic).[9] All else equal, a higher demand elasticity increases the effectiveness of subsidies.

In the probit formulation above, the price elasticity of market share will vary across the space of observed prices and demographic attributes. We choose a value of α so this elasticity is equal to the targeted value at the mean market share. Formally, if $S(y)$ is the market share of attribute y and $\bar{p}$ is the average price of a good with that attribute, the price elasticity of market share is

$$\frac{\partial S}{\partial \bar{p}} \frac{\bar{p}}{S} = \alpha\phi(\Phi^{-1}(S))\frac{\bar{p}}{S}.$$

Solving for α, we find the value of the price parameter that leads to the desired price elasticity (e) of market share at the mean:

$$\alpha^* = \frac{e \cdot S}{\phi(\Phi^{-1}(S)) \cdot \bar{p}}.$$

We then estimate the remaining model parameters $(\beta$ and $z)$ from observed purchase behavior using the probit, including the price effect $\alpha^* \cdot p$ as a fixed value with its coefficient constrained to one.

We estimate two functions mapping demographics to market shares. First, among all vehicle purchases, our "Vehicle Class" market share model ($S^T(\cdot)$) estimates the relationship between demographics and the market share of vehicles classified as "light trucks" (i.e., an SUV, pickup truck, or van) as $Y^T = 1$ or vehicles we will classify as "cars" (i.e., a coupe, sedan, or hatchback) as $Y^T = 0$. Second, among only purchases of cars, we estimate the relationship between demographics and the market share of EVs (i.e., a BEV or PHEV) as $Y^{EV} = 1$ or a vehicle with some other power train as $Y^{EV} = 0$ in the "Power Train" model ($S^{EV}(\cdot)$).

Combining these models allows us to predict the probability a consumer with a given set of demographic variables (X_i) would purchase a given vehicle—such as an EV car—as outlined in figure 6. We first apply the Vehicle Class model to determine the probability a consumer

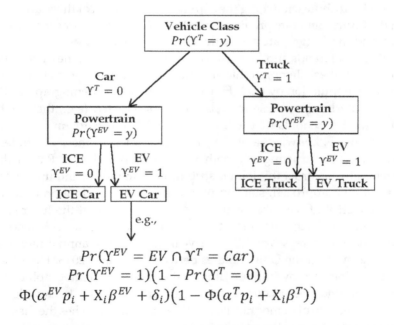

$$Pr(Y^{EV} = EV \cap Y^T = Car)$$
$$Pr(Y^{EV} = 1)\bigl(1 - Pr(Y^T = 0)\bigr)$$
$$\Phi(\alpha^{EV}p_i + X_i\beta^{EV} + \delta_i)\bigl(1 - \Phi(\alpha^T p_i + X_i\beta^T)\bigr)$$

Fig. 6. Market share model outline. Color version available as an online enhancement. Notes: Outline of the probit model used to predict vehicle market shares. The parameters α^{EV} and α^T are price effects for electric vehicles (EVs) and trucks, respectively. These parameters are fixed prior to estimation of the model to achieve an assumed price elasticity of market share at the average consumer. The parameter δ_i in the power train component is the intrinsic preference for EVs and is constant across all consumers in a given year. Is it zero in 2020 and increases over time so business as usual EV market share (absent price effects and demographic change) matches the assumed growth rate. ICE = internal combustion engine.

would elect to purchase a vehicle in the car class, and then apply the Power Train model to determine the likelihood, conditional on purchasing a vehicle, they elect to purchase one with an EV power train.[10]

B.   Future EV Adoption Scenarios

Based on the estimates from current patterns of adoption, we examine several scenarios to understand how EV entry into the light-duty truck segment and government subsidies might play a role in achieving national adoption targets. Equipped with estimates of the Vehicle Class and Power Train models, we are able to generate counterfactual probabilities of vehicle purchase for hypothetical consumers across the space of possible combinations of demographic variables. To simulate future vehicle purchases, we construct a population of individuals with demographic attributes matching the expected distribution of those attributes in the future, generate predicted purchase probabilities for each individual, and then aggregate across the entire population.

Historical trends and forecasts can allow us to predict the distribution of some of these demographic variables into the future (e.g., household income, population by age). However, many of the demographic attributes entering into these models are not forecasted (e.g., the number of future households that will value a vehicle for its towing capacity). Furthermore, knowledge of the *joint* distribution of these attributes is critical for constructing a hypothetical future population. Rather than attempt to construct this joint distribution from the ground up, we take a top-down approach, starting with the current distribution of demographic attributes as observed in our data to construct the future joint distribution of demographic attributes. To do so, we assume real household income increases at 1.2% per year, the average annual rate of income growth in the United States between 1970 and 2018. Household incomes increase over time without altering other demographic attributes. Second, we account for changes in population by reweighing the distribution of demographic variables so that it matches the distribution of population in the state by 5-year age bins in forecasts from Demographics Research Group (2018).[11]

Specific to the market for EVs, we focus on three factors that shift the future path of EV adoption. The first of these relates to the continued growth rate of intrinsic EV demand. One may expect that as the quality, range, or set of EV available models increases consumers may be more likely to purchase an EV, regardless of the price. Furthermore, charging infrastructure density and range limitation perceptions may continue to evolve over time in ways that increase demand for EVs. The intrinsic growth rate reflects the subsidy-free rate of growth in EV adoption that may result from these and other nonprice factors. These may include improvements in EV technology, build-outs in EV charging infrastructure, supply-side mandates, extensions of the product suite, and any network externalities that may result from EVs becoming a greater fraction of the vehicle fleet.

The intrinsic growth parameter is one of the most glaring unknowns facing the vehicle industry, policy makers, and researchers. Figure 1 shows the 3-year moving average annual growth rate in EV sales for California (light) and the rest of the United States (dark). To date, year-over-year growth in sales has generally exceeded 20% per year but has been declining in a manner similar to the growth rates for many other new technologies. This is to be expected in a young and maturing industry. In our analysis, we calibrate year-over-year demand growth in 2020 to the observed value of 30%. Acknowledging demand for EVs cannot grow at this rate indefinitely, we assume this growth rate decreases over time. We construct three benchmark scenarios wherein the year-on-year *rate of growth* of the intrinsic demand for EVs declines by 5% (high growth), 10% (medium growth) or 15% (low growth) per annum.

Under these scenarios, intrinsic demand for (and the resulting market share of) EVs will initially grow quickly, but at a rate that decreases and approaches zero over time. Figure 7 shows how these scenarios predict EV market shares will evolve over time, holding all other factors constant. Panel A shows EV market shares through our forecast horizon of 2035. Because growth of EV market share is compounding, it is clear that small changes in the assumed rate of EV market share growth have large impacts on market shares in 2035. Panel B demonstrates the difficulty in using past data to predict future market share growth. Starting in 2020, we backcast market shares from each of these scenarios to 2011 and plot them along actual EV market shares. Each of the high, medium, and low growth rate scenarios is consistent with the history of observed market shares. Finally, panel C shows the assumed year-over-year growth rates for each scenario in each year through 2035. EV market shares are assumed to be increasing at nearly 15% per year in 2035 under the high-growth scenario and at around 4% per year under the low-growth scenario.

We allow for the role of these time-varying preferences for EVs to enter into our market shares through the intrinsic preference parameter δ_i. This parameter is assumed to be zero during and before 2020 but is

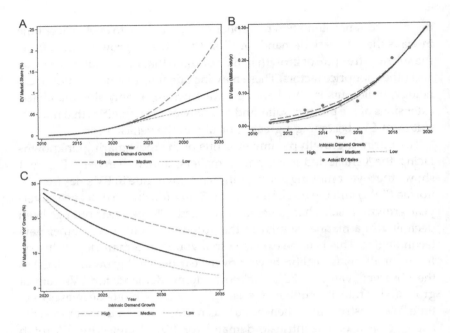

Fig. 7. Future business as usual electric vehicle (EV) sales growth scenarios. Color version available as an online enhancement.

Notes: Absent other intervention, EV sales grow at 30% year over year (YoY) in 2020. That rate of increase decreases by 5%, 10%, and 15% in the high–, baseline–, and low–EV growth scenarios. The full path of EV market share through 2035 is shown in panel A. EV sales following this pattern are backcasted to 2010 and contrasted with actual sales (dots) in panel B. The rate of YoY sales growth in each scenario is shown in panel C.

allowed to change in future years as consumer preferences for EVs change. We compute the value of this intrinsic preference parameter as the value δ_i^*, which rationalizes the assumed growth in EV market shares under a business as usual (no subsidies or demographic change) scenario. We then use this value of δ_i^* as the value of intrinsic preference when forecasting EV market shares.

The second factor is continued reductions in the price of EVs, driven either by falling production costs (e.g., as a result of economies of scale in battery production) or through continued or new government subsidies. Recall that we precondition the impact of prices out of decisions and demographic attributes prior to estimating the purchase models. After computing predictions from these models, we reincorporate price effects based on the composition of future prices. We assume consumers respond only to the net price of a vehicle (i.e., inclusive of any subsidies) and present several scenarios for the future evolution of EV prices. In all scenarios, we assume prices of non-EVs are constant in real terms.

As a starting point, we assume that the sedan and light truck EV markets reach price parity with gasoline cars in 2030 and 2040, respectively.[12] At that point, the average (unsubsidized) price of EVs will equal that of gasoline counterparts. In the intervening years, the EV price premium relative to the compatible internal combustion engine (ICE) vehicle falls at a constant rate. The decline in EV prices primarily reflects falling battery costs. This also underlies the rationale for light trucks to reach price parity later, because battery capacity requirements are much higher for these vehicles. In addition, we consider the impact of an extension of the federal subsidy of $7,500 per vehicle.[13]

Finally, we assume that, over time, the EV offerings available in the light truck market expand to saturate the product space. Although it is not possible to forecast the evolutionary path (i.e., range, power, and other attributes) of EV light trucks, we make the assumption that by 2035 EV light trucks have reached "quality parity" with EV sedans, such that the conditional probability of a buyer of choosing an EV when purchasing a light truck is equal to the conditional probability of the same buyer of choosing an EV when purchasing a sedan.

V.   Results and Discussion

A.   *Factors Correlated with EV Adoption*

We employ a single set of demographic variables to estimate both the Vehicle Class and Power Train market share models. Our selection of candidate variables was driven by two factors. First, no question in the Maritz survey requires a response, so we considered only demographic factors that were supplied by at least 80% of survey respondents. Second, our methodology in forecasting future purchase behavior allows for common demographic factors to change over time. The survey includes an array of questions on the underlying reasons for purchasing a vehicle (e.g., did the consumer purchase the vehicle because they value fuel economy). Although these attitudes are likely strong drivers of purchase behavior, there are scant projections of how these attitudes may convolve with other demographic factors over time. Consequently, we exclude responses designed to elicit attitudes underlying purchase reasons. Because we allow demographic factors to enter into these models flexibly, the effect of evolving attitudes will be reflected in forward forecasts to the extent attitudes are correlated with demographic factors included in our model.

The demographic factors included in the purchase model are annual vehicle miles traveled, annual household income, family size, portion of vehicles owned by the household falling into each of four classes (cars, pickups, SUVs, and vans),[14] age of the primary driver, income of the primary driver, and race of the primary driver. The true relationship underlying our market share models may be nonlinear or depend on interactions of these variables. We consider a space of candidate models of up to third-order interactions of all these candidate variables and select preferred models as the specification that minimizes mean square out-of-sample prediction error using 10-fold cross-validation. Using this procedure, the full set of these demographic factors and their second-order interactions form the controls in the Vehicle Class model and the full set of demographic factors absent interactions form the set of demographic variables in the Power Train model.[15]

We evaluate the predictions of these models by forecasting purchase probabilities and comparing to realized purchase behavior. Histograms from out-of-sample predicted probabilities from each model, grouped by the actual purchase behavior, are shown in figure 8. The Vehicle Class model strongly predicts observed behavior. Very few individuals with low predicted probabilities of purchasing a truck actually do so. Likewise, few individuals with large predicted probabilities of purchasing a truck actually purchase a car instead. The Power Train model is not as strongly discriminating between EV and ICE purchases, revealing the extent to which unobservable factors drive the EV adoption decision. However, the model still clearly has predictive power, with a substantially higher density predicting EV purchases among the population of consumers who actually purchased EVs.

B.   Future EV Adoption Paths

The primary goal of our paper is focus attention on three important drivers of future EV adoption: (1) assumptions about the intrinsic (subsidy-free) rate of growth of EV sales, (2) the role of subsidies or further production efficiency gains that push EVs below the point of cost parity with conventional vehicles, and (3) the importance of a robust portfolio of electric light trucks that complement the slate of electric sedans.

As discussed above, we model future adoption by combining the cross-sectional variation from the Maritz data (reflecting preferences for EVs

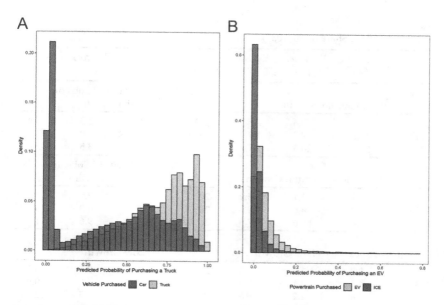

Fig. 8. Purchase behavior model predictions by Vehicle Class model (*A*) and Power Train model (*B*). Color version available as an online enhancement.

Notes: Histogram of the predicted purchase probability by the actual purchase behavior of consumers in the Maritz survey. Densities are weighted by survey weights. Perfect predictions would result in a single dark bar at zero and a single light bar at 1. EV = electric vehicle; ICE = internal combustion engine.

and preferences for light trucks), with a projection of how intrinsic preferences have changed since the inception of the industry. Table 2 presents six panels, each of which presents the market share of EV sedans, EV trucks, and the totals for the EV market through 2035 for one of the considered scenarios. Each row of scenarios corresponds to one of the three assumptions about the future rate of intrinsic growth in the demand for EVs.[16] The left column of scenarios assumes that EVs reach price parity in 2030 and remain there. The right column of scenarios assumes, in addition to price parity, a continuation of the federal subsidy of $7,500 per vehicle. Although we frame these scenarios as a continuation of the federal subsidy, because the consumer only cares about the subsidy-inclusive price of the vehicle, the right column of scenarios could also be thought of as arising from productivity gains that push the sticker price of EVs $7,500 below price parity with conventional vehicles.

Table 2 illustrates the relative importance of the three drivers of future EV adoption. Perhaps unsurprisingly, the most important of the three factors is the rate at which intrinsic growth declines going forward. As

Table 2
Predicted Market Share (2020–2035)

Year	EV Sedans (%)	EV Trucks (%)	EV Total (%)	Year	EV Sedans (%)	EV Trucks (%)	EV Total (%)
	(a) No Subsidies—High			(b) Continued Federal Subsidies—High Growth			
2025	3.7	2.6	6.3	2025	4.9	3.5	8.4
2030	10.0	7.9	17.9	2030	12.1	9.9	22.1
2035	21.4	20.3	41.7	2035	24.1	23.5	47.6
	(c) No Subsidies—Medium Growth			(d) Continued Federal Subsidies—Medium Growth			
2025	3.1	2.1	5.2	2025	4.1	2.9	7.0
2030	6.2	4.6	10.8	2030	7.9	6.0	13.8
2035	9.4	7.6	17.0	2035	11.5	9.6	21.1
	(e) No Subsidies—Low Growth			(f) Continued Federal Subsidies—Low Growth			
2025	2.7	1.8	4.5	2025	3.6	2.5	6.1
2030	4.4	3.1	7.5	2030	5.7	4.2	9.9
2035	5.6	4.2	9.8	2035	7.2	5.5	12.7

Note: Intrinsic demand growth of 30% in 2020 declines at a rate of 5%, 10%, and 15% per year in the high-, medium-, and low-growth cases, respectively. Electric vehicle (EV) cars reach cost parity with their internal combustion engine counterparts in 2030, and trucks in 2040.

illustrated in figure 7, even a relatively modest change in the intrinsic growth rate leads to very significant differences in the rates of future EV growth. In the "high" scenario, where intrinsic rates of EV adoption decline by only 5% per year, the growth rate declines slowly from approximately 30% in 2020 to roughly 15% per year in 2035, whereas in the "low" scenario, the per year growth rate in EV adoption quickly dips into the single digits. These differences translate into large differences in adoption in panels (a), (c), and (e). In the more optimistic of the scenarios, EV market share rises to more than 40%, split roughly equally between EV sedans and EV light trucks, by 2035. In the least optimistic case, in which the growth rate falls to single digits later this decade, the market share of EVs stays below 10% through 2035. Figure 9 provides a graphical illustration of the evolution of predicted market shares over time.

Although we remain agnostic as to which of the three assumptions about intrinsic growth rates is the most appropriate, the data suggest that the intrinsic growth rate is both central to any projection and likely difficult to estimate from historical data. Notably, when "backcasting" the historical market share of EVs in figure 7, panel B, all three growth

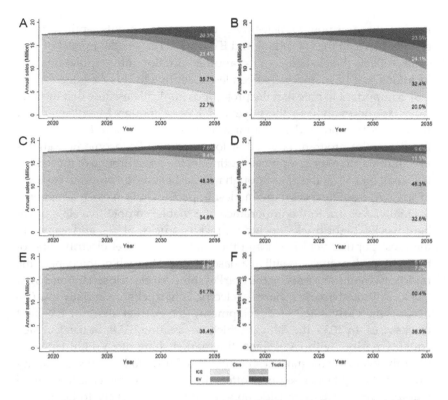

Fig. 9. Sales by vehicle type, with and without subsidies. Color version available as an online enhancement.

Notes: (A) No-subsidy, high EV demand growth; (B) federal subsidy, high EV demand growth; (C) no-subsidy, medium EV demand growth; (D) federal subsidy, medium EV demand growth; (E) no-subsidy, low EV demand growth; and (F) federal subsidy, low EV demand growth. Intrinsic electric vehicle (EV) demand growth is 30% in 2020 and the growth rate declines by 5% (high growth), 10% (medium growth), or 15% (low growth) each year. ICE = internal combustion engine.

rate scenarios do a reasonable job. This suggests that, although the rate of intrinsic growth is a very important driver of the future adoption path, historical data do not provide a clear guide as to how intrinsic growth might evolve over the next 2 decades.

Next, we consider the impacts of a continuation of the $7,500-per-vehicle federal subsidy. The left-hand and right-hand columns of scenarios in table 2 contain the projections without and with the federal subsidy, respectively.[17] Relative to the impact of the intrinsic growth rate, the impact of subsidies is more modest, although still considerable. Across the low-, medium-, and high-growth-rate scenarios, subsidies increase the market share of new vehicles by 3–6 percentage points, split roughly equally between the EV sedans and EV trucks. The smaller impact of subsidies reflects the challenge of expanding adoption into populations and locations that have generally been less receptive to EVs to date.

It is important to note that the projections implicitly assume that the subsidies accrue entirely to the buyers of EVs. Although Muehlegger and Rapson (2018) find evidence of rates of pass-through close to one for the EFMP, a pilot program targeted at low- and middle-income households in California, no paper empirically estimates the pass-through of the federal tax credit on EVs. If the pass-through rate declines as the program expands in size, we would expect more modest impacts of subsidies on adoption.

Finally, we turn to the importance of a viable, competitive slate of EV light trucks. Light trucks (including pickup trucks, SUVs, and vans) are the most popular vehicle class in the United States. Yet electrification of the light truck segment is still at a nascent stage. In each of the panels, the middle two columns present the market shares of electric sedans and light trucks. Although market shares of electric light trucks are initially low (reflecting the early stage of development), the market share of EV light trucks rises. In 2035, the date at which we assume EV light trucks reach "quality parity" with EV sedans, the market share of EV light trucks is roughly level with the market share of EV sedans. Mathematically, expansion into the light truck segment offers the potential to increase the overall market shares of EVs considerably, an outcome unlikely to be accomplished through EV sedan sales alone.[18]

The roughly equivalent market shares of EV light trucks and EV sedans by 2035 reflect two competing forces. Light trucks, as a class, are more popular than sedans. As illustrated in figure 2, panel B, the light trucks command the majority of the new vehicle sales in virtually every state in the United States.[19] Thus, the overall potential for EV light trucks is greater than that for EV sedans, barring a major shift in consumer preferences (table 3). But the higher market share of light trucks is tempered by the characteristics of the truck buyers, who tend to have less strong preferences for EVs, all else equal, than sedan buyers (see figure 4, panels A and B).

C. Implications for Achieving National EV Goals

As an alternative way of evaluating the feasibility of reaching different adoption targets, we calculate the necessary reductions in the subsidy-inclusive price of EVs, and the implied cumulative government subsidy bill, required in each of our scenarios. Again, despite our framing of the

Table 3
EV Market Share in 2035 by State

State	Intrinsic Demand Growth		
	High (%)	Medium (%)	Low (%)
District of Columbia	64.8	39.9	29.3
California	54.8	26.5	16.6
Connecticut	54.1	26.0	16.2
New Jersey	54.3	25.9	16.1
Maryland	53.8	25.8	16.1
Massachusetts	53.5	25.4	15.8
Hawaii	53.2	25.4	15.9
Rhode Island	52.6	24.3	14.8
Illinois	50.7	23.2	14.2
Virginia	50.1	23.0	14.1
. . .			
Louisiana	40.0	15.8	8.9
West Virginia	39.2	15.4	8.7
South Dakota	38.3	15.0	8.5
Arkansas	38.5	14.8	8.3
North Dakota	38.0	14.5	8.1
Alaska	36.9	14.2	8.0
Idaho	37.9	14.2	7.8
Mississippi	37.4	14.1	7.8
Montana	33.8	12.4	6.8
Wyoming	31.7	11.1	6.0

Note: Intrinsic demand growth of 30% in 2020 declines at a rate of 10% per year. Electric vehicle (EV) cars reach cost parity with their internal combustion engine counterparts in 2030, and trucks in 2040. Market shares assume a $7,500-per-vehicle subsidy on EVs.

"subsidy effect" that will follow, our model does not distinguish between the role of subsidies and the role of falling production costs. From the perspective of the consumer purchasing an EV, a dollar of savings arising from lower production costs is equivalent to a dollar of savings arising from more generous government support received at the time of purchase. Thus, we focus on how much the subsidy-inclusive price must decline to meet different adoption targets in our model. Whether these price reductions are feasible in a "no-subsidy" world is left to the reader's judgment.

A consensus does not exist about the desirable EV market share in the future, or the expected share. California has stated an intention to achieve 100% EV market share by 2035. Under the International Energy Agency's Sustainable Development Scenario, the worldwide market share of EVs will need to reach 30% by 2030 (International Energy Agency 2020). Milovanoff, Posen, and MacLean (2020) estimate that EVs must comprise 90% of the US vehicle fleet by 2050 to limit warming to under 2 degrees Celsius.

Private sector predictions range from 50% EV market share in 2030 (UBS), roughly 50% in 2035 (BNEF), and 18% in 2030 (IHS Markit).

To frame the discussion, we focus on the subsidy requirements to achieve 20% and 35% nationwide US market share in 2035 under our low-, medium-, and high-intrinsic-growth-rate scenarios. These targets represent a substantial increase from the present EV market share in the United States (table 4). Higher targets, although potentially desirable, are either infeasible or prohibitively expensive under our low- and medium-intrinsic-growth-rate scenarios.

Figures 10 and 11 show the relationship between EV market share in 2035 and the required level of government subsidies, where the latter are reported both in per car terms (figure 10) and as the cumulative subsidy bill required from 2020 to 2035 (figure 11).[20] We estimate that, to achieve a 20% EV market share in 2035, the cumulative subsidy bill

Table 4
EV Market Share in 2035 by Model Assumptions

		Intrinsic EV Demand Growth		
Average EV Price ($)	Price Response	High (%)	Medium (%)	Low (%)
40,000	High	36.5	14.6	8.4
40,000	Medium	39.2	15.5	8.8
40,000	Low	42.0	16.7	9.4
37,500	High	39.3	16.2	9.5
37,500	Medium	41.3	16.8	9.6
37,500	Low	43.1	17.4	9.9
35,000[a]	High	42.0	18.1	10.8
35,000[a]	Medium	43.1	18.0	10.5
35,000[a]	Low	44.0	18.0	10.3
32,500	High	44.9	20.0	12.1
32,500	Medium	45.3	19.4	11.5
32,500	Low	45.2	18.7	10.8
30,000	High	47.6	22.1	13.8
30,000	Medium	47.1	20.8	12.5
30,000	Low	46.1	19.4	11.3
27,500	High	50.7	24.3	15.3
27,500	Medium	49.3	22.3	13.5
27,500	Low	47.2	20.2	11.8

Note: Comparison of electric vehicle (EV) market share in 2035 across model assumptions and average EV prices. Average price is the average price paid for all EVs in 2035. Price responses are measured at the consumer with the average valuation and are selected so the price elasticity of market share for that consumer is −3 (high), −2 (medium), or −1 (low). Intrinsic demand growth of 30% in 2020 declines at a rate of 5%, 10%, and 15% per year in the high-, medium-, and low-growth cases, respectively.
[a]Denotes the average price where EVs are at approximate parity with comparable internal combustion engine vehicles.

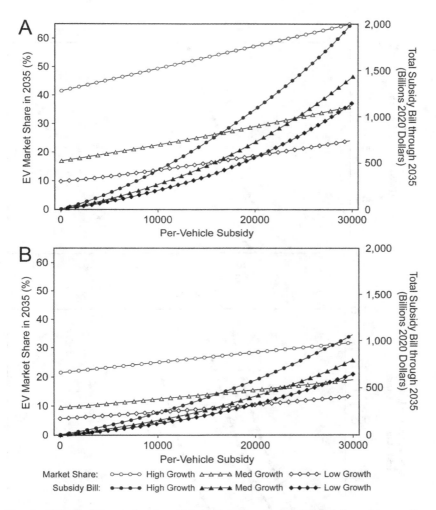

Fig. 10. Subsidy bill and electric vehicle (EV) market share in 2035. Color version available as an online enhancement.

Notes: Total subsidy bill and 2035 EV market share for a range of per-vehicle subsidies. (A) EV cars and trucks available and (B) EV cars only. Present value of the total subsidy bill through 2035 in 2020 dollars, at a 3% discount rate. Scenarios assume intrinsic EV demand growth is 30% in 2020 and declines by 5% (high growth), 10% (medium growth), or 15% (low growth) each year.

under the low– and medium–intrinsic growth scenarios will be $710 and $140 billion, respectively (table 5). To achieve 35% EV market share in 2035, the cumulative subsidy bill increases to $2.7 and $1.3 trillion, respectively, in the low- and medium-growth scenarios. If high intrinsic growth is achieved, the 2035 market share will exceed 40% in the absence of subsidies, so no subsidies would be required.

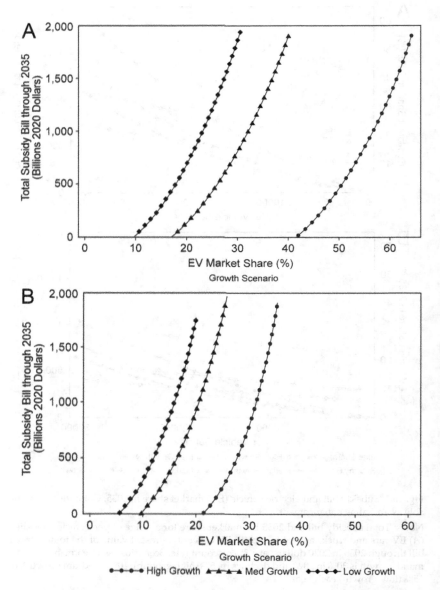

Fig. 11. Subsidy bill to achieve electric vehicle (EV) market share targets in 2035. (*A*) EV cars and trucks available and (*B*) EV cars only. Color version available as an online enhancement.

Notes: Relationship between EV market share in 2035 and the total subsidy bill required to achieve that market share. Present value of the total subsidy bill through 2035 in 2020 dollars, at a 3% discount rate. Scenarios assume intrinsic EV demand growth is 30% in 2020 and declines by 5% (high growth), 10% (medium growth), or 15% (low growth) each year.

Table 5
Total Subsidy Bill to Achieve Target EV Market Shares in 2035

2035 Target EV Market Share (%)	Intrinsic EV Demand Growth		
	High (in billion dollars)	Medium (in billion dollars)	Low (in billion dollars)
20	0	140.2	710.4
35	0	1,356.1	2,735.5
50	481.3	3,562.5	N/A

Note: Comparison of the total subsidy bill required to achieve electric vehicle (EV) market share targets in 2035. Subsidy bills in billions of 2020 dollars with a 3% discount rate. The subsidy is assumed a constant between 2020 and 2035. Intrinsic demand growth of 30% in 2020 declines at a rate of 5%, 10%, and 15% per year in the high-, medium-, and low-growth cases, respectively. No subsidy less than the price of an EV results in the target market share of 50% under the low-EV-demand growth scenario.

Achieving the higher level of EV market share of 50% in 2035 would require dramatically higher subsidies, all else equal. In the low-growth scenario, it would be practically infeasible, requiring subsidies in excess of $30,000 per car. Intrinsic demand in the medium-growth scenario would need to be augmented by $3.6 trillion in total subsidies to achieve 50% market share in 2035, a figure that falls to roughly $480 billion if high intrinsic growth is achieved.

In summary, the cost of reaching ambitious EV market share targets may easily reach trillions of public dollars. These subsidy estimates reinforce one of the main conclusions of this paper: that, although it is possible for subsidies to increase the market share of EVs, subsidies are expensive and have less impact on the rate of EV adoption than other factors that influence intrinsic growth in demand. One such factor may be the density of charging infrastructure. Indeed, some papers have argued that a dollar spent on charging infrastructure will induce more EV demand than a dollar spent on consumer purchase subsidies (e.g., Li et al. 2017). The availability of EV light trucks is likely to be even more important and has the benefit of being a feature that the market is likely to provide even in the absence of government support.

D. Implications for Subnational Adoption

Although the focus of this paper is on national adoption trends, we examine whether EV market share rises evenly across all states or whether some states (e.g., California) remain persistently ahead, even after light truck EVs are well established. As we are not including any state-level

incentives, patterns of EV adoption speak to the importance of the underlying preferences of vehicle buyers. In essence, we ask whether, once a
slate of attractive, electric light trucks exists, adoption patterns in much
of the interior of the United States rise to meet adoption patterns on the
East and West Coasts. Or will adoption in the interior of the United States
continue to lag behind, due to the mix of potential buyers?

In figure 12, we overlay the projected market share of EVs (in total),
electric sedans, and electric light trucks on maps of the United States
in panels A, B, and C, respectively. Panel A illustrates the substantial
variation in adoption across states, even after a competitive slate of light
truck EVs exists. Although market shares have risen in all states, the
market share of EVs remains much higher on the coasts than in the interior of the country, reflective that buyer demographics are more
"EV friendly" on the coasts than in the interior.

From the perspective of environmental policy, relatively lower rates
of adoption in the upper Midwest are beneficial, at least in a future
world in which the marginal unit of the electricity grid in the upper Midwest remains more carbon intensive than the marginal unit of electricity
on the coasts. Holland et al. (2016) document that EVs are generally beneficial from an environmental perspective on the West Coast, due to low
carbon-intensity sources of electricity. In contrast, EVs are significantly
less beneficial relative to a comparable conventional vehicle in many
other parts of the country, although as Holland et al. (2020) note, the
gap between the Midwest and other parts of the country has been closing over the last decade. Yet uneven rates of adoption also raise potential concerns of environmental equality, if rates of EV adoption are significantly higher in more affluent states and cities.

Separating sedan and light truck EV sales further reveals why adoption
rates vary substantially across states. In panel B, state-level variation in
market share of EV sedans is similar to the variation that exists today.
States with buyers who have a relative preference for sedans and are more
"EV friendly" (e.g., California) have higher rates of adoption than states
with buyers who prefer trucks. In panel C, which maps the market share
of EV light trucks in 2035, we see much more heterogeneity. Particularly
instructive is the comparison between Colorado and Wyoming. Both Colorado and Wyoming have populations that prefer light trucks, yet Colorado is higher income and more progressive than Wyoming and, hence,
has a population that is more receptive to EV light trucks.

Figures 13 and 14 both suggest that the impacts of the intrinsic growth
rate and federal subsidies tend to spread the distribution of market

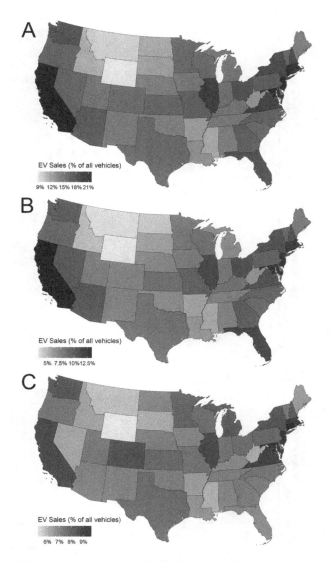

Fig. 12. Electric vehicle (EV) adoption by state, with and without light truck EVs, 2035. (*A*) All EVs, (*B*) sedan EVs, and (*C*) light truck EVs. Color version available as an online enhancement.

Notes: Forecast EV market share by state in 2035. Assumes medium EV demand growth, EV sedans reach price parity with comparable ICEs in 2030, EV trucks reach price parity in 2040, and no federal EV subsidies. Washington, DC, excluded from the scale.

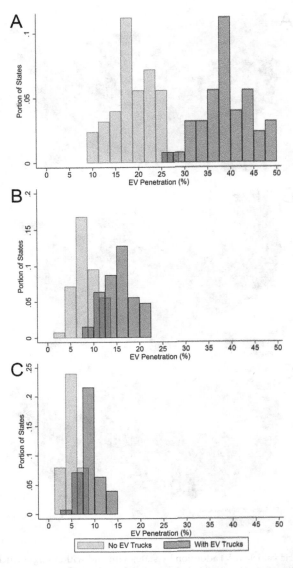

Fig. 13. Heterogeneity in electric vehicle (EV) penetration across states, 2035. Color version available as an online enhancement.

Notes: (*A*) No-subsidy, high EV demand growth; (*B*) no-subsidy, medium EV demand growth; and (*C*) no-subsidy, low EV demand growth. Distribution of the state-by-state EV market share accounting for EV sedans only (light) and EV sedans and trucks (dark). Excludes Washington, DC. Intrinsic EV demand growth is 30% in 2020, and the growth rate declines by 5% (high growth), 10% (medium growth), or 15% (low growth) each year.

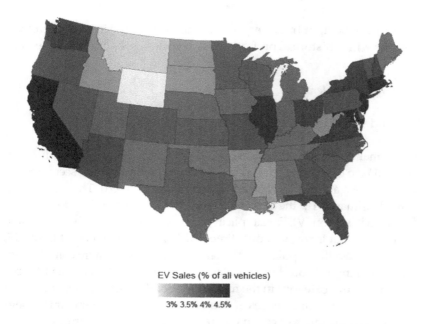

EV Sales (% of all vehicles)

3% 3.5% 4% 4.5%

Fig. 14.   Additional impact of subsidies on electric vehicle (EV) penetration in 2035. Color version available as an online enhancement.

Notes: Additional market share of EVs in each state in 2035 induced by a $7,500-per-vehicle subsidy. Assumes intrinsic demand growth of 30% in 2020 that declines at a rate of 10% per year; EV cars reach cost parity with their ICE counterparts in 2030 and trucks in 2040. Washington, DC, excluded from the scale.

shares rather than compress it. Figure 13 counts of states by different values of EV market share in 2035, under the high, medium, and low adoption scenarios. In each panel, the dark and light histograms illustrate the distribution with and without electric light trucks, respectively. High growth rates mechanically pull states with historically high adoption away from states with lower rates of current adoption, at least through 2035. Figure 14 suggests that subsidies act in a similar fashion. Because sedans tend to have slightly lower costs than light trucks, a $7,500 subsidy is a higher fraction of the overall purchase price for a sedan. Hence, we see slightly higher rates of subsidy-induced adoption along the East and West Coasts.

The differential impact of the expansion of electric power trains into the light truck segment is mapped in figure 12. Panels A and B illustrate the market shares of EVs with and without expansion into the light truck segment, and panel C maps the difference between the market shares in A and B. Although for all states, adoption increases with the expansion of EVs into the light truck segment of the market, the impact is greatest in states with a historical preference for vehicles types other than sedans.

E. Other Considerations

Demand Elasticities

The demand elasticity determines how sensitive the quantity of EVs demanded is to changes in consumer EV prices. The forecasting scenarios described above assume an elasticity in the range of 1.0–3.0. This range is informed primarily by the recent literature that estimates EV demand (as described in section IV). For simplicity, the scenarios that we present assume an elasticity that is constant over time and (with the exception of figure 15, panel D) across the population. The reality is likely to be more complicated.

Future demand could be less elastic than current demand as EVs become a broader category in the market for goods (Berry, Levinsohn, and Pakes 1995). Also, differences in demand are likely between market segments. Early adopters of cars have traditionally been thought to be more price elastic (Goldberg 1995), although one wonders whether this is true of wealthier EV early adopters (Borenstein and Davis 2016). The elasticity of less expensive cars is typically higher than that of more expensive cars (Goldberg 1998), allowing the possibility that EV cost declines will lead to an increase in price elasticity.

To the extent that EV subsidies are means tested, as they are currently in California under the Clean Vehicle Rebate Project, there will be theoretically ambiguous effects on the overall price elasticity. On the one hand, means testing will reduce "free-riding" by directing subsidies away from the subpopulation for which subsidies are inframarginal. This is consistent with Muehlegger and Rapson (2018), who find that low- and middle-income households have relatively elastic demand for EVs. With all else equal, this would cause means testing to increase subsidy cost-effectiveness. On the other hand, if latent demand for EVs is higher among wealthier households, targeting subsidies exclusively toward lower-income households may induce only a modest increase in demand. This would be likely to the extent low-income households perceive low-cost gasoline cars as preferable to subsidized EVs.

Other factors may also affect the EV elasticity, such as the demand for used EVs in a functioning secondary market. Chevalier and Goolsbee (2009) present evidence of forward-looking buyers in primary durable goods markets, where demand for the new durable increases in the

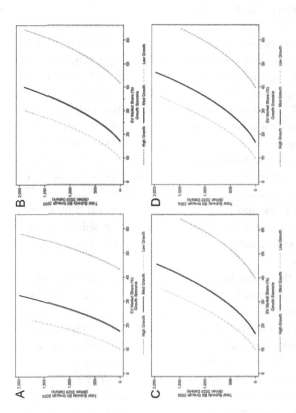

Fig. 15. Sensitivity of market shares to price elasticity. (*A*) Low price response, (*B*) medium price response, (*C*) high price response, and (*D*) income-dependent price response. Color version available as an online enhancement.

Notes: Relationship between EV market share in 2035 and the total subsidy bill required to achieve that market share across a range of potential consumer price responsiveness. Price responsiveness (α^{EV} in the EV market share model) is selected so that the price elasticity of EV market share for the average vehicle purchaser is −1, −2, or −3 (low, medium, and high price responsiveness, respectively). Medium price responsiveness is assumed in other figures. Panel *D* assumes consumers in the top income quartile have low price responsiveness, with the average consumer in this group having an elasticity of −1, and all other consumers have high price responsiveness, with the average consumer in this group having an elasticity of −3. The vertical axis shows the present value of the total subsidy bill in 2035 in 2020 dollars, at a 3% discount rate, and the horizontal axis shows the resulting EV market share in 2035. Scenarios assume intrinsic EV demand growth is 30% in 2020 and declines by 5% (high growth), 10% (medium growth), or 15% (low growth) each year.

option to sell it later in the secondary market. This channel is also important for those concerned with market access, as lower-income households typically purchase used, not new, cars. In summary, the range of constant EV demand elasticities that we present is a deliberate simplification of demand in a complex consumer marketplace, but the intention is for readers to see the potential implications of an elasticity that falls in the range that they believe is realistic.

Plug-in Hybrid and Battery Electric Vehicles

In the projection above, we do not distinguish between BEVs and PHEVs, although both will likely play an important role in meeting future adoption goals. From the perspective of the buyer, the private costs of the two different power train technologies are different and will plausibly evolve along different trajectories. PHEVs allow for a buyer to substitute between gasoline and electricity as the primary fuel and to overcome potential range challenges that might be more important for light trucks. Furthermore, their upfront costs are closer to those of conventional vehicles as a result of a smaller battery. Yet, at present gasoline prices, BEVs offer lower operational costs than PHEVs (under typical use) for much of the country. The relative future mix of PHEVs and BEVs largely depends on how energy prices evolve (as the demand and supply of electricity shift outward) and the degree to which falling battery costs close the upfront price gap between BEVs and PHEVs.

Whether the future path of adoption favors one power train technology over the other also has important implications for the public benefits of EVs. The difference in public benefits depends primarily upon the composition of the electric grid and the relative use of electricity and gasoline by PHEVs. To a lesser extent, the public benefits of BEVs also depend on whether future battery technology better overcomes efficiency losses associated with low-temperature operation as discussed in Archsmith, Kendall, and Rapson (2015). Although it is difficult to predict how the grid (and particularly how the marginal generating unit) will evolve over the next decade and a half, Holland et al. (2020) find that EVs have become cleaner over the past decade relative to comparable conventional vehicles.

VI. Conclusion

Policy makers view electrification of the vehicle fleet as one of the primary strategies for reducing carbon emissions and have set ambitious future adoption targets to help achieve this vision. Yet the cost (and more broadly feasibility) of meeting those targets depends on the degree of organic growth in the future demand for EVs. Although credibly predicting future technological innovation, trends, or adoption is a challenging exercise (at best), our goal in this paper is to understand underlying drivers of organic adoption that might hinder or aid progress toward the ambitious vision of a less carbon-intensive transportation sector.

In this paper, we focus upon determinants of future EV adoption: (1) the introduction of electric power trains into the light truck segment of the EV market, and (2) the supplementary impact of future subsidies. Our scenarios suggest that both may be necessary to meet ambitious future targets, even with all but the most "aggressive" assumptions of the continuous growth of the intrinsic demand for EVs. We also observe that the intrinsic growth is substantially more important to future EV market share than government subsidies.

Intuitively, introducing an equally attractive slate of EV offerings for the roughly 70% of new car buyers who currently purchase SUVs, crossovers, vans, and trucks has a demonstrably larger impact on the feasibility of reaching future EV targets than a subsidy. In our main scenario, we assume that the light truck market reaches "quality parity" toward the end of our forecast period, at which time the suite of light truck EV offerings is viewed as equally attractive to light truck buyers as sedan EVs are to sedan buyers. This convergence drives our prediction of the market share of EV light trucks to surpass the market share of EV sedans toward the end of our study period. Yet whether "quality parity" is reached depends centrally on the ability of automakers to design light truck EVs that capture the attention of buyers who differ from buyers who have been traditionally attracted to EV sedans and who rank different attributes as important in their purchase decisions. And relative to the lower-priced sedan market, the market for light trucks, with their attendant higher prices, might be less easy to influence with subsidies than the lower-priced sedan market.

We also note that the two levers operate along different margins and have important implications for whether adoption patterns in future years are more or less balanced across regions of the country. "Quality parity" of light truck EVs plays a role in balancing EV adoption between regions of the United States with relative preferences for light trucks (e.g., the Midwest) and regions with relative preferences for sedans (e.g., the West and East Coasts). In contrast, an extension of the federal subsidy tends to increase heterogeneity in adoption patterns across states, as a flat subsidy has a larger impact in percentage terms on lower-priced sedans than higher-priced light trucks.

Endnotes

Author email addresses: Archsmith (archsmit@umd.edu), Muehlegger (emuehlegger@ucdavis.edu), Rapson (dsrapson@ucdavis.edu). We thank Joshua Linn and Resources for the Future for providing access to data and computing. We gratefully thank Reid Taylor for excellent research assistance and the editors of this volume for their helpful comments and suggestions on early versions of the paper. All errors are our own. For acknowledgments, sources of research support, and disclosure of the authors' material financial relationships, if any, please see https://www.nber.org/books-and-chapters/environmental-and -energy-policy-and-economy-volume-3/future-paths-electric-vehicle-adoption-united -states-predictable-determinants-obstacles-and.

1. https://www.coltura.org/world-gasoline-phaseouts.

2. Throughout the paper, "EV" refers to both battery electric (BEV) and plug-in hybrid vehicles (PHEV), and "EV market share" refers to the share of new car sales in the US light-duty market.

3. Throughout, we use the term "light trucks" to include sport utility vehicles (SUVs), minivans, and pickup trucks.

4. See Muehlegger and Rapson (2021) for a deeper, complementary discussion of this observation.

5. https://afdc.energy.gov/laws.

6. A detailed overview of the population forecasting methods can be found here: https://demographics.coopercenter.org/sites/demographics/files/2019-02/NationalProjections _MethodologyOverview_Dec2018.pdf.

7. As one example, the MSRP of an entry-level 2021 Nissan Leaf EV is $31,670 (before incentives), whereas the starting price of its gasoline counterpart, the 2021 Nissan Versa, is roughly $15,000.

8. As a point of reference, the 2021 Nissan Leaf, Tesla Model 3, and Tesla Cybertruck currently list battery capacities of 40–62, 50–82, and 100–200 kWh, respectively.

9. Li et al. (2017) uses gasoline prices as an independent variable (IV) and estimates a demand elasticity of –1.3. Springel (2021) and Li (2017) both use IVs following those in Berry, Levinsohn and Pakes (1995) to retrieve estimates of –1.0 to –0.5 (Springel) and –2.7 (Li), respectively. Muehlegger and Rapson (2018) use variation from a low- and middle-income EV subsidy program to estimate an elasticity of –3.3 in that subsegment. We also present alternative scenarios with elasticities ranging from –3.0 to –1.0 and heterogeneous elasticities by income.

10. To be clear, the lack of EV light trucks to date prevents us from estimating the probability with which a light truck buyer would purchase an EV light truck from revealed preference data. Thus, as outlined in figure 6, we use the observable data on EV sedan purchases as a guide for the conditional probability that a future light truck buyer chooses to purchase an model with an electric power train.

11. Demographics Research Group (2018) forecast population in each state and 5-year age bin at 10-year intervals. We interpolate forecast population in the intervening years using a constant growth rate.

12. Larger mass and increased aerodynamic drag increase the battery capacity required to achieve a given range in EV trucks relative to EV cars. As batteries represent the bulk of the increased cost of EVs, we assume EV trucks will take longer to achieve cost parity than cars.

13. We also consider a range of alternative tax-inclusive prices in table 4.

14. These shares mechanically sum to one, so the portion of vehicles classified as vans are treated as the excluded category in estimation.

15. We performed this cross-validation procedure using three empirical models: the standard probit, a regularized probit using a lasso penalty selected via cross-validation, and a post-regularized probit using the set of variables selected by the regularized probit without

the lasso penalty. Each approach preferred the same specification for each model. The standard probit produced the lowest out-of-sample forecast error and is the basis of our forecasts.

16. As stated above, in all six scenarios we assume that the intrinsic (i.e., subsidy-free) growth rate starts at 30% per annum in 2020. The rate then declines by 5%, 10%, or 15% per annum thereafter, in the high-, medium-, and low-growth scenarios.

17. Alternatively, as the consumer does not distinguish between a subsidy and a reduction in the subsidy-exclusive sticker price, the right-hand column can be interpreted as a scenario in which efficiency gains lead the sticker price of EVs to be well below price parity with comparable ICE vehicles by 2035.

18. If potential buyers of EV light trucks would have purchased a conventional light truck in the absence of an electric option, EV market share would fall by the entire market share of EV light trucks in a world in which they were not available. If some of these buyers would purchase an EV sedan instead, though, the lack of EV light trucks would have a more modest effect on EV market share.

19. Collectively, trucks, SUVs, crossovers, and vans command more than 70% of the US new car market. https://www.nada.org/nadamarketbeat/.

20. The cumulative bill is expressed as a present value in 2020 dollars, and future expenditures are discounted at a 3% discount rate.

References

Archsmith, James, Alissa Kendall, and David Rapson. 2015. "From Cradle to Junkyard: Assessing the Life Cycle Greenhouse Gas Benefits of Electric Vehicles." *Research in Transportation Economics* 63 (3): 397–421.

Berry, Steven, James Levinsohn, and Ariel Pakes. 1995. "Automobile Prices in Market Equilibrium." *Econometrica* 63 (4): 841–90.

Borenstein, Severin, and Lucas W. Davis. 2016. "The Distributional Effects of US Clean Energy Tax Credits." *Tax Policy and the Economy* 30 (1): 191–234.

Chevalier, Judith, and Austan Goolsbee. 2009. "Are Durable Goods Consumers Forward-Looking? Evidence from College Textbooks." *Quarterly Journal of Economics* 124 (4): 1853–84.

Demographics Research Group. 2018. "National Population Projections." Weldon Cooper Center, University of Virginia. https://demographics.coopercenter.org/national-population-projections.

Goldberg, Pinelopi Koujianou. 1995. "Product Differentiation and Oligopoly in International Markets: The Case of the U.S. Automobile Industry." *Econometrica* 63 (4): 891–951.

———. 1998. "The Effects of the Corporate Average Fuel Efficiency Standards in the U.S." *Journal of Industrial Economics* 46 (1): 1–33.

Holland, Stephen, Erin Mansur, Nicholas Muller, and Andrew Yates. 2016. "Are There Environmental Benefits from Driving Electric Vehicles? The Importance of Local Factors." *American Economic Review* 106 (12): 3700–3729.

———. 2020. "Decompositions and Policy Consequences of an Extraordinary Decline in Air Pollution from Electricity Generation." *American Economic Journal: Economic Policy* 12 (4): 244–74.

Howe, Peter D., Matto Mildenberger, Jennifer R. Marlon, and Anthony Leiserowitz. 2015. "Geographic Variation in Opinions on Climate Change at State and Local Scales in the USA." *Nature Climate Change* 5 (6): 596–603.

International Energy Agency. 2020. "Global EV Outlook 2020." Technical Report, International Energy Agency, Paris.

Li, Jing. 2017. "Compatibility and Investment in the U.S. Electric Vehicle Market." Working Paper, Massachusetts Institute of Technology, Cambridge, MA.

Li, Shanjun, Lang Tong, Jianwei Xing, and Yiyi Zhou. 2017. "The Market for Electric Vehicles: Indirect Network Effects and Policy Design." *Journal of the Association of Environmental and Resource Economists* 4 (1): 89–133.

Milovanoff, Alexandre, I. Daniel Posen, and Heather L. MacLean. 2020. "Electrification of Light-Duty Vehicle Fleet Alone Will Not Meet Mitigation Targets." *Nature Climate Change* 10 (12): 1102–7.

Muehlegger, Erich, and David Rapson. 2018. "Subsidizing Mass Adoption of Electric Vehicles: Quasi-Experimental Evidence from California." Technical Report, NBER, Cambridge, MA.

———. 2021. "The Economics of Electric Vehicles." Technical Report, NBER, Cambridge, MA.

Springel, Katalin. 2021. "Network Externality and Subsidy Structure in Two-Sided Markets: Evidence from Electric Vehicle Incentives." *American Economic Journal: Economic Policy* 13 (4): 393–432.

Designing Fuel-Economy Standards in Light of Electric Vehicles

Kenneth T. Gillingham, *Yale University and NBER,* United States of America

Executive Summary

Electric vehicles are declining in cost so rapidly that they may claim a large share of the vehicle market by 2030. This paper examines a set of practical regulatory design considerations for fuel-economy standards or greenhouse gas standards in the context of highly uncertain electric vehicle costs in the next decade. The analysis takes a cost-effectiveness approach and uses analytical modeling and simulation to develop insight. I show that counting electric vehicles under a standard with a multiplier or assuming zero upstream emissions can reduce electric vehicle market share by weakening the standards. Furthermore, there are trade-offs from implementing a backstop conventional vehicle standard along with a second standard that also includes electric vehicles, but such a backstop offers the possibility of ensuring that low-cost conventional vehicle technologies are exploited.

JEL Codes: H23, Q48, Q53, Q54, Q58, R48

Keywords: electric vehicles, fuel-economy standards, greenhouse gases, climate change

"The period from 2025–2035 could bring the most fundamental transformation in the 100-plus year history of the automobile."
— National Academies of Science, Engineering, and Medicine (2021), page S-1

I.   Introduction

In the United States, regulations on the fuel economy or carbon dioxide emission rate of light-duty vehicles are the most prominent policies used to address greenhouse gas emissions from the transportation sector,

Environmental and Energy Policy and the Economy, volume 3, 2022.

which generates nearly a third of US greenhouse gas emissions.[1] The regulations were first promulgated as corporate average fuel-economy (CAFE) standards in 1975 by the US Department of Transportation's National Highway Traffic Safety Administration (NHTSA). In addition, in 2012, the US Environmental Protection Agency (EPA) began regulating vehicle greenhouse gas emissions under emissions standards.[2] The regulations are complicated and governed by multiple statues. But they were not designed for the massive transition that appears to be occurring in the automotive sector.

In the past decade, electric vehicles have gone from a curiosity to a widely recognized alternative to conventional internal combustion engine vehicles, with as many as 100 new electric vehicle models coming to showrooms by 2025.[3] Lithium-ion battery packs, which store the energy use for propulsion of electric vehicles, have dropped in price from more than $1,000 per kilowatt-hour (kWh) in 2010 to roughly $125/kWh today and are estimated to drop to $65–$80/kWh by 2030. Such a dramatic decline in battery prices could mean that electric vehicles achieve cost parity in upfront costs by 2030 (National Academies of Science, Engineering, and Medicine 2021). And some analysts even forecast a faster decline in battery costs (BNEF 2021).

Electric vehicles also tend to be much less expensive to operate, with the cost of electricity usually well below the cost of gasoline or diesel for comparable vehicles. Furthermore, the maintenance costs of electric vehicles are much lower than for conventional vehicles due to far fewer engine parts that can break. In addition, electric vehicles have superb low-speed torque and acceleration. For example, the *New York Times* states: "Even the new Shelby GT500—history's mightiest Mustang, with 760 horsepower—won't equal the 3.5-second 0-to-60 mph blast of this summer's Mach-E GT Performance version" (Ulrich 2021). Indeed, many analysts have forecast extremely rapid growth in electric vehicle sales over the next decade with battery cost declines and increased construction of charging infrastructure (e.g., BNEF 2020).

This study examines the trade-offs inherent in several major decisions relating to the design of standards regulating vehicle fuel economy or carbon dioxide emissions in light of a potential transition from a dominantly conventional vehicle fleet to a mostly electric vehicle fleet over the coming decade. What are the ramifications of more generously crediting electric vehicles under the standards, either through a multiplier or by ignoring all upstream emissions from the generation of electricity used to power the electric vehicles? What are the effects of a combined standard that includes electric vehicles and conventional vehicles rather than a separate standard for each vehicle technology? Because policy makers must decide today how to design standards when faced with uncertain developments in electric vehicle costs, I consider the effects of policy decisions in the context of uncertainty about future battery costs and electric vehicle uptake.

The analysis in this study is based on analytical models and illustrative simulations to provide a conceptual understanding of the forces at work. My first major set of findings relates to generous crediting. One clear result is that if electric vehicles receive generous crediting under the standards, either through a multiplier or by ignoring upstream emissions, selling more electric vehicles will allow less-efficient conventional vehicles to be sold. This can be thought of as an example of "leakage" of emissions from electric vehicles to conventional vehicles, analogous to the leakage that might occur if subnational actors, such as California, implement their own more stringent standard at the same time as a binding national standard (Goulder, Jacobsen, and van Benthem 2011).[4]

Furthermore, although one might expect more generous crediting to act as an incentive for electric vehicles, I find that it is likely to actually reduce the incentive for automakers to sell electric vehicles. The intuition for this result is that the multipliers weaken the standard sufficiently that fewer electric vehicles are needed to enable the automakers to meet the standard while selling the (currently) more profitable conventional vehicles. This counterintuitive finding appears to hold under reasonable assumptions and can even hold if induced innovation in electric vehicle technology is considered.

But the counterintuitive finding does not necessarily hold all the time. When electric vehicles are a nascent technology and are very far from competitive with conventional vehicles in terms of the profits they generate for automakers or have extremely strong innovation potential, then the standard may be more tightly binding on conventional vehicles and the generous crediting could be beneficial enough to lead to greater electric vehicle market share. But as soon as electric vehicles are even remotely close to competitive with conventional vehicles, more generous electric vehicle crediting appears to lead to reductions in electric vehicle market share. This is a useful finding because electric vehicle deployment is a stated policy goal of the Biden administration (White House 2021).

For broader context, these findings imply that even if generous crediting increases the market share of electric vehicles, it could still increase overall carbon dioxide emissions in the short run by allowing less-efficient conventional vehicles to be sold under the standard. But even in this (less likely) case, there is a long-run trade-off: More electric vehicles could reduce emissions as the electricity system is decarbonized, but this would have to outweigh the increased short-run emissions. Clearly, if overall carbon dioxide emissions increase on net, then including the generous crediting will unequivocally not be a cost-effective approach for emission reductions. Moreover, even if overall emissions decline over both periods, the generous crediting may still be a costly approach to reduce emissions because the direct emission reductions from the electric vehicles would be offset by increased emissions from conventional vehicles. Stepping back, if policy makers want to ensure that generous crediting increases electric vehicle market share and reduces emissions, one logical approach would be to tighten the standard when implementing the generous crediting to offset the standard-weakening effect of the generous crediting.

The second major set of findings of this study relates to uncertainty in regulation design. There is substantial uncertainty about future electric vehicle costs, and this uncertainty means that ex ante policy can deviate even more from what would have been the ex post optimal policy than is usual for standards. With greater uncertainty about future technology costs than usual, it will be especially difficult to set a standard in advance, as is required by law. I show that if electric vehicles become inexpensive, but there is still at least some demand for conventional vehicles, then averaging in the numerous electric vehicles into the sales-weighted average used for compliance will allow automakers to sell more inefficient conventional vehicles. This may leave low-cost emission reductions in the conventional fleet untapped.

With low-cost emission reductions in mind, I examine a standard that includes electric vehicles and conventional vehicles combined with a separate "backstop conventional vehicle standard." Such a complementary backstop standard could be nonbinding in expectation for most automakers and would only play an important role if electric vehicles become very inexpensive. In the context of very inexpensive electric vehicles, I find that adding this backstop standard could lead to substantially more deployment of electric vehicles. It also would likely improve the cost-effectiveness of the policy in reducing emissions, with the caveat that this depends on there being at least some low-cost conventional vehicle emission-reduction technologies continually available. On the downside, if the decline in electric vehicle costs is not quite as dramatic, adding the separate backstop standard could modestly reduce electric vehicle deployment and increase emissions. It also adds further complexity to an already complicated regulation. However, the statutory basis for these complementary standards appears to be strong.

This study focuses on real-world policy-maker objectives, such as incentivizing greater electric vehicle deployment and achieving emission reductions cost-effectively. It examines policy-relevant metrics such as emissions and costs. Although unquestionably important, analyzing the full welfare effects of standards is outside of the scope of this paper. Overall welfare effects depend on a wide variety of issues, including new vehicle purchasing decisions, the cost of new vehicle technologies, automaker vehicle design decisions, automaker long-run research and development investment decisions, strategic pricing decisions and other interactions, equilibrium in the used vehicle market, decisions about how much to drive more efficient vehicles, and even the scrappage of old vehicles. Among these numerous issues, perhaps the most important is whether consumers fully internalize the operating costs when making new vehicle purchase decisions or if there are features of consumer behavior that lead to an undervaluation of future fuel savings (Bento et al. 2018).

There are also other details that are important for standards setting that are outside the scope of this study, such as allowing or limiting trading between automakers, designating standards based on the "footprint" (a rough measure of vehicle size calculated as the wheelbase times track length) of new vehicles (Gillingham 2013; Ito and Sallee 2018), or offering credits for alternative-fuel vehicles (Anderson and Sallee 2011).[5] By focusing on cost-effectiveness and simplifying from some of these details, I aim to provide concise conceptual guidance to policy makers on the trade-offs inherent in different approaches to designing standards in light of uncertain electric vehicle uptake in the coming decade.

The paper is organized as follows. The next section provides some brief background placing this work in the policy context. Section III examines the implications of generous crediting of electric vehicles under the standards. Section IV explores how uncertainty in electric vehicle costs influence the effects of difference standards designs. Section V provides a concluding discussion of the policy and legal issues raised by the analysis in this study.

II.   Policy Background

Fuel-economy standards originate with the Energy Policy and Conservation Act of 1975 and have been updated several times since, most notably by the Energy Independence and Security Act of 2007. The statutory authority for regulating fuel economy under these laws is assigned to NHTSA. Specifically, NHTSA is required to set "maximum feasible" fuel-economy standards that regulate the sales-weighted averaged fuel economy for each automaker's passenger car and light truck fleet. Automakers can comply with the standards by achieving the target fuel economy, paying a fine, or using crediting approaches (e.g., trading credits across fleets or automakers). However, NHTSA argues that it cannot consider compliance credits in setting the standards, so if trading occurs between automakers that lowers the cost of the regulation, the lower costs cannot be accounted for in setting the standards. In addition, NHTSA also argues that it cannot consider alternative-fuel vehicles, such as electric vehicles, in setting the standards, but is required to average in electric vehicles for compliance with the standards based on a "petroleum-equivalence factor" set by the US Department of Energy.[6] There is a limit to the number of credits that can be traded across automakers under NHTSA's authority, although most automakers do not appear to hit this limit (National Academies of Science, Engineering, and Medicine 2021).

Vehicle greenhouse gas standards regulate tailpipe carbon dioxide emissions from vehicles. In 2007, the Supreme Court ruled that EPA must determine whether greenhouse gas emissions from vehicles are required to be regulated under Section 202 of the Clean Air Act of 1970 (updated in 1990). EPA determined affirmatively. Because fuel economy can be mapped quite well to carbon dioxide emissions, EPA and NHTSA have been aligning their standards as closely as possible under the statutes, starting with vehicle model year 2012. EPA faces fewer constraints in using the Clean Air Act than NHTSA faces under its statutory authority. EPA is permitted to allow for greater compliance flexibilities, such as flex-fuel credits or credits for less-polluting air conditioning materials, and has no limits on trading between fleets and automakers. EPA is also permitted to consider alternative-fuel vehicles in setting its standards and has substantial flexibility in how the standards are designed. These differences in the statutory authority of EPA and NHTSA add to the complexity of developing standards with a higher market share of electric vehicles in the fleet.

For historical perspective, figure 1 shows the US fleet-wide fuel-economy standard, achieved fuel economy in miles per gallon (mpg), and percent improvement in vehicle energy efficiency from 1975 levels. Prior to the standards for model year 2012, there was a separate standard for the passenger vehicle and light truck fleets. Starting with the model year

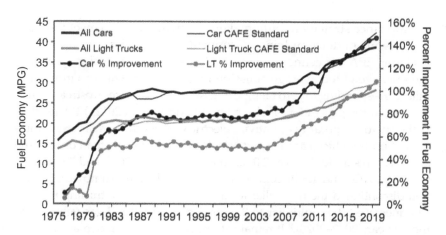

Fig. 1. Historical data for the period 1975–2018 showing fuel-economy standards, achieved fuel economy in miles per gallon (mpg), and percent improvement from 1975 levels. Color version available as an online enhancement.
Source.—National Academies of Science, Engineering, and Medicine (2021).

2012 standards, EPA and NHTSA converted to a system with separate standards for predetermined footprint bins in each of the passenger vehicle and light truck fleets, so that larger vehicles face a less-stringent standard. Credits for overcomplying in one fleet's footprint can be applied to permit undercompliance in other footprints or fleets.

The most recent standards set by EPA and NHTSA were developed in the Trump administration's Safer Affordable Fuel-Efficient (SAFE) Vehicles Rule, which set standards for the model years 2021–2026. The rule has standards increasing by 1.5% per year through 2026. This is a substantial rollback from the Obama administration's model year 2017–2025 standards, which had the standards rising by 5% per year over the same set of model years (National Academies of Science, Engineering, and Medicine 2021). The Biden administration has already indicated that it plans to reassess the SAFE Rule and will likely promulgate a new set of more stringent standards than the SAFE Rule in the next year (Davenport 2021).

III. Effects of Generous Crediting Electric Vehicles

Under the current standards, a conventional vehicle enters into the sales-weighted average used to determine automaker compliance as a single vehicle. Under NHTSA's fuel-economy standards, electric vehicles are treated the same as conventional vehicles with the miles-per-gallon equivalent of the electric vehicle averaged in. Thus, adding electric vehicles is a compliance strategy for automakers, allowing them to meet the standards while undercomplying on conventional vehicles.[7]

Under EPA's greenhouse gas standards, electric vehicles enter into the sales-weighted average emission rate with a rate of zero grams per mile, corresponding to zero tailpipe emissions. This ignores upstream emissions from the generation of electricity. In addition, in 2012, EPA used its authority to temporarily incentivize electric vehicles through a "credit multiplier" under which each electric vehicle is counted more than once in the average.[8] This multiplier was 2.0 for model years 2017–2019, and it dropped to 1.75 in 2020 and 1.5 in 2021. In the SAFE Rule, the Trump administration discontinued the multiplier for all electric vehicles, returning it to 1.0 (but increased the multiplier to 2.0 for dedicated natural-gas vehicles for model years 2022–2026).[9] It remains to be seen how the Biden administration will handle the crediting.

The vision behind the generous crediting for electric vehicles under EPA's greenhouse gas standard is that it would encourage automakers to develop and sell electric vehicles. Jenn, Azevedo, and Michalek (2016) note that because the standards fix the sales-weighted average greenhouse gas emissions for each footprint and there is trading by automakers within their fleet and across fleets, the generous crediting serves to weaken the standards and can lead to additional emissions by allowing automakers to sell some less-efficient vehicles. Jenn et al. (2016) hold the number of electric vehicles in the fleet fixed, but the stated policy goal of including the generous crediting is to induce innovation in electric vehicles and incentivize automakers to sell more of the nascent technology. Thus, a key unanswered question for policy makers is how the generous crediting from the credit multipliers and the ignoring of upstream emissions affects electric vehicle deployment and overall emissions.

The focus of my analysis is on EPA's greenhouse gas standards, but the insights also apply if generous crediting of electric vehicles is permitted under NHSTA's fuel-economy standards through the very high petroleum-equivalent fuel-economy values assumed for electric vehicles. In the following subsections, I build intuition by considering the automaker's profit maximization problem first in a single-period model and then in a two-period model to allow for the dynamic effects of innovation.

A.   Static Modeling of the Effects of Generous Crediting

Consider an automaker's decision problem when faced with the choice of how much to invest in developing and selling electric vehicles to maximize profits while still complying with the standards. There are many possible margins of adjustment to comply with the standards, including improving the fuel economy of new conventional vehicles, selling more electric vehicles, selling more efficient electric vehicles, and changing the relative prices of new vehicles based on their fuel economy. To provide insight on the research questions at hand, I model automakers choosing their sales of electric vehicles, represented by the market share, s_{EV}, and the average carbon dioxide emission rate for conventional vehicles, e_C. The electric vehicle market share and conventional vehicle emission rate will come about from numerous pricing and research investment decisions, but focusing on the net result of these decisions as the choice variables allows for greater transparency and clarity in the analysis.

Intuition from the Standard Itself

Under the current crediting approach used by EPA, the electric vehicle credit multiplier is applied such that each electric vehicle counts as some multiple of a vehicle in both the calculation of the achieved average emission rate used for compliance and the target standard itself. This implies that the multiplier not only makes electric vehicles more attractive by averaging in more electric vehicles than there actually are (with a currently assumed zero-emission rate) but also directly adjusts the stringency of the standard itself. Specifically, for the passenger vehicle and light truck fleets separately, carbon dioxide credits are calculated based on a sales-weighted average of the targets and a sales-weighted average of the assumed emission rates. This implies that the standard can be understood as the following, where the left-hand side is the sales-weighted average used for compliance and the right-hand side is the sales-weighted average target standard:[10]

$$\frac{\sum_{i\in C}e_{C,i}V_i + \sum_{i\in EV}e_{EV,i}V_iM}{\sum_{i\in C}V_i + \sum_{i\in EV}V_iM} \leq \frac{\sum_{i\in C}S_{GHG,i}V_i + \sum_{i\in EV}S_{GHG,i}V_iM}{\sum_{i\in C}V_i + \sum_{i\in EV}V_iM}. \quad (1)$$

Here C is the set of conventional vehicle offerings, EV is the set of electric vehicle offerings, $e_{C,i}$ is the emission rate for conventional vehicle type i, $e_{EV,i}$ is the emission rate for electric vehicle type i, V_i are the sales of vehicle i, $S_{GHG,i}$ is the standard facing vehicle i, and M is the multiplier. Note that M is on both the left-hand side and right-hand side. On the left-hand side, if the assumed emission rate for electric vehicles is zero, as is the current practice, the term in the numerator that includes M drops out and the multiplier only affects the denominator (and right-hand side of course).

To analyze the consequences of adding the multiplier, I simplify by using the average emission rate for conventional vehicles (e_C) and electric vehicles (e_{EV}), and assume a single combined standard (S_{GHG}). A single combined standard is consistent with full trading across fleets and is also consistent with how the EPA greenhouse gas standard allows for electric vehicles. Additional statutory authority would have to be given NHTSA for this exact representation to hold, due to limits to trading and the prohibition on setting standards considering electric vehicles. After some rearranging of the terms, the sales volumes drop out, and I can rewrite equation (1) in terms of the market share of electric vehicles (s_{EV}) as follows (see appendix Subsec. I.A for details):

$$s_{EV}e_{EV}M + (1 - s_{EV})e_C \leq S_{GHG}(1 + (M - 1)s_{EV}). \tag{2}$$

The left-hand side here is the sales-weighted average emission rate adjusted by the multiplier and the right-hand side is the target standard adjusted by the multiplier. This inequality immediately suggests some of the trade-offs inherent in including a multiplier greater than 1. Specifically, $M > 1$ not only helps automakers with compliance on the left-hand side (providing an incentive to sell more electric vehicles) but also directly relaxes the standard on the right-hand side. This can be seen most easily if one assumes that $e_{EV} = 0$ as EPA does. Then we can focus on the effect of M on the right-hand side and observe that $M > 1$ implies that $(M - 1)s_{EV} > 0$, so the carbon dioxide grams/mile emission rate required increases. A higher grams/mile rate implies a more relaxed standard.

Thus, a first finding of this study is the following:

Finding 1: An electric vehicle credit multiplier greater than 1 relaxes the standard when the assumed emission rate for electric vehicles is zero, as it is currently.

There is an analogous finding to this one in Jenn et al. (2016), although the formulation is different here. One takeaway from this formulation is that the policymaker would have to simultaneously tighten the standard by a value that depends on the multiplier and the electric vehicle share when $e_{EV} = 0$ and a credit multiplier is greater than 1 to assure that the effective stringency of the policy remains the same. This can be seen in equation (2) by setting $e_{EV} = 0$ and noting that if the standard is tightened by exactly $(M - 1)s_{EV}$ (i.e., there is a new S'_{GHG} that is equal to $S_{GHG} - (M - 1)s_{EV}$)), then the effect of relaxing the standard would be perfectly mitigated and the effective stringency of the policy would remain the same.

If the assumed emission rate for electric vehicles is greater than zero, so $e_{EV} > 0$, then increasing $M > 1$ increases the left-hand side, which makes compliance more difficult, and thus serves to effectively tighten the standard. This would have to be weighed against the relaxing of the standard from the inclusion of $M > 1$ on the right-hand side, so the net effect may be ambiguous. Increasing the assumed emission rate (e_{EV}), with s_{EV} and M held constant, will make compliance more difficult by averaging in a higher emission rate.

To build intuition on how the choice of credit multiplier and e_{EV} affect automaker incentives to sell electric vehicles and choose the emission rate of conventional vehicles, we now turn to the automaker's profit maximization problem.

Automaker Profit Maximization

Let the per-vehicle profits from electric vehicles and conventional vehicles be given by π_{EV} and $\pi_C(e_C)$ respectively, where it is assumed that today $\pi_{EV} < \pi_C(e_C)$, so there is an opportunity cost for the automaker to develop and sell more EVs rather than conventional vehicles. Thus selling more EVs reduces the automaker profits in the short run, although this may change in the future.[11] For simplicity, I assume away competitive interactions between automakers, allowing me to focus on a single representative automaker. Similarly, I also assume that the choice of how many electric vehicles to sell does not influence the total number of vehicles sold on the market, V.

I write the representative automaker's stylized profit maximization problem as the weighted average per-vehicle profits across electric vehicles and conventional vehicles times the total vehicles sold by the automaker, subject to the constraint of the greenhouse gas standard:

$$\max_{s_{EV}, e_C} V[s_{EV}\pi_{EV} + (1 - s_{EV})\pi_C(e_C)]$$

$$\text{subject to } s_{EV}e_{EV}M + (1 - s_{EV})e_C \leq S_{GHG}(1 + (M - 1)s_{EV}).$$

This formulation immediately provides insight. As discussed above, it is clear that the constraint is relaxed if e_{EV} is reduced (e.g., upstream emissions are ignored) and M is increased (e.g., a credit multiplier greater than 1 is applied). Thus, if $\pi_{EV} < \pi_C(e_C)$ in the range of the conventional vehicle emission rate, e_C, being considered (as is likely because electric vehicles are a newer technology) and automakers make greater profits from less-efficient vehicles (i.e., $d\pi_C(e_C)/de_C > 0$), then one might expect reducing e_{EV} and increasing M to lead to higher emission rates for conventional vehicles (e_C) in the profit-maximizing solution. This is the basic intuition in Jenn et al. (2016), and I will show the assumptions necessary for it to hold.

Let λ denote the shadow price on the greenhouse gas standard constraint. The first-order conditions of optimality from differentiating with respect to s_{EV} and e_C are given as follows:

$$V(\pi_C(e_C) - \pi_{EV}) + \lambda[e_{EV}M - e_C - S_{GHG}(M - 1)] = 0$$

$$-V\frac{d\pi_C(e_C)}{de_C} + \lambda = 0. \tag{3}$$

Rearranging for λ, and noting that the shadow price must be the same across the two first-order conditions, yields

$$e_C^* = e_{EV}M - S_{GHG}(M - 1) - \frac{\pi_{EV} - \pi_C(e_C^*)}{\frac{d\pi_C\left(e_C^*\right)}{de_C^*}}. \tag{4}$$

This equation implicitly defines the optimal emission rate for conventional vehicles, which is seen to be a function of the electric vehicle emission rate, credit multiplier, adjusted standard, and difference between electric vehicle and conventional vehicle profits divided by the marginal profits from a change in the conventional vehicle emission rate. Assuming a binding constraint, we can similarly rearrange the constraint for an equation that defines the optimal market share of electric vehicles as a function of the optimal emission rate of conventional vehicles, the standard, the electric vehicle emission rate, and the credit multiplier:

$$s_{EV}^* = \frac{S_{GHG} - e_C^*}{e_{EV}M - e_C^* - S_{GHG}(M - 1)}. \tag{5}$$

Comparative Statics for the Conventional Vehicle Emission Rate

To proceed, I first examine comparative statics at the optimum for the chosen conventional vehicle emission rate when the credit multiplier and assumed electric vehicle emission rate are changed. I rearrange equation (4) to set it equal to zero and then employ the implicit function theorem to obtain:

$$\frac{\partial e_C^*}{\partial M} = \frac{(S_{\text{GHG}} - e_{\text{EV}})\left(\frac{\partial \pi_C(e_C^*)}{\partial e_C^*}\right)^2}{(\pi_{\text{EV}} - \pi_C(e_C^*))\frac{\partial^2 \pi_C\left(e_C^*\right)}{\partial e_C^{*2}}}.$$

This comparative static shows that the optimal conventional vehicle emission rate depends on several intuitive terms. First, there is the difference between the standard and the assumed electric vehicle emission rate, which is important because it influences how much in the way of worse conventional emission rates each electric vehicle will allow. Electric vehicles are more useful for automaker compliance if their emission rates are much lower than the standard. Second, it depends on the additional per-vehicle profits from increasing the conventional vehicle emission rate (squared, which perhaps emphasizes the importance of this term). Third, in the denominator, it depends on the difference in the per-vehicle profits between conventional vehicles and electric vehicles, which again is important for determining the loss from using electric vehicles to allow for less-efficient conventional vehicles. Finally, it depends on the convexity or concavity of the per-vehicle profit function for conventional vehicles, which indicates what the marginal gain in profits might be from adjusting the conventional vehicle emission rate to take advantage of the credit multiplier.

The first two terms (the two terms in the numerator) are both expected to be positive, as the standard (S_{GHG}) should be larger than the assumed emission rate of electric vehicles (e_{EV}) and a square term is always positive. The third term is expected to be negative, as the profits from electric vehicles are likely to be less than those from conventional vehicles in the near term. The fourth term is a little less clear. However, one might expect that profits increase with higher emission rates (and thus lower fuel economy), but do so with diminishing returns. This would suggest a concave function, so that $\partial^2 \pi_C(e_C^*)/\partial e_C^{*2} < 0$.

Making these reasonable assumptions implies that $\partial e_C^*/\partial M > 0$, so that the optimal emission rate for conventional vehicles is increasing with the credit multiplier. Put simply, the automakers will have an incentive to sell less-efficient vehicles with a higher electric vehicle credit multiplier.

This leads to the second analytical finding:

Finding 2: In a static setting and under the assumptions discussed above used to sign the terms of the comparative static, the emission rate for conventional vehicles will increase with the electric vehicle credit multiplier.

This finding points to the "leakage" effect from using a credit multiplier to incentivize electric vehicles—it will likely lead to less-efficient conventional vehicles on the road.

There is a similar finding for how the emission rate of conventional vehicles changes with the assumed emission rate for electric vehicles. The assumed emission rate for electric vehicles is currently zero in current regulations, but would increase if upstream emissions from electric vehicle charging are accounted for.

Using the implicit function theorem again, the comparative static is the following:

$$\frac{\partial e_C^*}{\partial e_{EV}} = \frac{M\left(\frac{\partial \pi_C(e_C^*)}{\partial e_C^*}\right)^2}{(\pi_C(e_C^*) - \pi_{EV})\frac{\partial^2 \pi_C\left(e_C^*\right)}{\partial e_C^{*2}}}.$$

There is an economic interpretation to this comparative static as well. In the first term, we observe that if the electric vehicle credit multiplier M is increased, then the assumed emission rate for electric vehicles will have a greater impact on the automaker's choice of emission rate for conventional vehicles. This is intuitive because the credit multiplier exacerbates the effect of the assumed electric vehicle emission rate in the constraint (recall [2]). In the second term in the numerator, the additional per-vehicle profits from increasing the conventional vehicle emission rate increase the effect on the conventional vehicle emission rate. This logic is the same as in the previous comparative static.

In the denominator, the difference between the conventional vehicle and electric vehicle per-vehicle profits is important because it influences how many more electric vehicles may be sold in the optimum, which affects how important the assumed electric vehicle emission rate is. Finally, the concavity or convexity of the per-vehicle profit function for conventional vehicles is important, as before, because it determines the added profits from changing the emission rate for conventional vehicles due to the relaxing of the standard from the electric vehicle emission rate.

Both terms in the numerator are positive. In the denominator, the per-vehicle profits for conventional vehicles should be higher than for electric vehicles in the near term, so $\pi_C(e_C^*) - \pi_{EV} > 0$. If the profit function is concave as discussed above, so that $\partial^2 \pi_C(e_C^*)/\partial e_C^{*2} < 0$, then the denominator is negative.

Thus, under these reasonable assumptions, $\partial e_C^*/\partial e_{EV} < 0$. This implies that if the assumed emission rate for electric vehicles is increased, then the automaker's optimal emission rate for conventional vehicles will decrease and conventional vehicles will become more efficient. Hence, we have the third analytical finding:

Finding 3: In a static setting and under the assumptions discussed above used to sign the terms of the comparative static, the emission rate for conventional vehicles will decrease with the assumed electric vehicle emission rate.

The intuition for this finding is that if electric vehicles become less beneficial toward meeting the standards due to the assumed electric vehicle emission rate increasing, then conventional vehicles will have to make up the slack and become more efficient.

Comparative Statics for the Electric Vehicle Market Share

I now turn to exploring how the market share of electric vehicles is affected. For this analysis, I rely directly on the solution for the optimal electric vehicle market share as function of the optimal conventional vehicle emission rate given in equation (5). Differentiating with respect to the credit multiplier M yields the following comparative static:

$$\frac{\partial s_{EV}^*}{\partial M} = \frac{\frac{\partial e_C^*}{\partial M}}{e_{EV}M - e_C^* - S_{GHG}(M-1)} - \frac{(S_{GHG} - e_C^*)\left(e_{EV} - \frac{\partial e_C^*}{\partial M} - S_{GHG}\right)}{(e_{EV}M - e_C^* - S_{GHG}(M-1))^2}.$$

This equation is somewhat long, but has economic intuition. Whether electric vehicle market share increases with the credit multiplier depends on several factors. First, it depends on how the optimal conventional vehicle emission rate changes with the credit multiplier because this influences how stringent the standard is going to be. We showed above in Finding 2 that under reasonable assumptions, this should be positive. In the denominator of the first term, we see that the comparative static also depends on the assumed emission rate of electric vehicles relative to the adjusted standard (i.e., $S_{GHG}(M-1)$) and the conventional vehicle emission rate. If the assumed $e_{EV} = 0$, as is current practice by EPA, this denominator will definitely be negative. But it is very likely to be negative even if $e_{EV} > 0$ because the electric vehicle emission rate should be smaller than either the standard or the conventional vehicle emission rate. Thus, the first term should be negative.

In the numerator of the second term, we observe that the comparative static depends on the difference between the standard and the conventional vehicle emission rate. The intuition here is that if the conventional vehicle emission rate is far off, increasing the credit multiplier is more important because conventional vehicle emission rates need to be substantially reduced, which is costly. This difference should always be (weakly) negative because the optimal conventional vehicle emission rate will be at or above the standard due to the electric vehicles allowing for less-efficient conventional vehicles. This difference is multiplied by the difference between the electric vehicle emission rate and the optimal conventional vehicle emission rate changes with the credit multiplier plus the standard itself. The intuition here is somewhat more difficult to discern, but it is capturing how the electric vehicle emissions rate compares with the conventional vehicle emission rate changes and the standard. If $e_{EV} = 0$, this simplifies further and makes it easier to sign. Based on Finding 2, the derivative is positive, and the standard itself is positive, so $- \partial(e_C^*/\partial M) - S_{GHG} < 0$.

Because the electric vehicle emission rate is likely to be small, it is also very reasonable to assume that $e_{EV} - \partial(e_C^*/\partial M) - S_{GHG} < 0$. The denominator is the square of the assumed electric vehicle emission rate relative to the adjusted standard and conventional vehicle emission rate, just as before. Because it is squared, it must be positive.

Signing each of the terms suggests that as long as the reasonable assumptions $e_{EV} \leq \partial(e_C^*/\partial M) + S_{GHG}$ and $e_{EV}M - e_C^* - S_{GHG}(M - 1) < 0$ hold, then the second term is negative. Thus, the overall comparative static $\partial s_{EV}^*/\partial M$ is negative. This implies that the market share of electric vehicles will be decreasing with increases in the credit multiplier, which provides our first analytical finding focusing on electric vehicles:

Finding 4: In a static setting and under the assumptions described above, the electric vehicle market share will decline with an increase in the credit multiplier.

This finding indicates that instead of incentivizing electric vehicles, the credit multiplier may actually reduce the market share of electric vehicles. The core intuition is that although the credit multiplier may make it more advantageous for the automakers to sell electric vehicles to meet the standard, the credit multiplier also relaxes the standard, and this relaxing force appears to dominate under reasonable assumptions.

This finding, although based on reasonable assumptions, may not hold all the time. For example, if the assumptions described above do not hold (e.g., the one suggesting that $\partial e_C^*/\partial M > 0$), then one could find that electric vehicle market share increases along with the credit multiplier. In the illustrative simulation, I explore combinations of parameters when this result does not hold.

I next examine the comparative static on how the electric vehicle market share changes with the assumed electric vehicle emission rate. Differentiating equation (5) with respect to e_{EV} gives the following:

$$\frac{\partial s_{EV}^*}{\partial e_{EV}} = \frac{(e_C^* - S_{GHG})\left(M - \frac{\partial e_C^*}{\partial e_{EV}}\right)}{(e_{EV}M - e_C^* - S_{GHG}(M - 1))^2} - \frac{\frac{\partial e_C^*}{\partial e_{EV}}}{e_{EV}M - e_C^* - S_{GHG}(M - 1)}.$$

This comparative static is somewhat more difficult to interpret and sign. It shows that whether the electric vehicle market share increases or decreases with the emission rate depends on several factors. First is the difference between the optimal conventional vehicle emission rate and the standard (to capture the stringency on conventional vehicles and thus need for electric vehicles). Second, the difference between the credit multiplier and derivative of the conventional emission rate with respect to the electric vehicle emission rate (again capturing how electric vehicles are needed). Third, the relative difference between the adjusted electric vehicle emission rate and the conventional vehicle emission rate and adjusted standard. Finally, the derivative of the conventional emission rate with respect to the electric vehicle emission rate also comes in separately.

Because we showed above that $\partial e_C^*/\partial e_{EV}$ is most likely negative (Finding 3), following the same assumptions made before, the first of the two large terms on the right-hand side is going to be positive. The second is also going to be positive, but is being subtracted off, leaving the sign of the comparative static ambiguous. It is difficult to sign the two terms without parameterization, but it seems quite possible that the first term is larger because the terms in the numerator are likely to be much larger than the derivative (although they are divided by a square in the denominator). Thus, the next finding is the following:

Finding 5: In a static setting, electric vehicle market share may be increasing with the assumed electric vehicle emission rate.

Put differently, this finding states that ignoring upstream emissions from electric vehicles when calculating the fleet-wide average greenhouse gas emissions rate for compliance with the EPA greenhouse gas standard could reduce the electric vehicle market share, counter to the intention. This counterintuitive result holds when $(e_C^* - S_{GHG})(M - \partial e_C^*/\partial e_{EV})/(e_{EV}M - e_C^* - S_{GHG}(M - 1))^2 > \partial e_C^*/\partial e_{EV}/e_{EV}M - e_C^* - S_{GHG}(M - 1)$.

For some intuition, we can see that the result is more likely to occur when the optimal emission rate for conventional vehicles is substantially above the standard (S_{GHG}), so that the automaker is far from meeting the standard based on their conventional vehicle fleet alone. Thus, the finding would be less likely hold in the very early stages of electric vehicle penetration when there are so few electric vehicles that compliance must be largely based on the emission rate of the conventional vehicle fleet on its own.

These two findings on electric vehicles point to possible unintended consequences of regulatory design features that were expected to promote electric vehicles but instead can weaken the standards sufficiently that they reduce the incentive to sell electric vehicles.

B. Effects of Generous Crediting Allowing for Innovation

The analysis so far has been a static analysis, but at least part of the policy rationale for the generous crediting may have been to induce innovation in electric vehicles and bring down their costs. I extend the static model above to a two-period setting, in which the profits from electric vehicles in the second period are a function of the market share of electric vehicles in the first period. Under this framework, it is also possible to allow the conventional vehicle profits to depend on the market share of conventional vehicles or the emission rate of conventional vehicles in the first period. For example, if automakers invest heavily in reducing the emission rate in the first period, this may influence the cost of emission-rate reductions in the second period. I allow for this by writing the second-period profits from conventional vehicles as a function of first-period outcomes, but focus on the induced innovation channel for electric vehicles because they are the newer technology with the most scope for innovation.

For this analysis, I assume that automakers have perfect foresight and optimize over both periods. To simplify notation, I set up the problem ignoring any discounting of the second period. With a slight addition to the notation to refer to period 1 and period 2 in subscripts, this extended profit maximization problem can be written as follows:

$$\max_{s_{EV,i}, e_{C,i} \forall i \in \{1,2\}} V_1[s_{EV,1}\pi_{EV,1} + (1 - s_{EV,1})\pi_{C,1}(e_{C,1})] +$$

$$V_2[s_{EV,2}\pi_{EV,2}(s_{EV,1}) + (1 - s_{EV,2})\pi_{C,2}(1 - s_{C,1}, e_{C,1}, e_{C,2})] \tag{6}$$

$$\text{subject to} \quad s_{EV,1}e_{EV,1}M_1 + (1 - s_{EV,1})e_{C,1} \leq S_{GHG,1}(1 + (M_1 - 1)s_{EV,1})$$

$$s_{EV,2}e_{EV,2}M_2 + (1 - s_{EV,2})e_{C,2} \leq S_{GHG,2}(1 + (M_2 - 1)s_{EV,2}).$$

By adding the link between the two time periods, the automaker has an incentive to sell more electric vehicles in the first period to raise the profits from selling electric vehicles in the second period as long as the profits in the second period from selling electric vehicles are increasing in the market share of electric vehicles in the first period ($d\pi_{EV,2}/ds_{EV,1} \geq 0$), as would be expected.

The first-order conditions described in the previous subsection are identical for the second period in this problem (i.e., for $s_{EV,2}$ and $e_{C,2}$). However, in the first period, the first-order conditions will contain a new term that captures the incentive to sell more electric vehicles in the first period. Thus, the first-order condition from differentiating with respect to $s_{EV,1}$ is

$$V_1[\pi_{C,1} - \pi_{EV,1}] - V_2 s_{EV,2} \frac{d\pi_{EV,2}}{ds_{EV,1}} + \lambda_1[e_{EV,1}M_1 - e_{C,1} - S_{GHG,1}(M_1 - 1)] = 0.$$

Comparing this with equation (3), we observe a new middle term, with $V_2 \geq 0$, $s_{EV,2} \geq 0$, and $d\pi_{EV,2}/ds_{EV,1} \geq 0$ (the latter due to lowered costs from additional experience), so the first-order condition subtracts off a positive term. Accordingly, the addition of this term to the first-order condition implies that the automaker will sell more electric vehicles in the first period than without the term. The intuition is straightforward: There are additional profits to be had in the second period if the automaker sells more electric vehicles in the first period to bring down the costs.

A straightforward rearrangement of the first-order condition also suggests that, all else equal, the shadow price on the constraint (λ_1) decreases due to the addition of the new term. In other words, the choice to sell more electric vehicles makes it easier to meet the standard. This also then implies that the automakers can raise the vehicle emission rate of their conventional vehicles in the first period.

Of course, if more electric vehicles are sold in the first period, automakers can sell more inefficient conventional vehicles while still meeting the standard, which would partly or entirely offset any emission reductions from the increased electric vehicles sold in that period. Having more electric vehicles sold in the first period may or may not affect innovation in conventional vehicles that influences the second period, depending on how reduced numbers of conventional vehicles (which are also less-efficient conventional vehicles) affect profits for conventional vehicles in the second period. It is possible that with fewer conventional vehicles being sold in the first period, the profits from selling conventional vehicles will be lower in the second period (due to less innovation and higher costs). If the automakers recognize this "reduced innovation" effect, they may choose to invest in lowering the emission intensity of conventional vehicles or to sell more conventional vehicles in the first period, perhaps offsetting the electric vehicle innovation effect.

The research question at hand, however, is whether generous crediting of electric vehicles in the first period can influence the electric vehicle market share when there is an electric vehicle innovation effect and automakers are forward looking. It turns out that the assumptions that lead to the relatively clean findings in the static setting may still hold, but are slightly less likely to hold. This is stated in the following:

Finding 6: In a dynamic setting with perfect foresight where electric vehicle innovation can be induced by electric vehicle sales today, electric vehicle market share in the first period may increase or decrease when the first-period credit multiplier is increased or the first-period emission rate assumed for electric vehicles in ascertaining compliance with the standards is decreased.

This finding comes about because the assumptions underlying the previous findings are somewhat less likely to hold. The intuition for this result is that in a dynamic setting with induced innovation in electric vehicles, there is greater value to sales of electric vehicles in the first time period due to the benefits in the second time period. Thus, at low levels of electric vehicle market share, the more generous crediting can make electric vehicles worth selling for the automaker even if they are less profitable in the short run, although not substantially affecting compliance with the standards by conventional vehicles. Note that this phenomenon may also occur in the static setting, but that the assumptions required are less likely without the added innovation benefit in the second period from the first period's electric vehicle sales.

In short, the analysis suggests that at very low levels of electric vehicle market share (which can be somewhat higher as the innovation effect for electric vehicles is strengthened), the generous crediting in the EPA greenhouse gas standards can increase electric vehicle market share by making some additional electric vehicles worth selling. But at higher levels of electric vehicle market share, the weakening of the standard dominates and the generous crediting decreases the electric vehicle market share. The next section provides simulation results to illustrate this relationship.

There is a corollary here to carbon dioxide emissions as well. More generous crediting would only reduce emissions if the innovation effect is strong and the second-period upstream emissions from electricity generation to power the electric vehicles do not appreciably weaken the standards and allow for less-efficient vehicles. This will depend on the emission rates, strength of the innovation effect, the exact specifications of profits, and the level of the standard itself. A simulation approach is well suited for exploring this.

C. Simulation Results

This section develops a simple simulation to illustrate how these effects may play out in a transparent setting. Although this simulation is stylized to build intuition, the building blocks here could readily be implemented in a carefully parameterized modeling framework by EPA and NHSTA. For example, NHTSA could run their Volpe CAFE model that is used for rule-makings with different crediting approaches for electric vehicles to see which effects dominate. The goal of this exercise is to use parameterizations that are reasonable and can provide insight across a broader range of parameter values than could be readily implemented in a much more complex model.

For the primary simulation results presented here, I implement a two-period model with perfect foresight. Just as in equation (6), automakers choose the electric vehicle market share and emission rate of conventional vehicles in both periods to maximize the sum of profits over the two periods while meeting the standards in each period. The model allows for an electric vehicle induced innovation effect; however, if this effect is removed, the model reduces to two separate static models.

I assume that the per-vehicle profits for conventional vehicles are a fixed value minus a concave function of the difference between a starting or baseline emission rate and the chosen emission rate. If this difference is larger, then the automakers must have invested more to reduce the emission rate (either directly in technologies or indirectly through reduced levels of other attributes), thus lowering the per-vehicle profit. The per-vehicle profit for electric vehicles is an assumed constant in the first period and is a linear function of the first-period electric vehicle sales in the second period. The constraint in each period is just the weighted average emission rate across the fleet.

I choose parameterizations to give values for outcome variables that are at least generally realistic, and the details of these, along with the exact equations used, are given in appendix Subsection II.A. The greenhouse gas standard in the first period is assumed to be 165 grams/mile (g/mi), which is a modest decrease from today's standard. The greenhouse gas standard for the second period is assumed to be 100 g/mi, which is an ambitious standard that goes well beyond the Obama-era standards. It may be a possible standard for 2028 or 2030, though. For calculating total emissions, I assume this representative automaker sells 500,000 vehicles per year. I solve the model using a nonlinear solver with different values of the electric vehicle credit multiplier and emission intensity assumed for electric vehicles for compliance with the standards.[12]

Figure 2 shows the first-period share of electric vehicles—a key policy objective—over different values of the electric vehicle credit multiplier (*x*-axis) and assumed electric vehicle emission intensity (the three different lines). This figure uses the baseline values, which assume that electric vehicles are modestly less profitable than conventional vehicles (an average profit per vehicle of $4,000 rather than just more than $5,000). This is what we might expect to be the case in the next few years, although is likely to be optimistic today. Note that the market share of electric vehicles at the 1.6 multiplier and zero assumed emission rate for electric vehicles is about 8%, which is above the 2% market share of electric vehicles in the United States in 2020 (Statista 2021), likely because the profits per vehicle for electric vehicles are less than for conventional vehicles by a larger margin today (James-Armand 2021). This is projected to change in the upcoming years by many industry analysts (BNEF 2020).

In figure 2, we observe that the market share of electric vehicles is lower with higher electric vehicle credit multipliers. Similarly, the market share of electric vehicles is also declining with lower emission rates assumed for electric vehicles for compliance with the standards. Indeed, the lowest

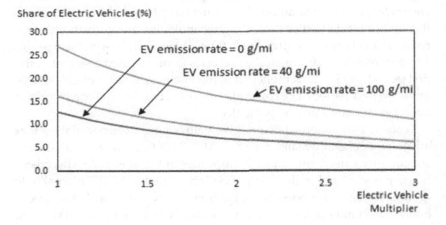

Fig. 2. Period 1 electric vehicle (EV) market share with different assumed EV emission rates and credit multipliers. Color version available as an online enhancement.

electric vehicle market share is with a high credit multiplier and zero-emission intensity. These results correspond quite closely with the analytical findings above. The result is coming about because increasing the multiplier and decreasing the emission intensity effectively relax the stringency of the standard.

What do the results imply for emissions? Panel A of figure 3 shows the first-period tailpipe emissions from the overall vehicle fleet and panel B

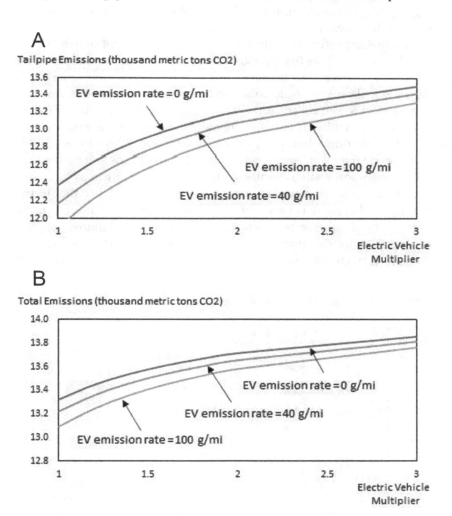

Fig. 3. Period 1 tailpipe emissions (panel *A*) and total emissions (panel *B*) with different assumed electric vehicle (EV) emission rates and credit multipliers. Color version available as an online enhancement.

of figure 3 shows the first-period total emissions, assuming a true up-stream emission rate for electric vehicles of 100 g/mi in the first period.[13] The results are clear: Carbon dioxide emissions are higher with higher credit multipliers and with lower assumed electric vehicle emission intensity. These results come about primarily from the reduced electric vehicle market share. The optimal emission rate for conventional vehicles does change very slightly across the scenarios due to the constraint being slightly relaxed with more electric vehicles, but this effect is very modest (less than 1% in these simulations).

Automaker profits are slightly affected as well. Figure 4 shows that automaker profits in the first period increase with the electric vehicle credit multiplier. This is mostly because it allows them to sell more higher-profit conventional vehicles. Automaker profits are also higher with a lower assumed electric vehicle emission rate, with the highest profits at a zero-emission rate, which relaxes the constraint the most. These simulation results are illustrative, but they provide suggestive evidence for why most automakers have not been opposed to generous electric vehicle credits.

The analytical results discussed above suggest that generous crediting could increase the market share of electric vehicles when the electric vehicle market share is very low and there is substantial induced innovation. The simulation results so far allow for induced innovation, but assume that electric vehicles are at least somewhat close to being as profitable as conventional vehicles in the first period. I adjust the assumed

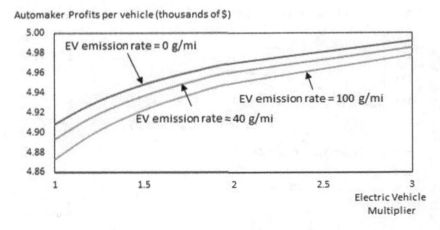

Fig. 4. Period 1 profits per vehicle for the representative automaker with different assumed electric vehicle (EV) emission rates and credit multipliers. Color version available as an online enhancement.

profitability of electric vehicles downward, reducing it to $1,000 per vehicle in the first period. This may even be more realistic today (although some Tesla models could be quite profitable). This change alone dramatically affects the results.

Panel A of figure 5 shows the share of electric vehicles with this lower profitability of electric vehicles in the first period. We observe that the

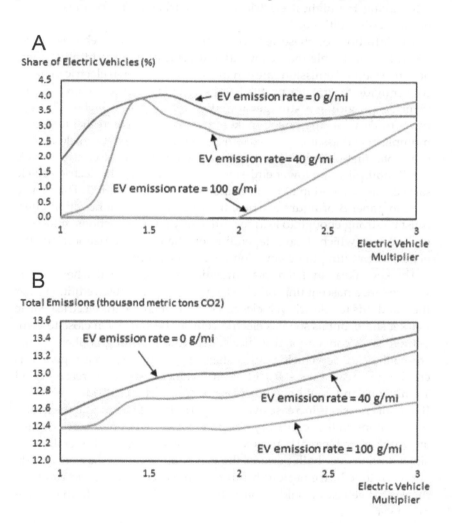

Fig. 5.   Period 1 electric vehicle (EV) market share (panel *A*) and total emissions (panel *B*) with different assumed EV emission rates and credit multipliers when electric vehicles are very far from cost-competitive with conventional vehicles. Color version available as an online enhancement.

overall market shares, regardless of the values of crediting or emission intensity, are less than half of those in figure 2, as would be expected if electric vehicles are much less profitable. Notably, there is overall an increase in the electric vehicle market share with higher credit multipliers. Along the same lines, there is also an increase in electric vehicle market share as the emission rate decreases, with the zero assumed emission rate having the highest electric vehicle market share for most values of the credit multiplier.

The intuition for these results is that when electric vehicles are so much less profitable than conventional vehicles, the credit multipliers or zero assumed emission rate can mean that additional electric vehicles sold provide for greater profits from selling less-efficient conventional vehicles, providing a stronger incentive for electric vehicles. This appears to be what the policy makers had in mind when including the multipliers and assuming a zero-emission rate for electric vehicles. However, total first-period emissions increase with the higher electric vehicle credit multiplier and lower emission rate, so this boost to electric vehicle sales comes at a cost in terms of emissions in the first period. This can be seen in panel B of figure 5. Thus, the electric vehicle innovation effect must be strong enough to lead to sufficiently large reductions in the second period (which it can, depending on the parameterization) for the generous crediting to be emission-reducing overall.[14]

The key takeaway from this simulation analysis is that when electric vehicles are a nascent unprofitable technology, generous crediting under the standards for electric vehicles can serve to increase the electric vehicle market share, but as soon as electric vehicles become even close to competitive with conventional vehicles, generous crediting is likely to decrease the electric vehicle market share. Furthermore, even if generous crediting increases the share of electric vehicles, it will increase period 1 emissions and could even increase overall carbon dioxide emissions. If overall emissions increase over both periods, then including the generous crediting in the regulatory design will clearly not be a cost-effective approach to reduce carbon dioxide emissions. But even if overall emissions decline over both periods, the generous crediting may be a costly approach to reduce emissions because the direct emission reductions from the electric vehicles would be offset by increased emissions from conventional vehicles.

One aspect of the analysis thus far is that using a multiplier greater than 1 and assuming a zero-emission rate from electric vehicles effectively serves to reduce the effective stringency of the standards. Put in terms of the notation in equation (3), this means that the shadow price on the constraint, λ, is lower with these assumptions in place. This goes a long way toward explaining the simulation result. The effective stringency of standards is important because it determines how much the standards influence automaker decisions. One could also consider a case where the standard is adjusted along with the multiplier or electric vehicle emission rate to hold the shadow price constant. I explore this scenario by adding a constraint that holds the shadow price to a fixed value and allows the standard itself to vary. I fix the shadow price at its value with the multiplier $M = 1.6$ for each electric vehicle emission rate separately (e.g., 0, 40, 100 g/mi). See appendix Subsection II.B for more details.

One finding that emerges from this analysis is that the greenhouse gas standard necessary to keep the shadow price constant is decreasing in the electric vehicle multiplier, but not differing greatly across emission rates (see fig. A1). The simulation results also suggest that the resulting market share of electric vehicles in the first period does not change much with more generous crediting when λ is held constant—which makes sense because the reason generous crediting matters is that it changes the effective stringency.

These findings provide clear guidance to policy makers on the factors at work in the generous crediting of electric vehicles and show how timing matters for the cost-effectiveness of the regulatory design approach.

IV.   Standards with Uncertain Electric Vehicle Costs

Vehicle standards are always set with uncertainty about future technology improvements. But before electric vehicles, this uncertainty was at least somewhat constrained. Conventional vehicle technologies are relatively mature and the standards are typically only set for 5 years (by statute, NHTSA can only set fuel-economy standards for 5 years). Thus, the list of technologies and approaches to improve conventional vehicle fuel economy and reduce greenhouse gas emissions can be developed in advance and used in standard-setting.

In contrast to the costs of conventional vehicle technologies, there is substantial uncertainty about electric vehicle technology costs even 5 years from today. Some analysts foresee costs remaining high and only a modest market share for electric vehicles (EIA 2021). Others are much more optimistic and forecast electric vehicles rapidly declining in price over the next several years and reaching a relatively sizable market share by 2030 and nearly half of the market or more by 2035 (e.g., BNEF

2020). It is likely that the next standards being set under the Biden administration will cover much of this period of highly uncertain, but potentially rapid, development of electric vehicles.

A potential concern with having only a single combined standard is that, although many electric vehicles may be sold if they become very low cost, the electric vehicles sold will also enable automakers to sell highly inefficient conventional vehicles and still meet the standard. Indeed, the conventional vehicles could even have lower fuel economy on average than the current vehicles on the road today, which are constrained by today's standards. Thus, emissions from conventional vehicles could remain constant or even increase with the standard, offsetting some of the emission reductions from the increased electric vehicles.

If the policy-making goal is to reduce emissions, then having emissions from conventional vehicles increasing would be counterproductive. The welfare effects may be more complicated of course and would depend on the magnitude of the externalities from the emissions and on whether consumers gain or lose welfare from less-efficient conventional vehicles. If either the Trump administration's or the Obama administration's rule makings on standards are correct, then year-over-year improvements in conventional fuel economy have positive net benefits and thus are social welfare improving.[15] Thus, having conventional vehicle fuel economy and emissions backslide and become worse than today's would leave cost-effective emission reductions on the table.

How can policy makers ensure cost-effective improvements for conventional vehicles? It would not be possible under a combined standard alone. The regulatory design would have to be changed. One possibility is a "backstop" standard for conventional vehicles that is designed to be nonbinding unless electric vehicles quickly become quite inexpensive. This could be a weak conventional vehicle standard that requires only modest year-over-year improvements. For example, it could require the automakers to add new low-cost conventional vehicle technologies. And it could be implemented in concert with an ambitious combined standard that accounts for electric vehicles in the setting of the standard. No trading would be allowed between this backstop standard and the combined standard.

The automakers would not have to worry about this conventional vehicle standard under most circumstances, so the additional regulatory burden would only occur if inexpensive electric vehicles render the combined standard largely nonbinding and allow for highly inefficient conventional vehicles to be sold. These two standards should be permitted under existing statutes. For example, EPA has the flexibility to set a back-stop vehicle greenhouse gas standard alone. Alternatively, with a tweak to the statutes that NHTSA is working under, to remove the requirement that electric vehicles apply toward standard compliance (with the petroleum-equivalence factor), the NHSTA fuel-economy standard could serve as the conventional backstop and EPA's greenhouse gas standards could serve as the more ambitious combined standard. Such a tweak would of course require congressional action. It may also be possible to set the petroleum-equivalence factor for electric vehicles so that electric vehicles do not apply toward compliance, with an argument that the statute requires the Secretary of Energy to set the factor based on "the need of the United States to conserve all forms of energy and the relative scarcity and value to the United States of all fuel used to generate electricity" (US Congress 1994, 217).

An analytical treatment of the two standards looks similar to the analytical modeling in the previous section, and adding uncertainty—which is very possible to do—adds complexity without much additional intuition. Thus, I turn directly to a simulation to consider ex ante regulatory design under uncertainty.

A.   Simulation Results

The simulation analysis focuses on three scenarios of electric vehicle costs: high, medium, and low. The high-cost scenario assumes that the profits from electric vehicles remain well below the profits from conventional vehicles, even in the second period. The medium-cost scenario assumes higher profits for electric vehicles, but profits that are still below those for conventional vehicles. The low-cost scenario assumes that the profits for electric vehicles approach those for conventional vehicles.

For all three of these scenarios, I first explore what the scenarios would imply under a combined standard that covers conventional and electric vehicles and that has a stronger standard in the second period than the first. The basic framework is the two-period framework discussed above, but I use different assumptions about the profitability of electric vehicles. For realism, I assume that the electric vehicle credit multiplier is 1.6 in the first period and 1 in the second period, and that electric vehicles are assumed to have zero emissions when calculating compliance with the standards. Changing these assumptions changes the exact quantitative estimates, but does not alter the qualitative findings.

For the standards in this illustrative scenario, I assume a combined standard of 165 g/mi in the first period and 100 g/mi in the second period. When a backstop conventional standard is added, I assume this standard is set at 150 g/mi in the second period (with no backstop in the first period). The parameterizations of each of the three scenarios are laid out in appendix Subsection II.C.

Figure 6 illustrates how the two standards influence electric vehicle market share. Panel A shows the results for the first period, and panel B shows the results for the second period. In the high electric vehicle cost scenario, automakers have to improve conventional vehicle technology anyway to meet the binding combined standard, so the backstop conventional vehicle standard has no effect. In the medium-cost scenario, more electric vehicles come on the road anyway, but somewhat fewer are required to enable the automaker to meet the standard when there is a conventional vehicle backstop standard forcing improvements in the emission rate of conventional vehicles anyway. In the low-cost scenario, the addition of the backstop conventional vehicle standard considerably increases the electric vehicle market share because conventional vehicles are more efficient and thus less profitable, so it is profit-maximizing to switch over more quickly and completely to electric vehicles. These are the high-level findings and examining the full suite of results helps to clarify the mechanisms at work.

I thus present table 1, which includes all of the main results to enable a more complete explanation for the findings. Column 1 shows the results under high electric vehicle costs, column 2 under medium costs, and column 3 under low costs. Panel A shows the results with a single combined standard, whereas panel B shows the results with both a combined standard and a backstop. It is useful to look both across the panels and across the electric vehicle cost scenarios.

With high costs under the single standard (col. 1 in panel A), the electric vehicle market share is very small in the first period and increases in the second period due to the need for electric vehicles to meet an ambitious standard, just as in figure 6. The conventional vehicle emission factors are substantially above the standard in both periods because the electric vehicles are averaged in. Emissions decline in the second period due to the tighter standard, and correspondingly, automaker profits are reduced. When the profit maximization is performed with the backstop conventional standard as an additional constraint, the results are identical, as can be seen in panel B. This is because the backstop conventional

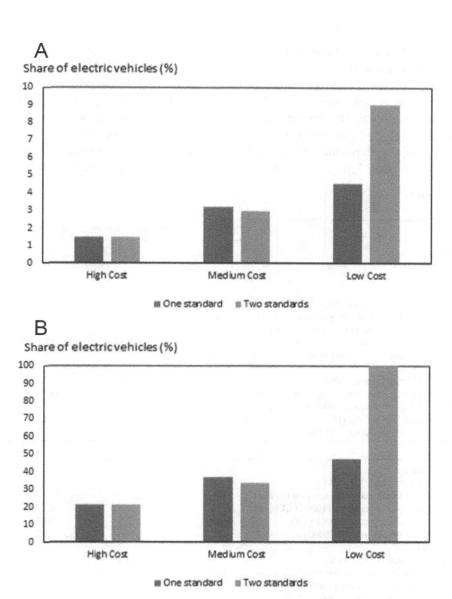

Fig. 6. Market share of electric vehicles under the three scenarios of electric vehicle cost with a single standard covering electric vehicles and conventional vehicles or two standards, which would consist of the single standard plus a backstop conventional vehicle standard. Note the very different *y*-axis scales in panel *A*, which shows the results for the first period, and panel *B*, which shows the results for the second period. Color version available as an online enhancement.

standard is not binding, and thus the representative automaker will effectively ignore it.

With medium costs under the single standard (col. 2 in panel A), the electric vehicle market share is slightly larger than with high costs, again as in figure 6. The market share increases in the second period, just as in the high-cost scenario. The conventional vehicle emission rate is also substantially above the standard in both periods because the electric vehicles are averaged in, just as under high costs. Emissions again decline in the

Table 1
Simulation Results

	High EV Cost	Medium EV Cost	Low EV Cost
	(1)	(2)	(3)
Panel A: Single Standard			
Period 1:			
EV market share (%)	1.5	3.2	4.5
Conventional emission rate (g/mi)	169	174	172
Tailpipe emissions (1000s t CO_2)	12.5	12.6	12.3
Total emissions (1000s t CO_2)	12.6	12.9	12.7
Profits per vehicle (1000s $)	4.8	4.8	4.7
Period 2:			
EV market share (%)	21.3	36.8	47.0
Conventional emission rate (g/mi)	127	158	189
Tailpipe emissions (1000s t CO_2)	7.5	7.5	7.5
Total emissions (1000s t CO_2)	7.8	8.1	8.2
Profits per vehicle (1000s $)	2.1	3.2	5.0
Panel B: Two Standards			
Period 1:			
EV market share (%)	1.5	3.0	9.0
Conventional emission rate (g/mi)	169	173	185
Tailpipe emissions (1000s t CO_2)	12.5	12.6	12.7
Total emissions (1000s t CO_2)	12.6	12.8	13.3
Profits per vehicle (1000s $)	4.8	4.8	4.6
Period 2:			
EV market share (%)	21.3	33.3	100.0
Conventional emission rate (g/mi)	127	150	150
Tailpipe emissions (1000s t CO_2)	7.5	7.5	0
Total emissions (1000s t CO_2)	7.8	8.0	1.5
Profits per vehicle (1000s $)	2.1	3.1	5.1

Note: The results in this table are from the illustrative simulation showing how the automaker profit-maximizing solution changes depending on whether electric vehicle (EV) costs are high, medium, or low. High costs are a situation where electric are very far from profitable relative to conventional vehicles, medium costs are when electric vehicles are still less profitable than conventional vehicles but are still somewhat profitable, and low costs are when electric vehicles are nearly as profitable as conventional vehicles.

second period, although they are even higher than in the high-cost scenario. Automaker profits are lower in the second period than the first, although higher in the second period than under the high-cost scenario.

When the backstop conventional standard is added under the medium-cost scenario, this standard is binding in the second period, so the conventional vehicle emission rate in the second period is exactly equal to 150 g/mi. This occurs because the increased electric vehicles allow for so many more less-efficient conventional vehicles that the backstop conventional standard becomes binding. With this binding backstop standard in the second period, total emissions do not increase as much relative to the high-cost scenario as they did with a single combined standard. But profits also do not increase as much. The electric vehicle market share is slightly lower in both periods when the backstop conventional standard is also in place. This is true in the second period because the automaker is required to improve the conventional vehicle emission rate to meet the backstop standard, so fewer electric vehicles are required. This effect in the second period also influences the first period through the electric vehicle innovation effect.

With low electric vehicle costs under the single standard (col. 3 in panel A), the electric vehicle market share is notably higher, just as was seen in figure 6. However, this higher electric vehicle market share enables automakers to sell less-efficient conventional vehicles in both periods, so the conventional vehicle emission rate increases substantially in both. This means that total emissions do not substantially decrease in period 1 and actually increase in period 2. However, note that a 100 g/mi emission rate is assumed for upstream electricity generation used to power the electric vehicles in both periods. If electricity is substantially decarbonized by the second period, total emissions could decline in this scenario relative to the medium- or high-cost scenarios.

The backstop conventional standard binds even more strongly when electric vehicle costs are low (col. 3 in panel B). Specifically, the conventional emission rate in the second period in panel A is 189 g/mi, which is substantially above the backstop standard of 150 g/mi. With that standard included, we observe a relatively extreme result: The automaker switches entirely to electric vehicles. Electric vehicles are similarly profitable to conventional vehicles and the 150 g/mi conventional vehicle standard is difficult to meet, so the profit-maximizing approach simply leads to all electric vehicles. The automaker profits are also higher and total emissions are much lower. I describe this as a relatively extreme result because there may be heterogeneity in consumers and certain vehicle types may be more expensive to shift to electric vehicles, so an average analysis, such as this one, would miss the heterogeneity. But the insight from the illustrative simulation is clear: Adding the backstop conventional vehicle standard can lead to a much higher market share of electric vehicles under the low-cost scenario.

These simulation findings underscore that a combined standard along with a backstop conventional standard set with small year-over-year increases in fuel economy has the potential to substantially increase electric vehicle uptake and reduce carbon dioxide emissions if electric vehicle technology continues to progress very rapidly. The trade-off is that if electric vehicle costs align more closely with the medium cost decline scenario, then electric vehicle uptake could slightly decrease and carbon dioxide emissions slightly increase. If electric vehicle costs remain much higher than conventional vehicle costs, the backstop conventional standard is entirely nonbinding and thus does not affect automaker decisions.

One possible caveat is the potential for the conventional vehicle standard to induce some innovation in conventional vehicle technology. In theory, if this effect is very strong, it could lead to more profitable conventional vehicles in the second period and reduced electric vehicle market share and emissions reductions in both periods. However, conventional vehicles are a quite mature technology and the backstop conventional vehicle standard would be set with small year-over-year increases or no increases at all, so there would not likely be a strong incentive for innovation in conventional vehicle technologies from the standard. This suggests such a conventional induced innovation effect may not appreciably affect the key findings.

V. Concluding Discussion

This study analyzes key aspects of ex ante policy design for standards that regulate the fuel economy or greenhouse gas emissions of light-duty vehicles. The technology pathway for the light-duty vehicle fleet appears to be at a crossroads, with many analysts forecasting much higher electric vehicle market share in the upcoming decade. However, this is highly uncertain and policy makers face challenging questions about how to design the regulation to meet policy objectives. One stated policy objective of the Biden administration is to encourage electric vehicle deployment.[16] Design details of standards have been leveraged in the recent past to try to encourage electric vehicles and there are open questions about how to encourage them cost-effectively going forward.

The first major result of this study points to trade-offs inherent in generous crediting of electric vehicles as part of the standard. When electric vehicles are a niche technology that is far from being profitable, generous crediting can serve to increase electric vehicle market share because automakers will find selling more unprofitable electric vehicles worth it to allow them to sell more profitable inefficient conventional vehicles. However, as electric vehicles become even remotely close to being profitable, generous crediting can quickly serve to relax the constraint imposed by the standard sufficiently that it reduces electric vehicle market share.

Furthermore, by relaxing the standard, the generous crediting can lead to less-efficient conventional vehicles and higher overall emissions from light-duty transportation. These basic findings hold both with and without induced innovation for electric vehicles based on the first-period market share, but induced innovation makes it more likely that electric vehicle market share will increase. Thus, policy makers may wish to be cautious in extending generous crediting for electric vehicles if the policy goals are to increase electric vehicle market share and reduce emissions. Indeed, by allowing for less-efficient conventional vehicles, the generous crediting is not likely to be a cost-effective approach to reduce emissions once electric vehicles are a competitive technology with conventional vehicles. Policy makers could of course tighten the standard at the same time as allowing generous crediting, which would ensure that the effective stringency of the standard remains the same.

This study also explores the trade-offs from implementing a weak backstop conventional vehicle standard in concert with a more ambitious standard that covers both electric vehicles and conventional vehicles. This approach with two standards appears possible under existing statutes, with one possibility being that EPA develops both standards under the Clean Air Act. Another possibility might be that the NHTSA CAFE standard serves as the backstop conventional vehicle standard and the EPA greenhouse gas regulation serves as the combined standard. This second possibility could be enabled with only a minor tweak to language by Congress and may even be possible without congressional action. The backstop standard will not be binding if electric vehicle costs remain high, so it is possible that it will not affect automaker decisions.

In a world with inexpensive electric vehicles, we would expect many more electric vehicles to be sold, which could lead the combined standard that includes both conventional vehicles and electric vehicles to become nonbinding. Thus, a backstop standard can serve to prevent automakers from selling highly inefficient conventional vehicles. This would imply that somewhat fewer electric vehicles will be sold than without the back-stop, but emissions will be lower on net. In addition, as long as there continue to be low-cost emissions reductions possible from the conventional fleet with steadily improving technology, the backstop standard ensures that these cost-effective emissions reductions occur, leading to greater overall cost-effectiveness of the regulation. With much lower electric vehicle costs that bring electric vehicles close to upfront cost parity with conventional vehicles, the backstop will mean that automakers are better off switching entirely to electric vehicles, leading to much larger emissions reductions (and higher profits for the automakers). Thus, under uncertainty, there are trade-offs in implementing a secondary backstop standard that depend on the exact path of electric vehicle technology costs.

The results of this study are illustrated for a representative automaker, but there will be heterogeneity in automakers and classes of vehicles. For example, General Motors has already indicated that it plans to sell only electric vehicles by 2035 (Boudette and Davenport 2021), likely due to a corporate leadership belief that electric vehicles will become inexpensive and highly profitable. In contrast, the management of Toyota has expressed much more skepticism about electric vehicles and plans to retain a focus on hybrid electric-conventional vehicles and explore hydrogen vehicles much more. In addition, there is substantial heterogeneity across states in the United States in electric vehicle policies (e.g., zero-emission vehicle policies) and electric vehicle sales. Such heterogeneity will likely prevent 100% market share of electric vehicles in the entire new vehicle fleet in the next decade, but it would not change the core insights of this paper. NHTSA and EPA could readily draw upon the intuition laid out in this paper to perform more detailed modeling of the light-duty fleet to trace out exactly when each of the findings will hold, allowing for regulatory development to meet policy-maker objectives as cost-effectively as possible.

Appendix

I. Mathematical Details on the Effects of Generous Crediting in a Static Model

A. Rewriting the Standard

This short appendix section explains how we can obtain the version of the standard in equation (2), which illustrates how including a multiplier greater than 1 can directly influence the standard. Recall, we begin with equation (1), which I rewrite here for completeness:

$$\frac{\sum_{i \in C} e_{C,i} V_i + \sum_{i \in EV} e_{EV,i} V_i M}{\sum_{i \in C} V_i + \sum_{i \in EV} V_i M} \leq \frac{\sum_{i \in C} S_{GHG,i} V_i + \sum_{i \in EV} S_{GHG,i} V_i M}{\sum_{i \in C} V_i + \sum_{i \in EV} V_i M}.$$

We can first note that the denominator is identical on both sides of the inequality, so the standard can be rewritten as

$$\sum_{i \in C} e_{C,i} V_i + \sum_{i \in EV} e_{EV,i} V_i M \leq \sum_{i \in C} e_C V_i + \sum_{i \in EV} e_{EV} V_i M.$$

We can then note that $\sum_{i \in C} e_{C,i} V_i = V(1 - s_{EV})e_C$, where V is the total number of vehicles sold, so $V(1 - s_{EV})$ is the number of conventional vehicles sold. This equality follows simply from the definition of an average. We can similarly replace the other summations, using the average for $S_{GHG,i}$ for the two on the right-hand side. This leads to the following inequality:

$$V(1 - s_{EV})e_C + V s_{EV} M e_{EV} \leq V(1 - s_{EV})S_{GHG} + V s_{EV} M S_{GHG}.$$

This much more compact equation is useful for providing quick intuition and provides the groundwork for the remainder of the analysis. We can divide both sides by V and rearrange to obtain

$$(1 - s_{EV})e_C + s_{EV} M e_{EV} \leq S_{GHG}(1 + (M - 1)s_{EV}).$$

This provides first intuition about how a multiplier greater than 1 serves to directly relax the standard, because $(M - 1)s_{EV}$ is positive, so a higher grams/mile emission rate is permitted if $M > 1$.

II. Details of the Simulation

A. Details for Generous Crediting Analysis

This appendix subsection describes further details of the illustrative simulation analysis. The basic framework of the simulation uses the same profit maximization approach laid out in the main text and I solve for the model explicitly using constrained optimization (rather than the first-order conditions, although using those would not change the result).

I will describe the two-period model equations, as those are the ones used in the simulation results presented.

The choice variables for the model are the electric vehicle share and conventional vehicle emission rate. For both, there is a period 1 and period 2 value, for a total of four choice variables. There also are several exogenous variables: the emission rate of electric vehicles in both periods, the credit multiplier in both periods, and the greenhouse gas standard itself in both periods.

I solve the maximization problem with values of the period 1 emission rate of electric vehicles in the following set: $\{0, 40, 100\}$. The units of these values are grams of carbon dioxide per mile. I fix the period 2 emission rate at zero, commensurate with a deep decarbonization of the electricity system. I solve the maximization problem with values of the period 1 credit multiplier in the set: $\{1, 1.2, 1.4, 1.6, 1.8, 2, 3\}$. I fix the period 2 credit multiplier at 1, so that electric vehicles and conventional vehicles will be treated the same in the second period. I set the period 1 greenhouse gas standard at 165 g/mi and the period 2 standard at 100 g/mi. These are both extremely ambitious relative to values today, which are on the order of 400 g/mi on average in 2018.[17] They should be considered illustrative examples in a future year with better technology. In that future year, I assume that the baseline no-standard average emission rate is 200 g/mi.

I calculate several variables of interest. Most simply, the market share of conventional vehicles is just one minus the market share of electric vehicles. I fix the per-vehicle profit for electric vehicles in the first period at $4,000 in my baseline runs. This can be thought of as an expected profit for all electric vehicles over a several-year period. Given that several automakers have announced a plan to go fully electric by 2035, clearly some automakers believe that they will be making profits from selling electric vehicles. Moreover, Tesla today is already earning a profit on each vehicle sold. In the second period, I model profits from selling electric vehicles as a function of the electric vehicle sales in the first period: $\pi_{EV,2} = 4000 + \gamma s_{EV,1}$. Here γ models the strength of the innovation effect. My baseline estimate for γ is 2,000. This leads to an electric vehicle profit that is higher in the second period than the first.

I model the conventional vehicle profits as a quadratic and concave function of the difference between the baseline average emission rate and the conventional vehicle emission rate. My baseline parameterization for period 1 is $\pi_{C,1} = 5000 + 8(\eta - e_{C,1}) - 0.4(\eta - e_{C,1})^2$. Here η is the baseline parameterization (200 g/mi). This equation gives a conventional vehicle profit on the order of $5,000 per vehicle in the first period. The period 2 parameterization for conventional vehicles is identical, only based on $e_{C,2}$. In side sensitivity runs, I also explored adding induced technological change to conventional vehicles as well, but do not include these in the primary results, as it is unclear how strong this induced innovation effect is (or even whether it exists at all).

I also constrain profits to be nonnegative and the electric vehicle shares to be between zero and one. The objective function and constraints are identical to those in the analytical modeling in Section III of the main text. For calculating emissions and profits, I assume the automaker sells 500,000 vehicles a year, which are driven 150,000 miles over their full lifetimes. The assumed upstream emission rate from charging electric vehicles is 100 g/mi in period 1 and 20 g/mi in period 2.

B.   Details on the Simulation Holding λ Constant

To perform the simulation holding constant the shadow price on the constraint, λ, the main change made is that I allow the standard $S_{GHG,1}$ to vary and set a new constraint that requires that the shadow price is equal to some fixed value. For each assumed electric vehicle emission rate, I first solve the model with the electric vehicle multiplier equal to 1.6 and calculate the shadow price by inverting the first-order condition with respect to the share of electric vehicles in the first period. I fix this shadow price for each of the other electric vehicle multiplier values I examine: 1.2, 1.4, 1.8, 2, and 3. All of the other equations, assumptions, and calculations are identical to those in the primary simulation results described above.

One of the key findings that emerges is how the multiplier reduces the effective stringency of the standards. Specifically, λ is much lower for higher values of the multiplier. Because the λ is somewhat harder to interpret, I instead present the greenhouse gas standard that would keep the stringency the same as when the multiplier is 1.6. This is shown in figure A1. The striking result in this figure is that the effective stringency is much higher at lower electric vehicle multipliers and much lower at higher electric vehicle multipliers. There is very little effect from changing the emission rate. In fact, it is likely that any differences across the emission rates are due to numerical or other optimization errors in the simulation. Notably, the nonlinear solver seems to be performing somewhat poorly with the added equality constraint that holds λ constant (especially for the 100 g/mi emission rate). A better solver may pin down the extremes more accurately.

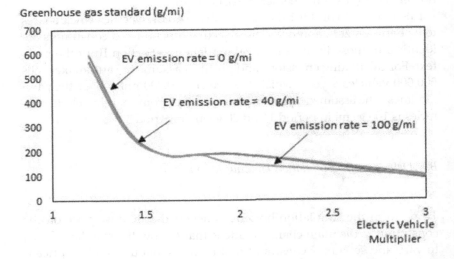

Greenhouse gas standard (g/mi)

Fig. A1. Plot of the isoquant of the greenhouse gas standard that would be necessary to keep the shadow price the same over different values of the emission rate and electric vehicle multiplier. The shadow price is fixed for each level of the emission rate at the value with the 1.6 multiplier. Color version available as an online enhancement.

C.   Details for the Uncertainty Analysis with a Backstop

For the analysis with uncertainty, I develop parameterizations for the high electric vehicle cost, medium-cost, and low-cost scenarios. The basic approach used is otherwise identical to that used for the crediting analysis, with exactly the same objective function and constraints.

Table A1 shows the full set of parameterizations used across the three scenarios in the baseline results presented in the main text. The term $S_{C,t}$ refers to the level of the conventional vehicle backstop standard in period t. The equations for the conventional vehicle profits ($\pi_{C,1}$ and $\pi_{C,2}$) are identical to those used in the generous crediting analysis described above. The equation for the per-vehicle profits in period 2 is $\pi_{EV,2} = v + \gamma s_{EV,1}$, and I show the values for v and γ in the table.

Table A1
Uncertainty Simulation Parameterizations

	High EV Cost	Medium EV Cost	Low EV Cost
	(1)	(2)	(3)
$e_{EV,1}$	0	0	0
$e_{EV,2}$	0	0	0
M_1	1.6	1.6	1.6
M_2	1	1	1
$S_{GHG,1}$	165	165	165
$S_{GHG,2}$	100	100	100
$S_{C,1}$	170	170	170
$S_{C,2}$	150	150	150
$\pi_{EV,1}$	−500	−100	0
v for $\pi_{EV,2}$	−3,000	500	4,760
γ for $\pi_{EV,2}$	4,000	4,000	4,000

Note: EV = electric vehicle.

Endnotes

Author email address: Gillingham (kenneth.gillingham@yale.edu). The author is grateful for constructive feedback from Jim Stock, Matt Kotchen, and Tatyana Deryugina. The author serves as an expert consultant on related issues for the California Air Resources Board and the Center for Applied Environmental Law and Policy, but has received no outside funding for this work. For acknowledgments, sources of research support, and disclosure of the author's material financial relationships, if any, please see https://www.nber .org/books-and-chapters/environmental-and-energy-policy-and-economy-volume-3 /designing-fuel-economy-standards-light-electric-vehicles.

1. See https://www.epa.gov/ghgemissions/sources-greenhouse-gas-emissions.

2. Vehicle fuel economy can be directly converted to a carbon dioxide emission rate, so fuel-economy standards and greenhouse gas standards are very closely related and this paper will refer generally to "standards" except where they differ.

3. The term "electric vehicles" is occasionally used to refer to both dedicated electric vehicles that have only an electric power source and plug-in hybrid electric vehicles (PHEV) that can run on both gasoline and electricity. This paper uses the term "electric vehicle" to refer to dedicated electric vehicles because automakers appear to be moving strongly in the direction of this class of electric vehicles due to the additional costs of having both a gasoline and electric supply chain. Source for the "100 new models" is https://www .nytimes.com/2021/04/22/business/electric-suvs-ford-volkswagen-volvo.html.

4. This leakage result from electric vehicles is also discussed in Jenn et al. (2016) using a different analytical and numerical framework and has been noted in subsequent papers as well, such as Carley et al. (2019).

5. There also could be interactions with other policies that affect automaker decisions and the stringency of standards, such as state-level zero-emission vehicle policies (Carley et al. 2019).

6. NHTSA points to a 1994 technical amendment passed by Congress that states that in developing fuel-economy standards, the Secretary of Transportation "may not consider the fuel economy of dedicated automobiles," where dedicated automobiles refer to any automobiles using only a fuel other than gasoline or diesel fuel. There is a similar clause for dual-fueled automobiles. See page 317 in Public Law 103-272 for further details (US Congress 1994). As well, page 319 of the same law states: "If a manufacturer manufactures

an electric vehicle, the Administrator shall include in the calculation of average fuel economy . . . equivalent petroleum based fuel economy values determined by the Secretary of Energy for various classes of electric vehicles." The statute also goes on to describe the factors that the Secretary of Energy needs to use to determine the "petroleum-equivalence factor." This factor greatly increases the number of compliance credits given to automakers for electric vehicles sold.

7. As mentioned above, NHTSA allows electric vehicles to be used for compliance with the standards, but they cannot be used in setting the standards.

8. The multiplier also applied to fuel-cell vehicles, and a lesser multiplier applies to PHEVs and dedicated natural-gas vehicles.

9. For details, see https://www.govinfo.gov/content/pkg/FR-2020-04-23/pdf/2020 -07098.pdf.

10. For details, see https://www.govinfo.gov/content/pkg/FR-2020-04-23/pdf /2020-07098.pdf. Technically, the actual calculation of the carbon dioxide credits is the difference between the left-hand side and right-hand side of equation (1) multiplied by the number of miles the vehicles are expected to be driven and total production (also adjusted for the multiplier) and normalized to be in the appropriate units.

11. This approach assumes that the electric vehicle profits are constant with the electric vehicle share. One could imagine profits from electric vehicles decreasing with electric vehicle sales if it requires more marketing or manufacturer discounts to sell more electric vehicles. Profits from conventional vehicles could even be affected as well. Exploring these details would be interesting for future work.

12. I use Generalized Reduced Gradient Nonlinear solver in Excel for most of the results, but confirm several in Matlab using fmincon.

13. The 100 g/mi estimate is a rough assumption. EPA upstream accounting currently reflects the difference between the electric vehicle's upstream emissions and the gasoline vehicle's upstream emissions. The 100 g/mi estimate may be on the high end depending on the exact assumptions used (GREET and eGRID use a current number closer to 75 g/mi), but is useful for illustrating the point.

14. In additional simulations, I find that increasing the strength of the electric vehicle innovation effect makes it slightly more likely that generous crediting will increase the share of electric vehicles in the first period, but the effect appears to be modest, even with a substantial innovation effect.

15. The automakers have supported year-over-year increases in conventional vehicle fuel economy, although generally they have only supported small increases. The economic rationale for the positive net benefits when we do not see consumers buying the more efficient vehicles in the market is that consumers undervalue future fuel savings from fuel-economy improvements by overweighting upfront costs. Several recent papers have suggested undervaluation (Allcott and Wozny 2014; Leard, Linn, and Zhou 2018; Gillingham, Houde, and van Benthem 2021), whereas others cannot reject perfect valuation (Busse, Knittel, and Zettelmeyer 2013; Sallee, West, and Fan 2016; Grigolon, Reynaert, and Verboven 2018) of fuel economy.

16. For example, see the April 22 White House Fact Sheet on advancing electric vehicle charging (White House 2021).

17. See https://www.epa.gov/greenvehicles/greenhouse-gas-emissions-typical-pas senger-vehicle.

References

Allcott, H., and N. Wozny. 2014. "Gasoline Prices, Fuel Economy, and the Energy Paradox." *Review of Economics and Statistics* 96 (5): 779–95.

Anderson, S., and J. Sallee. 2011. "Using Loopholes to Reveal the Marginal Cost of Regulation: The Case of Fuel-Economy Standards." *American Economic Review* 101:1375–409.

Bento, A., K. Gillingham, M. Jacobsen, C. Knittel, B. Leard, J. Linn, V. McConnell et al. 2018. "Flawed Analyses of US Auto Fuel Economy Standards." *Science* 6419:1119–21.

BNEF (Bloomberg New Energy Finance). 2020. "New Energy Outlook 2020." Technical report, BNEF, New York.

BNEF. 2021. "Hitting the EV Inflection Point." Report, BNEF, New York.

Boudette, N., and C. Davenport. 2021. "GM Will Sell Only Zero-Emission Vehicles by 2035." *New York Times*, January 28, 2021.

Busse, M., C. Knittel, and F. Zettelmeyer. 2013. "Are Consumers Myopic? Evidence from New and Used Car Purchases." *American Economic Review* 103 (1): 220–56.

Carley, S., N. Zirogiannis, S. Siddiki, D. Duncan, and J. Graham. 2019. "Overcoming the Shortcomings of US Plug-in Electric Vehicle Policies." *Renewable and Sustainable Energy Reviews* 113:109291.

Davenport, C. 2021, "Restoring Environmental Rules Rolled Back by Trump Could Take Years." *New York Times*, January 22, 2021.

EIA (US Energy Information Administration). 2021. *Annual Energy Outlook 2021.* Washington, DC: EIA.

Gillingham, K. 2013. "The Economics of Fuel Economy Standards Versus Feebates." Working paper, National Energy Policy Institute, New Haven, CT.

Gillingham, K., S. Houde, and A. van Benthem. 2021. "Consumer Myopia in Vehicle Purchases: Evidence from a Natural Experiment." *American Economic Journal: Economic Policy* 13 (3): 207–38.

Goulder, L. H., M. R. Jacobsen, and A. A. van Benthem. 2011. "Unintended Consequences From Nested State and Federal Regulations: The Case of the Pavley Greenhouse-Gas-per-Mile Limits." *Journal of Environmental Economics and Management* 63:187–207.

Grigolon, L., M. Reynaert, and F. Verboven. 2018. "Consumer Valuation of Fuel Costs and Tax Policy: Evidence from the European Car Market." *American Economic Journal: Economic Policy* 10 (3): 193–225.

Ito, K., and J. Sallee. 2018. "The Economics of Attribute-Based Regulation: Theory and Evidence from Fuel-Economy Standards." *Review of Economics and Statistics* 100:319–36.

James-Armand, T. 2021. "US Electric Vehicle Market Poised for Record Sales in 2021 According to Edmunds." *Edmunds*, February 2, 2021.

Jenn, A., I. Azevedo, and J. Michalek. 2016. "Alternative Fuel Vehicle Adoption Increases Fleet Gasoline Consumption and Greenhouse Gas Emissions under United States Corporate Average Fuel Economy Policy and Greenhouse Gas Emissions Standards." *Environmental Science and Technology* 50:2165–74.

Leard, B., J. Linn, and Y. Zhou. 2018. "How Much Do Consumers Value Fuel Economy and Performance? Evidence from Technology Adoption." Working paper, Resources for the Future, Washington, DC.

National Academies of Science, Engineering, and Medicine. 2021. *Assessment of Technologies for Improving Light-Duty Vehicle Fuel Economy—2025–2035.* Washington, DC: National Academies Press.

Sallee, J., S. West, and W. Fan. 2016. "Do Consumers Recognize the Value of Fuel Economy? Evidence from Used Car Prices and Gasoline Price Fluctuations." *Journal of Public Economics* 135:61–73.

Statista. 2021. "Plug-in Electric Vehicles as a Share of New Vehicle Sales in Selected Markets In 1st Half 2020." https://www.statista.com/statistics/267162/world-plug-in-hybrid-vehicle-sales-by-region.

Ulrich, L. 2021. "Three Electric SUVs with Tesla in their Sights." *New York Times*, April 26, 2021.

US Congress. 1994. Pub. L. No. 103-272, 108 Stat. 745 (1994).

White House. 2021. "Fact Sheet: Biden Administration Advances Electric Vehicle Charging." Technical report. https://www.whitehouse.gov/briefing-room/statements-releases/2021/04/22/fact-sheet-biden-administration-advances-electric-vehicle-charging-infrastructure.

Long-Term Resource Adequacy in Wholesale Electricity Markets with Significant Intermittent Renewables

Frank A. Wolak, *Stanford University and NBER,* United States of America

Executive Summary

Growing amounts of intermittent renewable generation capacity substantially increase the complexity of determining whether sufficient energy will be available to meet hourly demands throughout the year. As the events of August 2020 in California and February 2021 in Texas demonstrate, supply shortfalls can have large economic and public health consequences. An empirical analysis of these two events demonstrates that similar supply shortfalls are likely to occur in the future without a paradigm shift in how long-term resource adequacy is determined for an electricity supply industry with significant intermittent renewables. An alternative approach to determining long-term resource adequacy that explicitly recognizes the characteristics of different generation technologies is outlined and its properties explored relative to current approaches.

JEL Codes: Q4, L51, L94

Keywords: electricity markets, intermittent renewables, long-term resource adequacy

I. Introduction

Restructured electricity supply industries have one glaring weakness that is becoming increasingly apparent as the share of intermittent renewables in a region increases and more consumers shift to using electricity for space heating and personal transportation. There is no single entity responsible for ensuring that the supply of electricity equals demand under all possible current and future demand conditions. Generation unit

Environmental and Energy Policy and the Economy, volume 3, 2022.

owners can only supply electricity up to the available capacity of their generation units. Transmission network operators can only dispatch the set of available generation units or curtailable demands in the geographic region under their control. Electricity retailers can only withdraw the amount of energy produced by generation unit owners less any transmission network losses.

Under the vertically integrated monopoly regime, the geographic monopoly electricity supplier was the single entity responsible for ensuring supply equals demand under all possible current and future system conditions. Consequently, politicians and regulators knew precisely what entity to penalize if supply shortfalls occurred. In the restructured regime, generation unit owners, retailers, and the system operator can all shift blame to some other entity for a supply shortfall.

Fortunately, in a restructured electricity supply industry composed of dispatchable thermal generation units and predictable peak demands, ensuring that supply will equal demand throughout the year is relatively straightforward. The system operator first multiplies the installed capacity of each generation unit by its availability factor, the fraction of hours of the year the unit is expected to be available to operate. If the sum of the availability-factor-adjusted capacities across all generation units is greater than the annual demand peak by a 10%–15% margin, the system operator can be confident that there will be sufficient supply to meet demand throughout the year.

This process becomes more complicated if a substantial fraction of energy comes from hydroelectric resources because water availability determines how much energy these resources can produce at any time during the year. There are substantial unpredictable differences across seasons and years in the amount of water that is available to produce electricity, and many examples from hydro-dominated markets around the world where unexpectedly low water conditions have led to periods with supply shortfalls and/or extremely high prices in the short-term market.[1] The first evidence that the traditional capacity-based approach to long-term resource adequacy is inappropriate for regions with significant intermittent renewable resources is that these outcomes occurred because insufficient energy was available to be produced by the hydroelectric units, and not because there was insufficient hydroelectric generation capacity in the region.

As the share of intermittent renewable energy from wind and solar generation units in a region increases, it becomes even more difficult to ensure that supply equals demand during all hours of the year. Wind and solar resources can stop producing energy with little advance notice, produce very little energy during extreme hot and cold weather conditions, and have long durations of low energy output. These facts make it virtually impossible to determine the amount of energy wind and solar resources can reliably supply during any specific time interval during the year.

Many regions of the United States are transitioning to electricity and away from fossil fuels for space heating and personal transportation services. Charging of electric vehicles significantly increases both the level and variability of electricity demand. Electric space heating significantly increases the sensitivity of electricity demand to cold weather conditions. A significant share of space heating with electricity can change a region from one where the annual demand peak occurs during the summer to one where it occurs during the winter.

These facts imply the need for revisions to the existing approach to long-term *resource adequacy* (RA)—the process of ensuring that supply will equal demand during all hours of the year—in regions with significant amounts of wind and solar resources and goals to transition to electricity for space heating and personal transportation. The purpose of this paper is to propose a long-term RA mechanism that is more likely to achieve a reliable supply of electricity in this environment.

The first step in this process is a statement of why, unlike other product markets, all existing wholesale electricity markets require a long-term RA mechanism. This is because of what Wolak (2013) calls the *reliability externality*, caused by a regulator-mandated upper bound on the offer price a supplier can submit to the short-term market in all existing wholesale markets in the United States. This cap on offer prices creates an incentive for electricity retailers and consumers to underprocure their expected real-time demands in the forward energy market, which can result in energy shortfalls during high-demand conditions and expose customers to extremely high prices for sustained periods of time.

Empirical evidence from California during August 2020 is used to illustrate the increasing risk of relying on a capacity-based approach to address the reliability externality in a wholesale electricity market with a substantial share of intermittent renewables and policy goals to transition to electricity for space heating and personal transportation. The experience of Texas during February 2021 is used to illustrate the risk of not having a formal long-term RA mechanism in place in a wholesale electricity market with a significant share of intermittent renewables, even if there is an extremely high offer cap on the short-term market. The amount of energy supplied by renewable resources during high-demand periods in these two markets can be unexpectedly low, and for both markets this was a major factor determining the need to curtail demand during these two time periods.

The experience of California, Texas, and several international markets demonstrates that having adequate energy available to serve demand, not adequate generation capacity, is the fundamental long-term RA challenge in renewables-dominated regions. I propose a standardized fixed-price forward contract (SFPFC) approach to long-term RA to address this challenge. This approach assigns the risk of meeting system demand throughout the year to generation unit owners. It encourages cross-hedging of energy-supply risk between dispatchable generation units and intermittent renewable resource owners. It also fosters the active participation of final consumers and storage resources in managing the real-time supply and demand balance.

The SFPFC mechanism shares a key feature with the existing long-term RA mechanisms that exist in Chile and Peru, two regions with significant hydroelectric resources as well as growing shares of intermittent wind and solar resources, particularly in Chile. As outlined in Wolak (2021), both these regions assign the risk of meeting system demand throughout the year to generation unit owners by operating a supplier-only short-term market where electricity retailers and large consumers must purchase full-requirements contracts from participants in the short-term market to meet their hourly energy demands throughout the year. These regions have successfully served system demands with average annual growth rates in Chile of more than 7% since 1992 and more than 5% since 1990 in Peru. This outcome emphasizes the necessity of high-powered financial incentives for suppliers to ensure that system demand is met every hour of the year in regions with significant intermittent renewables. The goal of the SFPFC mechanism is to subject suppliers to this high-powered financial incentive while still maximizing the opportunities for active participation of final consumers in the short-term market.

The remainder of the paper proceeds as follows. The next section defines the reliability externality and argues that it exists in all markets with finite offer caps on the short-term market. Section III describes the conventional solution to the reliability externality—a capacity-based long-term RA mechanism. This section explains why such an approach to long-term RA is likely to work as intended in a system with dispatchable thermal generation units, and why it is has led to supply shortfall periods in regions with significant renewable energy shares. Section IV uses California and Texas market outcomes during each region's supply shortfall period to illustrate, for the case of California, the inappropriateness of a capacity-based long-term RA mechanism in renewables-dominated markets and, for the case of Texas, the need for a long-term RA mechanism even in a short-term market with an extremely high offer cap. Section V presents the SFPFC mechanism and explains why it is more likely to achieve long-term RA in a renewables-dominated market with electrification goals for space heating and transportation. This section uses the performance of the existing long-term RA mechanisms in Chile and Peru as empirical evidence in favor of the SFPFC mechanism. Section VI concludes and suggests directions for future research.

II. The Reliability Externality in Wholesale Electricity Markets

Why do wholesale electricity markets require a regulatory mandate to ensure long-term RA? Electricity is essential to modern life, but so are many other goods and services. Consumers want cars, but there is no regulatory mandate that ensures enough automobile assembly plants to produce these cars. They want point-to-point air travel, but there is no regulatory mandate to ensure enough airplanes to accomplish this. Many goods are produced using high fixed cost, low marginal cost technologies similar to electricity supply. Nevertheless, these firms recover their production costs, including a return on the capital invested, by selling their output at a market-determined price.

So, what is different about electricity that requires a long-term RA mechanism? The regulatory history of the electricity supply industry and the legacy technology for metering electricity consumption results in what Wolak (2013) calls a reliability externality.

Unlike the case of wholesale electricity, the markets for automobiles and air travel do not have a regulatory limit on the level of the short-term price. Airlines adjust the prices for seats on a flight over time in an attempt to ensure that the number of customers traveling on that flight equals the number of seats flying. This ability to use price to allocate the available seats is also what allows the airline to recover its total production costs and can result in as many different prices paid for the same flight as there are customers on the flight.

Using the short-term price to manage the real-time supply and demand balance in a wholesale electricity market is limited by a finite upper bound on a supplier's offer price and/or a price cap set by the regulator that limits the maximum market-clearing price. Although offer caps and price caps can limit the ability of suppliers to exercise unilateral market power in the short-term energy market, they also reduce the revenues suppliers can receive during scarcity conditions. This is often referred to as the *missing money problem* for generation unit owners.

However, this missing money problem is only a symptom of the existence of the reliability externality.

This externality exists because offer caps limit the cost to electricity retailers of failing to hedge their expected purchases from the short-term market. Specifically, if the retailer or large consumer knows the price cap on the short-term market is $250 per megawatt-hour (MWh), then it is unlikely to be willing to pay more than that for electricity in any earlier forward market. This creates the possibility that real-time system conditions can occur where the amount of electricity demanded at or below the offer cap is less than the amount suppliers are willing to offer at or below the offer cap.

This outcome implies that the system operator must be forced to either abandon the market mechanism or curtail firm load until the available supply offered at or below the offer cap equals the reduced level of demand, as occurred several times in California between January 2001 and April 2001, and most recently on August 14–15, 2020. A similar, but far more extreme, set of circumstances arose during February 14–18, 2021, in Texas, and this required significant demand curtailments during February 15–18.[2]

Because random curtailments of supply to different distribution grids served by the transmission network—also known as rolling blackouts—are used to make demand equal to the available supply at or below the offer cap under these system conditions, this mechanism creates a reliability externality because no retailer bears the full cost of failing to procure adequate energy to meet their demand in advance of delivery. A retailer that has purchased sufficient supply in the forward market to meet its actual demand is equally likely to be randomly curtailed as another retailer of the same size that has not procured adequate energy in the forward market. For this reason, all retailers have an incentive to underprocure their expected energy needs in the forward market. When short-term prices rise because of the supply shortfalls, retailers that do not hedge their wholesale energy purchases will go bankrupt. If they attempt to pass these short-term prices on to their retail customers, many are likely to be unable to pay their electricity bills. As we discuss in Subsection IV.B, both outcomes occurred in Texas following the events of February 14–18, 2021.

The lower the offer cap, the greater the likelihood that the retailer will delay their electricity purchases to the short-term market. Delaying more purchases to the short-term market increases the likelihood of insufficient supply in the short-term market at or below the offer cap. Because retailers do not bear the full cost of failing to procure sufficient energy in the forward market, there is a missing market for long-term contracts for energy with long enough delivery horizons into the future to allow new generation units to be financed and constructed to serve demand under all future conditions in the short-term market. Therefore, a regulator-mandated long-term RA mechanism is necessary to replace this missing market.

Regulatory intervention is necessary to internalize the resulting reliability externality unless the regulator is willing to eliminate the offer cap and commit to allowing the short-term price to clear the real-time market under all possible system conditions. There are no short-term wholesale electricity markets in the world that make such a commitment. All of them have either explicit or implicit caps on the offer prices suppliers can submit to the short-term market. The Electricity Reliability Council of Texas (ERCOT) has a $9,000/MWh offer cap, which is the highest in the United States. The National Electricity Market (NEM) in Australia has a A$15,000/MWh offer cap, which is currently the highest in world.

As the experience of February 14–18, 2021, in Texas demonstrated, an extremely high offer cap on the short-term market does not eliminate the reliability externality. It just shrinks the set of system conditions when random curtailments are required to balance real-time supply and demand. For the same reason, there have also been a small number of instances when the NEM of Australia has experienced supply shortfalls despite having an extremely high offer cap.

If customers do not have the ability to shift their demand away from these high-priced periods because a significant fraction of their demand for electricity is caused by space heating needs in response to the freezing outside temperatures, charging customers an extremely high wholesale price for their consumption is largely punitive. This was the case for many retail electricity customers in Texas during February 2021. They were committed to buy a substantial fraction of their wholesale electricity at the short-term price at a time when their demand for electricity for space heating is extremely price inelastic. This experience underscores the importance of a long-term RA mechanism in regions with significant intermittent renewables, growing electrification of space heating, and increasing adoption of electric vehicles.

III. Conventional Solution to Reliability Externality with Intermittent Renewables

Currently, the most popular approach to addressing the reliability externality is a capacity procurement mechanism that assigns a firm capacity value to each generation unit based on the amount of energy it can provide under stressed system conditions. Retailers are then required to demonstrate that they have purchased sufficient firm capacity to meet their monthly or annual demand peaks. Having sufficient firm capacity typically means that the retailer has purchased firm capacity equal to between 1.10 and 1.20 times its annual demand peak. The exact multiple of peak demand chosen by a region depends on the mix of generation resources and the reliability requirements of the system operator.

Under the current long-term RA mechanism in California, firm-level capacity procurement obligations are assigned to retailers by the California Public Utilities Commission (CPUC) to ensure that monthly and annual system demand peaks can be met. Electricity retailers are free to negotiate bilateral capacity contracts with individual generation unit owners to purchase firm capacity to meet these obligations. The eastern United States wholesale electricity markets in the PJM Interconnection, Independent System Operator (ISO) New England, New York ISO, and Midcontinent ISO each have a centralized market for firm capacity. These involve periodic capacity auctions run by the wholesale market operator where all retailers purchase their capacity requirements at a market-clearing price. ERCOT does not currently have a formal long-term RA mechanism besides its $9,000/MWh offer cap and an ancillary services scarcity pricing mechanism.

All capacity-based approaches to long-term RA rely on the credibility of the firm capacity measures assigned to generation units. This is a relatively straightforward process for dispatchable thermal units. As noted earlier, the nameplate capacity of the generation unit times its annual availability factor—the fraction of hours of the year a unit is expected to be available to produce electricity—is the typical starting point for estimating the amount of energy the unit can provide under stressed system conditions. As discussed below, if all retailers have met their firm capacity requirements in a sizable market with only dispatchable thermal generation, there is a very high probability that the demand for energy will be met during peak demand periods.

A simple model helps to illustrate the logic behind this claim. Suppose that the peak demand for the market is 1,000 MW and the market is composed of equal size generation units, each with a 90% annual availability factor, meaning that it is available to produce electricity any hour of the year with a .90 probability. Suppose that the event that one generation unit fails to operate is independent of the event that any other generation unit fails to operate. This independence assumption is reasonable for dispatchable thermal generation units because unavailability is typically due to an event specific to that generation unit. If each generation unit has a nameplate capacity of 100 MW, each has a firm capacity of 90 MW. If there are 13 generation units, then with probability .96 demand peak will be covered.[3] In this case, a firm capacity requirement of 1.17 times the demand peak would ensure that system demand is met with .96 probability. Assuming that each generation unit is one-tenth of the system demand peak is unrealistic for most electricity supply industries, but it does illustrate the important point that smaller markets require firm capacity equal to a larger multiple of peak demand to achieve a given level of reliability.

Suppose that each generation unit is now 50 MW and each still has the same availability factor, so the firm capacity of each unit is now 45 MW. In this case, the same firm capacity requirement of 1.17 times the demand peak, or 26 generation units, would ensure system demand is met with .988 probability. If each generation unit had a nameplate capacity of 20 MW with the same availability factor, each unit would have a firm capacity of 18 MW. This 1.17 times peak demand firm capacity requirement, or 65 generation units, would ensure that system demand is met with .999 probability. This example illustrates that in an electricity supply industry based on dispatchable thermal generation units, where each unit has a 10% chance of being unavailable, the system demand peak will be met with a very high probability with a firm capacity requirement of 1.17 times peak demand if all the generation units are small relative to the system demand peak.

Introducing renewables into a capacity-based long-term RA mechanism considerably complicates the problem of computing the probability of meeting system demand peaks for two major reasons. First, the ability to produce electricity depends on the availability of the underlying renewable resource. A hydroelectric resource requires water behind the turbine, a wind resource requires wind to spin the turbine, and a solar facility requires sunlight to hit the solar panels. Second, and perhaps most important, the availability of water, wind, or sunshine to renewable generation resources is highly positively correlated across locations for a given technology within a given geographic region. This fact invalidates the assumption of independence of energy availability across locations that allows a firm capacity mechanism to ensure system demand peaks can be met with a very high probability. For example, if the correlation across locations in the availability of generation units is sufficiently high, then a 0.9 availability factor at one location would imply only a slightly higher than a 0.9 availability factor for meeting system demand, almost regardless of the amount intermittent renewable capacity that is installed.

Hydroelectric facilities have been integrated into firm capacity regimes by using percentiles of the distribution of past hydrological conditions for that generation unit to determine its firm capacity value. However, this approach only partially addresses the problem of accounting for the high degree of contemporaneous correlation across locations in water availability in hydroelectric-dominated systems. There is typically a significant amount of data available on the marginal distribution of water availability at individual hydroelectric generation units. However, the joint distribution of water availability across all hydro locations is likely to be more difficult to obtain. The weather-dependent intermittency in energy availability for hydroelectric resources is typically on an annual frequency. There are low-water and high-water years depending on global weather patterns such as the El Niño and La Niña weather events, as discussed in McRae and Wolak (2016).

Incorporating wind or solar generation units into firm capacity mechanisms is extremely challenging for several reasons, and increasingly so as the share of energy produced in a region from these resources increases. The intermittency in energy supply is much more frequent than it is for hydroelectric energy. There can be substantial differences across and within days in the output of wind and solar generation units. Moreover, if stressed system conditions occur when it is dark, the firm capacity of a solar resource is zero. Similarly, if stressed system conditions occur when the wind is not blowing, a likely outcome on extremely hot days, the firm capacity of a wind resource is zero.

The contemporaneous correlation across locations in the output of solar or wind generation resources for a given geographic area is typically extremely high. There is even a high degree of correlation across locations in the output of wind and solar resources. Again, information on the marginal distribution of wind or solar energy availability at a location is much more readily available than the joint distribution of wind and solar energy availability for all wind and solar locations in a region. For these reasons, calculating a defensible estimate of the firm capacity of a wind or solar resource that is equivalent to the firm capacity of a dispatchable thermal generation resource is extremely difficult, if not impossible.

Wolak (2016) demonstrates the extremely high degree of contemporaneous correlation between the energy produced each hour of the year by solar and wind facilities in California. For each of the 13 solar locations and 40 wind locations in the California ISO control area studied, Wolak (2016) computes the hourly capacity factor—hourly output of the generation unit divided by its nameplate capacity—from April 1, 2011, to March 31, 2012. Let $F_h = (f_{1h}, f_{2h}, \ldots, f_{Kh})'$ equal the vector of locational capacity factors for K renewable energy locations for hour h, where f_{ih} is capacity factor for hour h at location i. Each of the locational capacity factors, f_{ih}, is a random variable that takes on values in the interval $[0, 1]$. Let the contemporaneous covariance matrix F_h equal Σ, a positive definite $(K \times K)$ matrix, where the (i, i) element is the variance of f_{ih} and the (i, j) element is the covariance between f_{ih} and f_{jh}. Using the singular value decomposition of a positive definite matrix implies that $\Sigma = S\Lambda S'$, where Λ is a diagonal matrix composed of the eigenvalues of Σ and S is an orthogonal matrix ($S'S = I$, a $K \times K$ identity matrix) composed of the eigenvectors of Σ. It can be shown that the sum of the eigenvalues of Σ, which is the sum of the diagonal elements of Λ, is equal to the sum of diagonal elements of Σ, which is also equal to the sum of the variances of f_{ih} for $i = 1, 2, \ldots, K$. The ratio of the largest eigenvalue to the sum of the diagonal elements of Σ (sum of the variances of the f_{ih}) is a measure of the extent of contemporaneous correlation between the elements of F_h.

For the case of the 13 solar locations in California, the largest eigenvalue is equal to 80% of the sum of the variances of the f_{ih} for all 13 solar locations, which indicates a substantial degree of contemporaneous correlation in hourly values of f_{ih} across the K locations. For the 40 wind locations in California, the largest eigenvalue is more than 50% of the sum of the variances of all 40 locations. For the 53 wind and solar locations, the first eigenvalue is equal to slightly less than 50% of sum of the variances of all these 53 locations. For comparison, if the f_{ih} for $i = 1, 2, \ldots, K$ were independently distributed random variables, all with the same variance, these percentages would equal $100 \times (1/K)$, where K is number of locations.

The high degree of contemporaneous correlation across locations in hourly capacity factors requires a methodology for computing firm capacity that accounts for the joint distribution of hourly capacity factors across locations throughout the year. Not only does this methodology need to account for the contemporaneous correlation in capacity factors across locations, but also the high degree of correlation of capacity factors over time for the same locations and other locations. California currently uses an effective load carrying capacity (ELCC) methodology for computing the firm capacity values of wind and solar generation units. The ELCC methodology was introduced by Garver (1966) and it measures the additional load that the system can supply from a specified increase in the MW of that generation technology with no net change in reliability. The loss of load probability, which is the probability that system demand will exceed the available supply, is the measure of reliability used in the ELCC calculation.

Consistent with the results of Wolak (2016), the ELCC values for solar generation resources in California have declined as the amount of solar generation capacity in the state has increased. For example, a recent study prepared for California's three investor-owned utilities (Carden, Dombrowsky, and Winkler 2020), Southern California Edison, Pacific Gas and Electric, and San Diego Gas and Electric, recommended ELCC values for a MW of fixed-mount solar photovoltaic capacity for 2022 of approximately 5% of the nameplate capacity. Their estimates for 2026 are less than half that amount, and those for 2030 are less than one-fourth that amount. These declines in ELCC values are due to the forecast increase in the amount of solar generation capacity in California.

To understand the computational and data compilation challenge associated with calculating the ELCC of a new generation unit, suppose there are K existing generation units in an electricity supply industry and C_i is the installed capacity at location i in MW, so that the MWh produced at location i in hour h is equal to $f_{ih} \times C_i$, where f_{ih} is the capacity factor at location i during hour h. Let L_h equal system load during hour h and $\lambda(F, L)$ equal the joint density of $(F'_h, L_h)'$, where F'_h is defined above. The loss of load probability during hour h is equal to $\mathrm{LOLP}_h = E_\lambda(I[\sum_{i=1}^K f_{ih} \times C_i < L_h])$, where $I[A]$ is equal to 1 if the event is true and equal to zero otherwise and $E_\lambda(.)$ denotes the expectation taken with respect to $\lambda(F, L)$. The annual loss of load expectation is defined as $\mathrm{LOLE} = \sum_{h=1}^{8760} \mathrm{LOLP}_h$. The "1 day in 10 years" criteria for the LOLE implies 2.4 hours per year or 0.00027397.

Let the current value of the LOLE equal LOLE(Current). To define the ELCC of a Q MW of intermittent renewable capacity at a new location, let Δ equal the increase in load that can be served by this additional Q MW and still maintain LOLE(Current) and $\Lambda(F, L, f(\mathrm{new}))$ the joint density of $(F', L, f(\mathrm{new}))'$, where $f(\mathrm{new})$ is the hourly capacity factor at the new generation unit location. The system load increment associated with the Q MW of new investment is the solution to the following equation in Δ,

$$\mathrm{LOLE(Current)} = E_\Lambda \left(I \left[\sum_{i=1}^K f_{ih} \times C_i + Q \times f(\mathrm{new})_h < L_h + \Delta \right] \right),$$

where $E_\Lambda(.)$ is the expectation with respect to $\Lambda(F, L, f(\mathrm{new}))$. The ELCC of this Q MW unit is defined as $\mathrm{ELCC} = \Delta/Q$. This expression illustrates the massive data and computational requirements associated with computing the ELCC. First, an estimate of the joint density of $\Lambda(F, L, f(\text{new}))$ is required for every hour of the year. Second, a $K + 2$ dimensional integration must be performed 8,760 times to compute the right-hand-side expression. Third, this equation must be solved numerically for Δ. Consequently, all implementations of this process make simplifying assumptions that can have a substantial impact on the resulting ELCC value as shown in Kahn (2004).

An additional problem with computing the firm capacity of a solar or wind generation resource using the ELCC methodology is that the same Q MW investment is likely to be able to serve different increments to system demand depending on the location of the investment, the location of the increment to demand, and the size and location of other renewable resources in the region. This leaves the system operator with two difficult choices for setting the value of firm capacity for solar and wind resources. The first would be to set different values of firm capacity for resources based on their location in the transmission network. This would likely be a very politically contentious process because of the many assumptions that go into computing the ELCC of a resource. The second approach would set the same firm capacity value for all resources employing the same generation technology. This means that two resources with very different ELCC values could sell the same product, to the potential detriment of overall system reliability.

These facts, and the fact that what is predicted to be the major source of electricity in the future in California has been estimated to have a little firm capacity value, imply that it would be prudent for California to consider alternatives to its capacity-based long-term resource mechanism if it intends to meet its goals of obtaining 50% of the state's energy from renewable sources by 2025 and 60% by 2030 and increase the use of electricity in space heating and personal transportation.

IV. Experience with Long-Term RA Mechanisms

This section presents an analysis of the performance of the California and Texas markets during stressed system conditions. These states are also the two regions of the continental United States with the largest shares of intermittent renewables in their energy mix. The experience of the California market during August 2020 provides an example of the shortcomings of the existing capacity-based long-term RA mechanism described in the previous section. The experience of Texas demonstrates that even a wholesale market with an extremely high offer cap still suffers from the reliability externality discussed in Section II.

A.   California

Figure 1*A* plots the time series of in-state generation capacity in MW by technology in California between 2001 and 2020. Figure 1*B* plots the time series of in-state electricity generation in gigawatt-hours (GWh) for the same time period. California's renewables portfolio standard (RPS) was established in 2002 with the requirement that California obtain 20% retail electricity sales from renewable resources by 2017. Figure 1*A* shows that the major increase in renewable generation capacity did not begin until later in the decade, and most of that came in the form of wind generation units. The RPS requirement was accelerated to 33% by 2020, starting in 2013. This was followed by a significant increase in investments in solar photovoltaic (PV) capacity.

Between 2013 and 2019, California retired 2,254 MW of nuclear capacity at the San Onofre Nuclear Generating Station (SONGS). Over the same time period, natural gas generation capacity in California fell by 8,529 MW. Solar PV and solar thermal capacity increased by 8,471 MW and wind generation capacity increased by 188 MW over this same period. It is important to bear in mind that the SONGS facility typically ran at annual average capacity factor of more than 90%, whereas solar facilities in California had an annual average capacity factor in 2020 of 24.67% and wind facilities had a 24.09% annual average capacity factor in 2020.[4] Natural gas facilities typically have annual availability factors greater than 85% but currently run at a significantly lower annual average capacity factors because of the large amount of renewable generation capacity in the state. Consequently, replacing the 10,750 MW reduction in thermal generation capacity with 8,712 MW of intermittent wind and solar capacity significantly reduces the amount of firm capacity available to the California ISO.

An important factor in allowing the California ISO to meet demand with significantly less firm capacity is that California has more than 18,000 MW of transmission capacity between it and the rest of the Western Interconnection, also called the Western Electricity Coordinating Council (WECC), which contains all western US states and Canadian provinces.[5] Historically, California obtains between 25% and 33% of its annual consumption from electricity imports from hydroelectric units in the Pacific Northwest and coal-fired and natural gas-fired generation units in the desert Southwest.

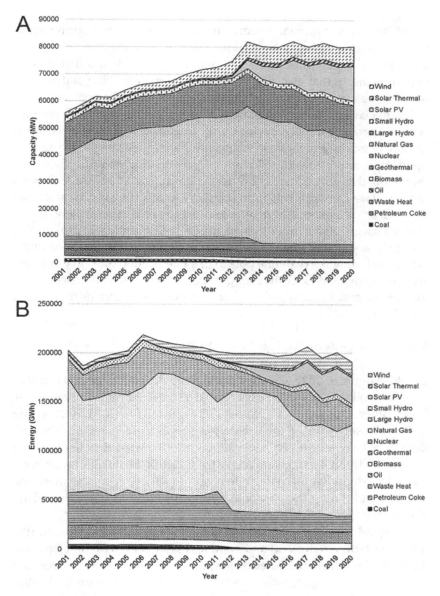

Fig. 1. *A*, In-state generation capacity in megawatts (MW) by fuel type 2001–2020. *B*, In-state generation in gigawatt-hours (GWh) by fuel type 2001–2020. Color version available as an online enhancement.

California's substantial import dependence is another strong argument against a capacity-based long-term RA mechanism. Kirchoff's laws governing the flow of electricity in transmission and distribution networks imply that electricity imports from neighboring states occur because these regions produce more electricity than they consume and California consumes more electricity that it is producing.[6] This requires system operators in neighboring states to ensure that the agreed-upon amount of excess generation in their states is produced, so that the agreed-upon imports will flow into California. Consequently, as a rule, California cannot purchase firm capacity from neighboring states. At best, California can purchase commitments from suppliers located outside the state that they will schedule specified quantities of energy imports into the state. Exactly which generation units located outside of California will provide this energy is largely unknown until real-time operation. It depends on many factors including the real-time output of all generation units in California and the rest of the WECC, the configuration of the transmission network in the WECC, and location and level of demand at all locations throughout the WECC.

Rolling Blackouts on August 14–15, 2020

In mid-August of 2020, California and neighboring states in the rest of the Western Interconnection experienced a sustained period of extremely hot weather. This led the California ISO to curtail firm load by declaring rolling blackouts during the late evening on August 14 and 15. The California ISO also came very close to having to curtail firm load during August 16–18. This section documents the failure of the state's firm capacity-based long-term RA mechanism to ensure sufficient energy to meet system demand during the portions of August 14 and 15 when the rolling blackouts occurred.

Figure 2A presents the 5-minute demand, 5-minute net demand (the difference between demand and wind and solar energy production), and the hour-ahead demand forecast for August 14, 2020. This net demand must be met by dispatchable generation resources in California or electricity imports. As shown in figure 1A, the vast majority of these dispatchable in-state resources are powered by natural gas. The rectangle between 18:00 and 19:00 denotes the time interval when the rolling blackout occurred. Figure 2B presents the same information for August 15, 2020, along with a rectangle denoting when rolling blackouts occurred. Figure 3A compares these demands to those on August 16–18. The dashed

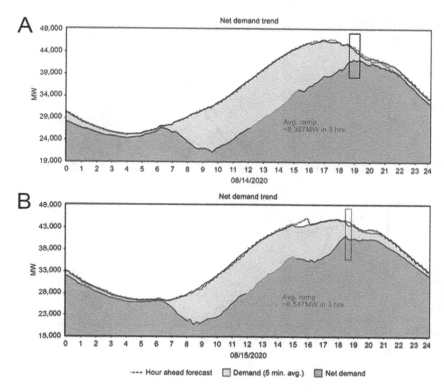

Fig. 2. *A,* System demand, net demand, and hour-ahead forecast demand in megawatts (MW) on August 14, 2020. *B,* System demand, net demand, and hour-ahead forecast demand on August 15, 2020. Color version available as an online enhancement.

line on the bottom of the graph plots the hourly demands on June 29, 2020, which is an ideal day for solar energy production, as shown in figure 3*B.* The hourly demands on August 18 were uniformly higher than the demands on August 14 and 15 and the demand on August 17 was higher than the demand on August 14, even though blackouts occurred on August 14 and 15.

The rolling blackouts on August 14 and 15 were necessitated by the fact that the net demand in California exceeded the amount of available dispatchable generation capacity in California and amount of electricity imports available during the evening hours. This outcome occurred for a variety of reasons. First, the demand for electricity in California was high because of the intensive use of air conditioning due to high in-state temperatures. Second, a reduced supply of intermittent renewable generation increased the net demand that must be met by dispatchable generation

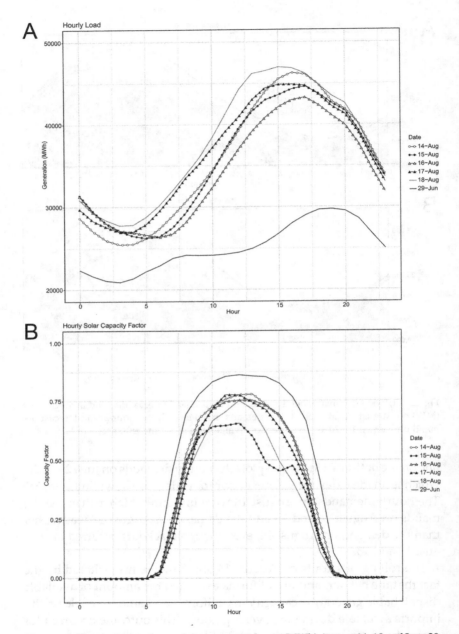

Fig. 3. *A,* Hourly system demands in megawatt-hours (MWh) August 14–18 and June 29, 2020. *B,* Hourly capacity factor of solar generation units August 14–18 and June 29, 2020. Color version available as an online enhancement.

units in California or electricity imports. Third, extreme temperatures in the rest of the western United States and Canada reduced the amount of electricity produced in the rest of the WECC that could be imported into California.

Figure 3B presents the first factor contributing to the events of August 14–18 by plotting the hourly capacity factor of solar generation units in California on these days. The dashed line is the hourly capacity factor for solar generation units in California for June 29, 2020. During much of the day on August 14 and 16–18, the hourly capacity factor of the solar generation units in California is lower than it was on June 29, 2020. This is particularly true for the evening hours when the rolling blackouts were declared.

Figure 4A provides one explanation for this outcome. It plots the hourly temperatures within the day in Barstow, California, for August 14–18 and for June 29, 2020. Barstow is located near a significant fraction of the solar generation capacity in California. Hourly temperatures during the day on August 14–18 were much higher than they were on June 29, which is close to an ideal day for electricity to be produced from a solar PV facility. Solar panels convert light into electricity, and this occurs with maximum efficiency at a panel temperature of 77°F. The efficiency of a solar panel declines linearly with every degree its temperature is above 77°F. The extremely high temperatures during the day on August 14–18 significantly reduced the efficiency at which the solar panels converted light into electricity. The solar panels were also likely to be significantly hotter later in the day than earlier in the day given the pattern of daily temperatures shown in figure 4A. Another contributing factor to the lower injections of electricity to the transmission grid from solar generation facilities during August 14–18 is the larger demand for electricity for on-site cooling on these days relative to June 29, 2020.

As shown in the next subsection, the firm capacity numbers assigned to solar generation units in California only vary by month, and do not depend on the outside temperature. However, as the share of solar energy increases in California, even a 5% reduction in solar output on high temperature days coupled with the likely increase in the demand for electricity for space cooling can lead to more days like August 14 and 15 in California.

Figure 4B plots the hourly capacity factors within the day for California's wind generation units for the same days as figure 4A. Consistent with the high temperatures throughout the state, the amount of wind energy produced was extremely low, particularly during the middle

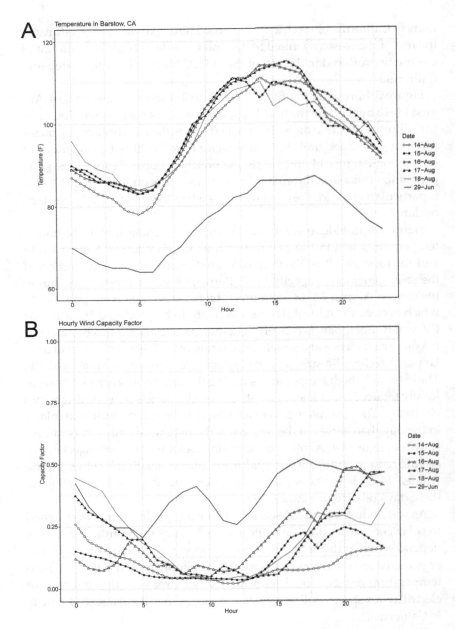

Fig. 4. *A*, Hourly temperature in Barstow, California, on August 14–18 and June 29, 2020. *B*, Hourly capacity factor of wind generation units on August 14–18 and June 29, 2020. Color version available as an online enhancement.

of the day, as well during the period of the rolling blackouts. This is consistent with the fact that wind blows because of temperature differentials between locations, and on extremely hot days in California and neighboring states temperatures are similar across locations. The hourly capacity factors on June 29, 2020, are significantly higher throughout the day, consistent with the milder temperatures throughout that day. The hourly capacity factors are significantly below the firm capacity values for August 2020 for wind generation capacity assigned by CPUC of 21% for the entire day on August 14 and for virtually all daylight hours for August 15–18.

To investigate the extent to which the various technologies used to produce electricity in California had statistically distinguishable lower or higher mean capacity factors during the extreme weather period of August 14–18 of 2020 than the remainder of the month of August, I ran the following regression for the hourly capacity factors for each technology for January 1, 2020, to December 31, 2020:

$$CF_{hdm} = \alpha_{hm} + \delta_d + I_{hdm}\beta + \varepsilon_{hdm}$$

where CF_{hdm} is the capacity factor in hour h of day d of month m, α_{hm} is an hour-of-day h for month m fixed effect, δ_d is the fixed effect for weekend days (Saturday and Sunday), I_{hdm} is an indicator variable that is equal to 1 if hour h of day d of month m is during the August 14–18 of 2020 period, and ε_{hdm} is a zero-mean disturbance.

Table 1 presents the 2020 annual mean hourly capacity factors for wind, solar, and natural gas generation units in California and the estimate of the change in the mean hourly capacity factor during the August 14–18 period for each technology. For the case of natural gas generation units, there was no statistically discernable change in the mean capacity factor during August 14–18, 2020. For the case of both solar and wind, the mean capacity factor was lower during the August 14–18 period relative to the remainder of the month of August. For solar it was 0.033 lower, which,

Table 1
Change in Mean Capacity Factor (CF) by Technology for August 14–18, 2020

	Solar_CF	Wind_CF	Natural Gas_CF
Sample Mean of Dependent Variable	.2467	.2409	.5946
β	−.0330	−.161	.000000649
Standard error	(.0140)	(.0336)	(.00000673)

Note: All regressions include hour-of-day fixed effects for each month of the year. Standard errors are clustered by day of sample.

when applied to an installed capacity of solar of close to 14,000 MW, implies an average hourly reduction in output of close to 500 MWh. For wind it was 0.161 lower, which, when applied to an installed capacity of close to 6,000 MW, implies an average hourly reduction in output of more than 900 MWh. This average shortfall in intermittent renewable output of 1,400 MWh (= 500 MWh + 900 MWh) is significantly larger than the amount of load that was curtailed during each of the rolling blackout events on August 14 and 15.

Given the similarities between hourly system demands on August 14–18 and the output of renewables on these days, an obvious question is why rolling blackouts occurred on August 14 and 15 but not on August 16–18. Figure 5 provides an answer to this question. Figure 5A plots the hourly net imports (imports minus exports) scheduled in the day-ahead market. These are commitments that market participants make to import energy into California the day before the energy actually flows. The day-ahead imports during the late afternoon and early evening are very low during August 14–17 relative to the day-ahead imports on June 29, 2020. This outcome is consistent with temperatures in neighboring states in the Western Interconnection being extremely high on these 5 days in August and relatively mild on June 29, 2020. This means the opportunity cost of scheduling an import into California, typically the highest priced region in the WECC, was extremely low on June 29, 2020. However, there were lucrative opportunities for selling electricity outside of California on August 14–18, because of the extremely high temperatures and high demand outside the state.

The high net imports scheduled in the day-ahead market on August 18 shown in figure 5A hint at what ultimately led to rolling blackouts on August 14 and 15, but not during the period August 16–18. Figure 5B presents the hourly real-time net imports into California for the same set of days as figure 5A. The real-time net imports on August 16–18 are uniformly higher by substantial margins during the late afternoon and early evening than the same magnitudes on August 14 and 15. The real-time net imports on August 14 are also significantly lower than those on August 15. After the events of August 14 and 15, the California ISO operators and entities throughout the Western Interconnection significantly increased the supply of imports willing to sell into the California market in real-time.

A final point about this 5-day period in August is particularly important to emphasize. That is the impossibility of preventing sellers of electricity from finding the highest possible price for their electricity. There

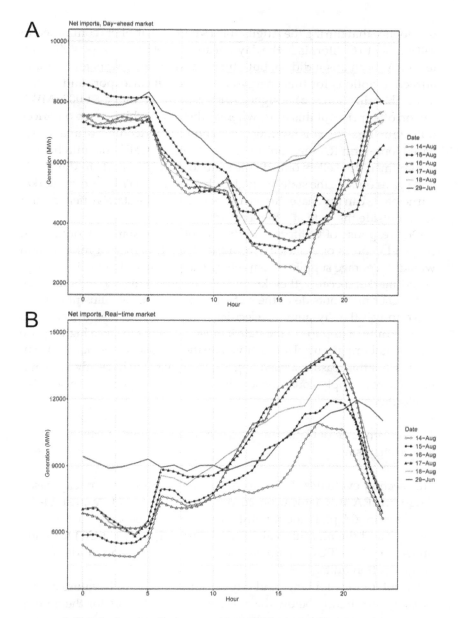

Fig. 5. *A,* Hourly day-ahead imports in megawatt-hours (MWh) on August 14–18 and June 29, 2020. *B,* Hourly real-time imports on August 14–18 and June 29, 2020. Color version available as an online enhancement.

is evidence that during the August 14–18 period, suppliers committed to sell energy to California in the day-ahead market under the state's long-term RA mechanism did so, but other market participants found more attractive options for this energy and bought it for export and sold it in neighboring states at a higher price. California had a $1,000/MWh cap on offer prices at this time, whereas there was a higher cap on prices outside of the state. This fact illustrates another shortcoming of a capacity-based long-term RA mechanism for California. If California purchases a commitment for sellers outside the state to supply imports to California and prices outside the state are higher than California's offer cap, market participants can purchase this energy at or below the state's offer cap and sell it outside the state at a higher price.

One response of California to this set of circumstances would be to suspend exports of electricity from the state. This market intervention would discourage suppliers from selling energy into California in the day-ahead market, because they know they are foregoing the option to sell at a higher price outside of the state if they do. This fact illustrates what I like to call the "tyranny of electricity imports," because if California wants to attract imports to the state it must be willing to pay a higher price than neighboring control areas or violate the integrity of its market mechanisms. For this reason, suspending exports is likely to have adverse long-term energy-supply consequences for an import-dependent region like California.

The Performance of California's Capacity-Based Long-Term RA Mechanism

This section evaluates the performance of California's capacity-based long-term RA mechanism based on the experience of August 14–18, 2020. Figure 6A plots the monthly average wind capacity factors (CF) for 2020 and the monthly values of the firm capacity (ELCC) for wind units set by the CPUC. Figure 6B plots these same to magnitudes for solar generation units.

Except for May for wind and July for solar, the monthly values of firm capacity are slightly below the average capacity factors for the month. However, it is important to bear in mind that the firm capacity of a generation unit is supposed to measure what the facility can reliably produce under extreme system conditions, not what it produces on average. Consequently, a monthly average capacity factor less than the firm capacity value assigned to wind or solar generation resources provides

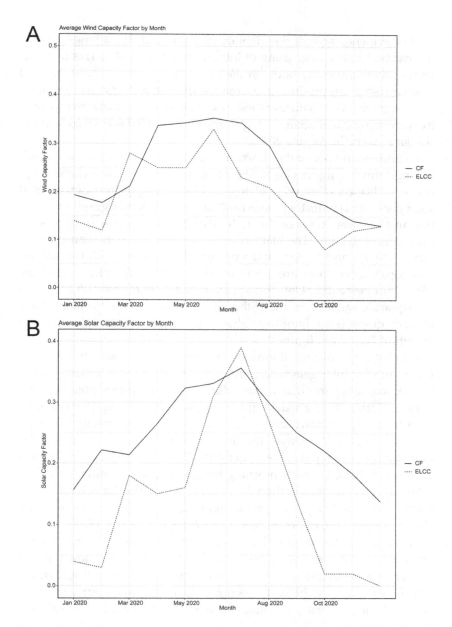

Fig. 6. *A*, Monthly average wind capacity factor (CF) and effective load carrying capacity (ELCC) value for firm capacity for 2020. *B*, Monthly average solar capacity factor and ELCC value for firm capacity for 2020. Color version available as an online enhancement.

further evidence against the viability of a capacity-based long-term RA mechanism with a large share of intermittent renewables. This outcome implies there are many hours in the month when the intermittent wind or solar resource is producing less than its firm capacity. Given the unpredictable intermittent nature of these resources, there is a nonzero probability this outcome will occur during a time with stressed system conditions, similar to those in August 2020.

To understand better the shortcomings of a capacity-based approach to long-term RA, figures 7 and 8 break down the information behind figure 6 into hourly within-day histograms of capacity factors of wind and solar generation units by month for 2020. Each monthly graph provides box and whiskers plots of the daily distribution of capacity factors for that hour of the day. The black bar for each box is the median capacity factor, the top and bottom of the box are the 75th and 25th percentiles, and top/bottom lines are 1.5 times the interquartile range from the 75th/25th percentile. Dots are values that are more than 1.5 times the interquartile range from the 75th/25th percentiles. The horizontal line on each graph is the monthly value of the firm capacity value for that month of 2020 from figure 6.

For all months of 2020, there are days when the firm capacity value for the month for solar generation units exceeds an hourly capacity factor. This outcome is particularly likely during the March to September time period. During the early daylight hours and late evening hours of these months, there are many days when there are hourly capacity factor realizations that are less than the firm capacity value assigned to solar units for that month. As shown in figure 3B, on all the days during August 14–18, 2020, the early morning hours and early evening hours had solar capacity factors less than the firm capacity value for solar units for August 2020 of 0.27. As shown in figure 2, rolling blackouts were declared during the early evening hours of August 14 and 15.

The situation for wind units is even worse. There are many months when the median capacity factor for an hour of the day is below the firm capacity value for the month for a substantial number of hours of the day. During August 2020, it was not unusual to have hourly capacity factors during the early evening that were below the monthly value of firm capacity of 0.21.

It is important to emphasize that the capacity factors plotted in figures 6–8 are on a fleet-wide basis. The hourly capacity factor values for specific generation sites are likely to be even more volatile. Moreover, for the reasons discussed in Subsection IV.A, there are likely to be significant

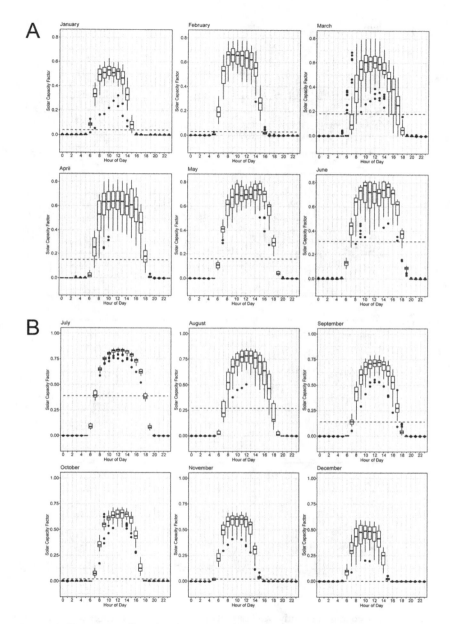

Fig. 7. A. Histograms of hourly solar capacity factors and monthly effective load carrying capacity (ELCC) value for firm capacity for 2020 (January–June). *B*, Histograms of hourly solar capacity factors and monthly ELCC value for firm capacity for 2020 (July–December).

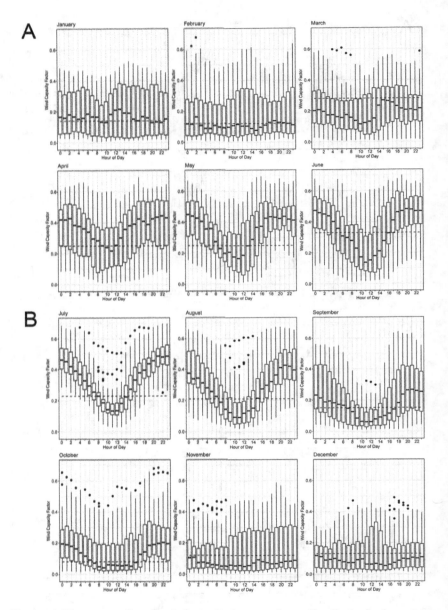

Fig. 8. *A,* Histograms of hourly wind capacity factors and monthly effective load carrying capacity (ELCC) value for firm capacity for 2020 (January–June). *B,* Histograms of hourly wind capacity factors and monthly ELCC value for firm capacity for 2020 (July–December).

differences in the distributions of hourly capacity factors across locations, even though the CPUC assigns all facilities of the same generation technology the same firm capacity factor value that changes each month of the year.[7]

These results suggest that events like August 14–15 are increasingly likely to occur under a capacity-based long-term RA mechanism in California with an increasing amount of intermittent wind and solar generation capacity. The state will increasingly need to rely on imports from neighboring states from dispatchable thermal generation resources when the net demand for electricity in California is high. Unless California builds additional controllable generation resources or makes substantial investments in energy storage, the state will be increasingly reliant on imported energy under these system conditions. These imports are also likely to be significantly more carbon intensive than electricity produced inside the state.

Figure 9 plots the mix of generation capacity in the WECC excluding California. Any available energy from the hydroelectric capacity shown in the figure will be used each year regardless of California's demand for electricity, because of its very low variable cost of production. Consequently, any marginal increase in electricity imports to California is likely to come from either natural gas-fired or coal-fired generation. This means that incremental imports will typically be more carbon intensive than electricity produced from natural gas-fired units in California, because California does not have any significant coal-fired generation capacity.

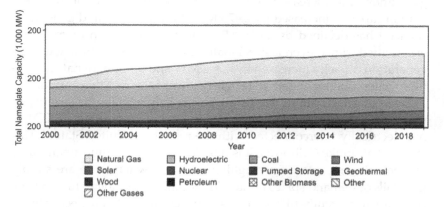

Fig. 9. Installed capacity in megawatts (MW) by technology in Western Electricity Coordinating Council (WECC) excluding California 2000–2019. Color version available as an online enhancement.

B. Texas

To illustrate the existence and consequences of the reliability externality even in a market with an extremely high offer cap, this section analyzes the performance of the ERCOT market during two periods with extreme cold weather in the state. A major difference between these two weather events was the mix of generation capacity available to meet demand during these two periods. The first period is February 1–5, 2011, and the second is February 14–18, 2021.

The significant increase in the share of energy supplied by intermittent wind and solar resources in February 2021 relative to February 2011 appears to be a major factor in explaining the difference in the performance of the ERCOT market across these two time periods. However, the more extreme weather during 2021 versus 2011 and the larger share of home heating supplied by electricity in Texas in 2021 versus 2011 cannot be ruled out as factors. As Doss-Gollin et al. (2021) note, the weather during the 2011 period was not nearly as severe at the weather during 2021 period. However, these authors also argue that the 2021 period was not as severe as a weather period of a similar length that occurred in December 1989. At that time Texas had very little wind generation and a significantly smaller fraction of households heated with electricity.

Figure 10A plots generation capacity in MW by fuel type in ERCOT from 2010 to 2020. Figure 10B plots the annual generation in terawatt-hours (TWh) by fuel type in ERCOT over this same time period. Three trends are immediately apparent. First, the installed capacity of wind generation units increased by 15,477 MW and the amount of solar generation capacity increased by 2,478 MW. Second, coal-fired generation capacity has declined by 4,619 MW and the production of coal-fired electricity declined even faster. Finally, the amount of natural gas-fired generation capacity increased by 3,356 MW and amount of natural gas-fired generation increased at a slightly lower rate over this period.

Two other facts about the Texas market help explain the severity of these two supply shortfall periods. First, legally speaking ERCOT is not electrically interconnected with the rest of the United States.[8] This means that unlike California, it is unable to rely on significant amounts of electricity imports from neighboring states when there are supply shortfalls or demand spikes in ERCOT. Second, according to the US Census Bureau, currently 61% of Texas housing units rely on electricity for heating, compared with 39.5% nationally.[9] This makes the electricity demand in Texas extremely sensitive to extreme cold-weather events.

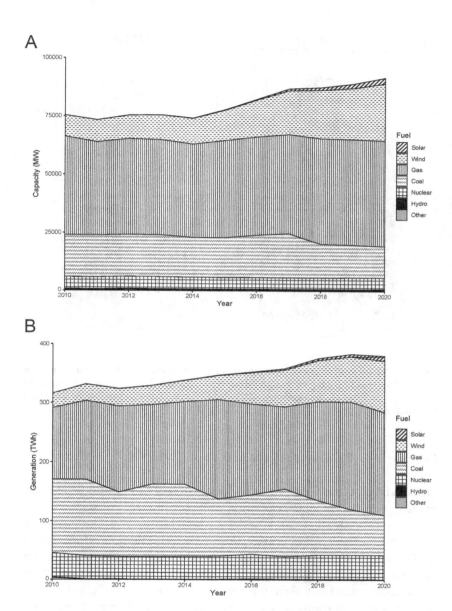

Fig. 10. *A*, Installed capacity in megawatts (MW) by technology in Electric Reliability Council of Texas (ERCOT) 2010–2020. *B*, Annual generation in terawatt-hours (TWh) by technology in ERCOT 2010–2020. Color version available as an online enhancement.

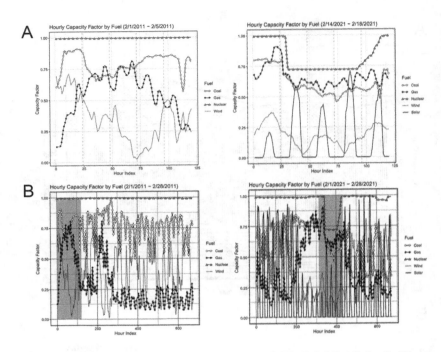

Fig. 11. *A*, Hourly capacity factors by technology in Electric Reliability Council of Texas (ERCOT) for selected 5-day periods in February, 2011–2020. *B*, Hourly capacity factors by technology in ERCOT for February, 2011–2020. Color version available as an online enhancement.

February 1–4, 2011, versus February 14–18, 2021

Figure 11*A* plots the hourly capacity factors of coal-fired, natural gas-fired, nuclear, wind, and solar generation units for the two extreme weather periods—February 1–4, 2011, and February 14–18, 2021. Because there were no solar generation units in 2011, this technology is omitted from the February 1–4 graph. Although there is significant variation in the hourly capacity factors during these two periods, two differences between them immediately stand out. First, the average capacity factor of wind generation units is significantly less during the February 2021 period relative to the February 2011 period. Recognizing that wind generation capacity increased by 15,472 MW between 2011 and 2021 implies a significant shortfall in renewable energy production throughout February 14–18, 2021. Second, there is a significant drop in the nuclear capacity factor during the second day of the 2021 period, whereas the nuclear capacity factor remains constant during the 2011 time period.

Figure 11B plots hourly capacity factors for the same technologies for the entire month of February 2011 and 2021 with the two extreme weather periods are shaded in the figure. These graphs demonstrate that the low capacity factors for wind generation units during February 14–18, 2021, were significantly lower than other hours during February 2021, whereas the average capacity factors of wind units during February 1–4 of 2011 was not different from that for remainder of February 2011. For the case of nuclear power, the average capacity factor during the period February 14–18 is significantly less than the mean capacity factor for remaining hours of the month. Finally, for solar units the average capacity is lower during February 14–18 of 2021 relative to the remainder of the month.

To investigate which technologies had statistically distinguishable lower or higher mean capacity factors during the extreme weather periods of February 2011 and February 2021, relative to the remainder of the month of February, I ran the following regression for the hourly capacity factor for each technology for the periods March 1, 2010, to February 28, 2011, and March 1, 2020, to February 28, 2021:

$$CF_{hdm} = \alpha_{hm} + \delta_d + I_{hdm}\beta + \varepsilon_{hdm}$$

where CF_{hdm} is the capacity factor in hour h of day d of month m, α_{hm} is an hour-of-day h for month m fixed effect, δ_d is the fixed effect for weekend days (Saturday and Sunday), I_{hdm} is an indicator variable that is equal to 1 if hour h of day d of month m is during the February time period of 2011 or 2021, and ε_{hdm} is a zero-mean disturbance.

Table 2 presents the estimates of the coefficient associated with I_{hdm} for each technology and each February period. The annual mean capacity factor for each sample period for each technology is also included in

Table 2
Estimated Change in Mean Hourly Capacity Factor (CF) by Technology during February 1–4, 2011, and February 14–18, 2021, Weather Events

Technology	2011 Mean CF	2011 Coefficient	2011 Std. Error	2021 Mean CF	2021 Coefficient	2021 Std. Error
Coal	.7793	.0189	.0258	.5993	.0167	.0572
Natural gas	.3155	.3159	.0638	.4056	.3061	.0521
Wind	.3198	−.0454	.0734	.3996	−.2236	.0443
Nuclear	.9214	.0005	.0026	.9152	−.1641	.0476
Solar	N/A	N/A	N/A	.2117	−.0763	.0283

Note: All regressions include hour-of-day fixed effects for each month of the year. Standard errors are clustered by day of sample.

the table. For coal-fired generation units there is a slight, but not statistically different from zero, increase in the mean hourly capacity factor during the extreme weather periods in February 2011 and 2021 versus other hours in the month. For natural gas units, there is a precisely estimated substantial increase in the mean hourly capacity factor during both February extreme weather periods. In both 2011 and 2021, the mean hourly capacity factor of natural gas units increased by more than 0.30 during these extreme weather periods.

For the wind generation units, the capacity factor is 0.2236 less during the extreme weather period in 2021 than in other hours of February. Because there is 24,593 MW of wind generation in ERCOT in 2020, this reduction in the average capacity factor implies an average MWh reduction of wind energy during the February 2021 extreme weather period of 5,410 MWh. The nuclear capacity factor fell by 0.1641 during the extreme weather period, which for an installed capacity of 4,973 MW implies an average hourly reduction in nuclear generation of 795 MWh. The solar energy capacity factor fell by 0.0763, which for an installed capacity of 2,478 MWs implies an average hourly reduction in solar energy of 173 MWh during the extreme weather period. The total of these average hourly supply shortfalls during February 14–18, 2021, was 6,400 MWh, with the vast majority coming from intermittent renewable resources.

These results emphasize the substantial risk of relying of intermittent renewable energy units to produce during extreme cold weather periods, even relative to system conditions that typically exist during the winter months. As the graphs for 2021 in figures 11A and 11B demonstrate, the average hourly reduction in wind energy production of 5,410 MWh implies significantly larger reductions for a number of hours during February 14–18. As shown in both figures, hourly capacity factors very close to zero occurred at least twice during this time period.

ERCOT and the Reliability Externality

Although the historical peak demand of 72,820 MWh in ERCOT occurred on August 12, 2019, during the 4 p.m. to 5 p.m. hour, demand during the February 14–18 period was expected to exceed that demand but did not because rolling blackouts were implemented.[10] From analysis of the previous subsection, it seems reasonable to expect that a similar supply shortfall could occur during future extreme weather events as Texas increases the share of wind and solar resources in the state.

These events demonstrate that having a $9,000/MWh offer cap on the short-term market does not eliminate the reliability externality; it only reduces the frequency of supply shortfall events. The implicit assumption of the ERCOT market that the supply of energy would always exceed demand at a price at or below $9,000/MWh turned out to be false for the weather conditions experienced during February 14–18, 2021. The large share of housing units heated with electricity makes the demand for electricity in Texas extremely sensitive to extremely cold temperatures because these households must increase their demand for electricity to keep warm.

Consistent with the logic of the reliability externality, there were many households that paid for their wholesale electricity according to the hourly short-term price. This decision clearly makes economic sense in vast majority of hours of the year because short-term wholesale prices typical reflect substantial amounts of wind and solar energy production. One company, Griddy, was well known for selling retail electricity in this manner. Early during the extreme weather event, Griddy told all its customers to switch retail suppliers.[11] Of those that did not switch, many were unable to pay their bills as a result of purchasing much of their wholesale electricity during this time period at $9,000/MWh ($9/KWh). Consequently, ERCOT removed Griddy's right to operate effective February 21, 2021.

There were also several retailers that failed to fully hedge the partial or fully fixed-price retail contracts they sold to customers. These retailers had to purchase energy at $9,000/MWh and sell it at a fixed price to these retail customers. There was at least one retailer offering customers a $100 credit off their final bill and waiving all early termination fees if they switched providers before February 15, 2021.[12] This would enable the retailer to avoid having to purchase wholesale energy at a loss and sell it to its customers or avoid the likelihood that their customers would be unable to pay their bills, two outcomes with adverse financial consequences for the retailer.

Given the substantial volatility in wind and solar energy production in ERCOT, the state's dependence on electricity for space heating, and the fact that Texas cannot rely on large amounts of net imports from neighboring states when renewable energy shortfalls occur, the events of February 2021 are not unexpected. Figures 12 and 13 repeat figures 7 and 8 for the case of ERCOT for the period March 2020 through February 2021. Each monthly graph gives the same box and whiskers graph of the histogram of hourly capacity factors within that month. Because ERCOT

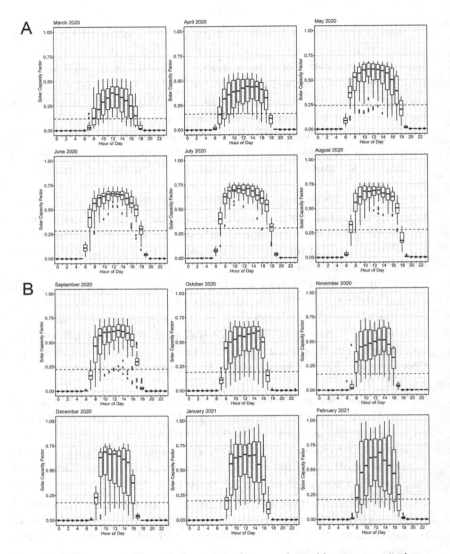

Fig. 12. *A*, Histograms of hourly solar capacity factors and monthly mean capacity factor in Electric Reliability Council of Texas (ERCOT) for March 2020–August 2020. *B*, Histograms of hourly solar capacity factors and monthly mean capacity factor in ERCOT for September 2020–February 2021.

does not have a firm capacity construct, the horizontal line on each graph is the monthly mean capacity factor for that technology. Figure 12 shows that the monthly mean capacity factor for solar resources is generally larger than the median hourly capacity factor for the early and late daylight hours of the day for many months of the year.

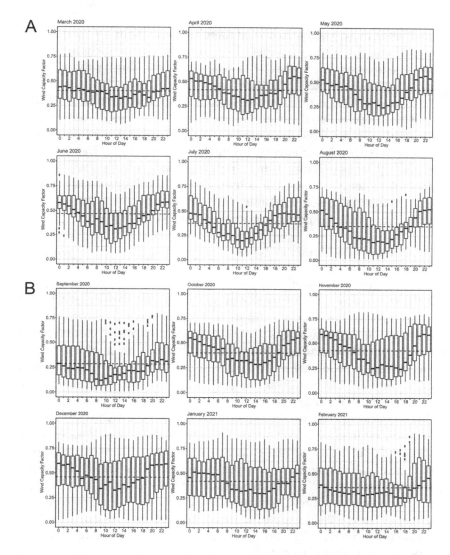

Fig. 13. *A*, Histograms of hourly wind capacity factors and monthly mean capacity factor in Electric Reliability Council of Texas (ERCOT) for March 2020–August 2020. *B*, Histograms of hourly wind capacity factors and monthly mean capacity factor in ERCOT for September 2020–February 2021.

From April to November 2020, the monthly mean capacity factor for wind units in ERCOT is above the median capacity factor for most hours in the middle of the day. During the December to March time period, the median hourly capacity factor is relatively constant across hours of the day. All of these graphs show that there are many hours of the day during all months when extremely low capacity factors for wind occur. These extremely low capacity factors can occur during the summer months as well as the winter months.

Because ERCOT is not interconnected with the rest of the United States grid, this implies that the region will need to invest in significant storage capacity or increase the amount of natural gas-fired generation capacity to meet the demand for energy during these time periods. These thermal generation units will run at smaller capacity factors as the share of wind and solar energy increases. It is unclear whether the necessary storage units or thermal generation units will be built and remain financially viable without a long-term RA mechanism in ERCOT.

The Natural Gas Market in Texas

The severity of the electricity supply shortfall during February 15–18, 2021, was exacerbated by events in natural gas markets caused by the extremely cold weather and curtailment of electricity to natural gas processing facilities, natural gas pumping stations, and compressors on natural gas pipelines and at power plants.[13] Because much of the natural gas currently produced in Texas is associated with the production of oil, it comes to the surface at low pressure along with other liquids, including water. This has two implications for the level of natural gas production during cold weather conditions. First, low temperatures can lead to well freeze-offs, where the raw natural gas stream freezes at the wellhead or in the natural gas gathering lines, which ultimately stops production of natural gas. Second, to pump the oil and associated natural gas to the surface, process it, and compress it for transportation to natural gas generation units requires electricity. Many of the natural gas processing facilities in Texas failed to apply for outage exemptions as essential facilities before the February 2021 extreme weather event, and as a result were curtailed in the rolling blackouts.[14]

It is difficult to determine precisely what fraction of the almost 50% decline in natural gas production during the February 2021 cold snap was due to freeze-offs versus electricity outages to natural gas processing facilities.[15] A significant amount of natural gas-fired generation capacity was unable to operate during the cold snap because natural gas could not be delivered to these units.

Requiring all natural gas processing and transportation facilities to be classified as critical infrastructure that is protected from power outages due to supply shortfalls should eliminate this cause of natural gas short-falls. One natural gas company found that all its natural gas facilities that had been registered as critical infrastructure did not have their power turned off during the February 2021 cold snap.[16]

A more controversial recommendation made by many observers is to winterize natural gas wells to prevent freeze-offs during cold weather conditions. This recommendation was made following the 2011 cold snap but was not implemented for the same reason it is unlikely to be implemented after 2021 cold snap without an explicit regulatory mandate. Only around 0.06% of total annual natural gas production in Texas freezes off on average, and winterizing can cost as much as $100,000 per well.[17] These two figures suggest that it was and continues to be expected profit-maximizing for Texas natural gas producers not to winterize. In addition, if the political process decides to mandate winterizing all wells, this would likely cause producers to abandon many wells rather than pay the cost to winterize them, which would ultimately reduce the supply of natural gas in Texas.

C. The Need for Long-Term Storage with Significant Renewables

This section identifies an important characteristic of electricity supply industries with significant intermittent renewable generation capacity that provides further evidence against a capacity-based long-term RA mechanism. This is the potential for long durations of low levels of renewable output, particularly in regions where a significant amount of the renewable energy comes from wind generation units, as is the case in Texas.

Table 3 presents summary statistics on the annual hourly distribution of wind, solar, and combined wind and solar output for California from 2013 to 2020. Although the mean hourly output for wind and solar generation increases across the years, so does the standard deviation of hourly output. For the case of combined wind and solar generation, the standard deviation of hourly output has increased more rapidly than the hourly mean output, as evidenced by the upward trend in the coefficient of variation (CV) across the years.[18]

This increased variability in wind and solar output has characteristics that make significant investments in storage capacity necessary if the share of renewables is increased significantly beyond current levels. There can be long durations of relatively low levels of energy production from the wind and solar generation units. Table 4 presents data

Table 3
Annual Moments of Hourly Wind, Solar, and Wind and Solar Output in California

	2013	2014	2015	2016	2017	2018	2019	2020
	Hourly Wind Output (MWh)							
Mean	1033.54	1131.32	999.26	1204.73	1235.28	1597.35	1581.63	1551.73
Median	973.79	1035.19	860.06	1092.49	1074.29	1496.55	1439.55	1378.13
Standard deviation	843.79	881.27	822.59	918.41	957.56	1161.22	1148.88	1149.84
Coefficient of variation	.82	.78	.82	.76	.78	.73	.73	.74
Standard skewness	.39	.49	.53	.41	.47	.34	.42	.45
Standard kurtosis	2.03	2.29	2.18	2.05	2.08	1.92	2.07	2.1
	Hourly Solar (MWh)							
Mean	315.39	1000.38	1510.80	1910.23	2633.99	2923.06	3035.64	3214.42
Median	11.98	55.50	90.08	101.91	150.53	174.16	209.95	186.55
Standard deviation	435.64	1290.47	1906.14	2391.94	3257.65	3587.68	3761.14	3907.56
Coefficient of variation	1.38	1.29	1.26	1.25	1.24	1.23	1.24	1.22
Standard skewness	1.22	.84	.83	.73	.69	.67	.72	.66
Standard kurtosis	3.50	2.14	2.63	1.86	1.78	1.75	1.85	1.78
	Hourly Combined Wind and Solar Output (MWh)							
Mean	1348.93	2131.57	2510.06	3114.96	3869.27	4520.41	4617.28	4766.15
Median	1364.04	1971.03	2030.58	2385.57	2595.63	3255.97	3150.32	3265.43
Standard deviation	883.40	1461.08	1983.06	2426.76	3258.25	3606.08	3818.19	3894.42
Coefficient of variation	.65	.69	.79	.78	.84	.80	.83	.82
Standard skewness	.19	.45	.63	.55	.6	.55	.62	.57
Standard kurtosis	2.32	2.50	2.95	2.07	1.97	1.96	2.03	1.95

Source: California ISO OASIS website.
Note: MWh = megawatt-hours.

on the distribution of durations of wind and solar energy production below a given threshold during each year from 2013 to 2020. For a given threshold, say 1,000 MWh, the following process is applied to compute each low energy production duration. The first hour in the year that wind and solar energy production falls below 1,000 MWh starts the duration. This duration ends the first hour that wind and solar energy production is above 1,000 MWh. The second duration is defined following the same process. For example, in 2013 there were 231 durations when total wind and solar production was less than 1,000 MWh. The mean length of these durations was 13.54 hours, but there was one duration of 288 hours or 12 days. By 2020, there were roughly the same number of durations of with solar and wind energy production less than 1,000 MWh— 210 durations—but the average length was 7.88 hours, and the longest was 17 hours.

Table 4
Combined Wind and Solar Output Shortfall Durations in California (Hours)

	2013	2014	2015	2016	2017	2018	2019	2020
Threshold value				1,000 MWh				
Number of durations	231	263	256	228	247	171	183	210
Mean	13.54	8.46	9.54	8.73	7.96	9.39	9.07	7.88
Standard deviation	27.43	6.08	5.70	5.79	5.49	5.65	5.33	5.31
Maximum	288	20	18	21	16	17	17	17
Threshold value				3,000 MWh				
Number of durations	53	298	356	364	388	380	396	386
Mean	160.47	21.42	15.85	14.29	12.51	10.72	10.55	10.62
Standard deviation	238.97	42.27	8.57	8.42	5.01	5.94	6.01	5.24
Maximum	1,283	684	140	141	65	44	44	21
Threshold value				5,000 MWh				
Number of durations	1	71	226	321	349	356	353	366
Mean	8,758	119.20	32.84	19.84	16.31	15.33	15.50	14.58
Standard deviation	NA	260.95	65.10	21.56	8.19	6.32	7.21	3.09
Maximum	8,758	1809	875	299	92	90	68	44
Threshold value				7,000 MWh				
Number of durations	1	1	19	131	284	318	318	349
Mean	8,758	8,759	457	61.89	23.36	19.38	19.16	16.94
Standard deviation	NA	NA	800.28	155.67	36.90	22.03	20.62	9.44
Maximum	8,758	8,759	3,177	1,363	478	226	239	116
Threshold value				10,000 MWh				
Number of durations	1	1	3	1	58	161	199	200
Mean	8,758	8,759	2918.33	8,784	146.53	48.91	37.92	37.64
Standard deviation	NA	NA	2793.92	NA	363.65	137.20	98.65	93.89
Maximum	8,758	8,759	5,583	8,784	2,145	1,173	876	849

Source: California ISO OASIS website.

In 2020 there was almost 20,000 MW of wind and solar generation capacity in California, yet for 50% of the hours of the year, 3,265.43 MWh or less energy was produced from these units. In 2020, the average length of the duration of energy production less than 5,000 MWh was 14.58 hours and the longest duration was 44 hours or slightly less than 2 days. For the 10,000 MWh threshold in 2020, the longest duration was 849 hours or more than 35 days.

Tables 5 and 6 repeat the information in tables 3 and 4 for ERCOT for 2018–20. Although ERCOT has almost 27,000 MW of wind and solar capacity in 2020, during 50% of the hours of the year less than 10,789 MWh is produced by this generation capacity. The advantage of the wind capacity

Table 5
Annual Moments of Hourly Wind and Solar Output in ERCOT (MWh)

	2018	2019	2020
Mean	8337.5	9258.6	10910.6
Median	8074.2	8996.5	10769.8
Standard deviation	4179.5	4360.7	4686.9
Coefficient of variation	.50	.47	.43
Standard skewness	.16	.16	.03
Standard kurtosis	1.99	2.00	2.02

Source: Electric Reliability Council of Texas (ERCOT).
Note: MWh = megawatt-hours.

in ERCOT is the significantly higher average capacity factors shown in figure 13 versus the average solar capacity factors shown in figure 12.

The downside of significant wind capacity in ERCOT is the substantially longer maximum durations of low output levels. For example, in 2020 the longest duration of wind and solar output less than 5,000 MWh

Table 6
Combined Wind and Solar Output Shortfall Durations in ERCOT (Hours)

	2018	2019	2020
Threshold value		5,000 MWh	
Number of durations	202	189	146
Mean	11.33	9.34	7.01
Standard deviation	13.40	10.05	8.09
Maximum	94	60	60
Threshold value		7,500 MWh	
Number of durations	222	221	242
Mean	18.21	15.62	10.30
Standard deviation	25.56	17.23	12.15
Maximum	239	133	97
Threshold value		10,000 MWh	
Number of durations	206	241	247
Mean	26.93	20.67	15.98
Standard deviation	45.26	25.16	21.30
Maximum	425	141	230
Threshold value		15,000 MWh	
Number of durations	83	143	207
Mean	99.99	53.83	32.29
Standard deviation	190.65	79.05	56.01
Maximum	1,310	428	387

Source: Electric Reliability Council of Texas (ERCOT).
Note: MWh = megawatt-hours.

is 60 hours or 2.5 days. Unlike solar energy, which relies on daily sunlight with varying levels of intensity, there are sustained periods with very low wind energy production.

The potential for multiday durations of low energy production implies the need for significant storage investments to ensure a reliable supply of energy so California and Texas can reduce significantly the amount of fossil fuel energy they consume. Although California still has the option to significantly increase its consumption of imported electricity from neighboring states during these system conditions, unless Texas interconnects with the rest of the United States this option is not available to ERCOT.

Storage generation units make money buying energy at low prices and selling it at high prices. Capacity-based long-term RA mechanisms typically suppress energy price volatility because of the mandates that retailers purchase multiples greater than 1 of their peak demand in firm capacity. Therefore, a capacity-based long-term RA mechanism provides less market revenue to the storage units necessary to manage sustained periods of low renewable energy production. Consequently, one key criterion for a long-term RA mechanism in a high renewables share market is allowing the short-term energy price volatility that will support the necessary storage investments.

V.   The SFPFC Approach to Long-Term RA

As the previous sections have demonstrated, a capacity-based approach to long-term RA mechanism is poorly suited to a region with significant intermittent renewables. The primary reliability challenge is not adequate generation capacity to serve demand peaks, but adequate energy available to serve realized demand during all hours of the year. As the example of California on August 14 and 15, 2020, demonstrates, supply shortfalls do not necessarily occur during system demand peaks, but during net demand peaks.

Because of the substantial contemporaneous correlation in hourly output across locations and across renewable energy technologies, ensuring sufficient supply to meet demand throughout the year will require taking full advantage of the mix of available generation resources. Intermittent renewable resources must reinsure the energy they sell in the forward market with dispatchable generation resources and storage devices. The long-term RA mechanism must also recognize the increasing weather dependence of electricity demand with more customers heating and cooling their homes with electricity.

The SFPFC mechanism results in the realized system demand each hour of the compliance period being covered by a fixed-price forward contract. The SFPFC approach to long-term RA recognizes that a supplier with the ability to serve demand at a reasonable price may not do so if it has the ability to exercise unilateral market power in the short-term energy market. As Wolak (2000) demonstrates, an expected profit-maximizing supplier with the ability to exercise unilateral market power with a fixed-price forward contract obligation would like to minimize the cost of supplying the quantity of energy sold in forward contract. The SFPFC long-term RA mechanism takes advantage of this incentive by requiring retailers to hold hourly fixed-price forward contract obligations for energy that sum to the hourly value of system demand. The SFPFC mechanism implies that all expected profit-maximizing suppliers would like to minimize the cost of meeting their hourly fixed-price forward contract obligations, the sum of which equals the hourly system demand for all hours of the year.

To understand the logic behind the SFPFC mechanism, consider the example of a supplier that owns 150 MW of generation capacity that has sold 100 MWh in a fixed-forward contract at a price of $25/MWh for a certain hour of the day. This supplier has two options for fulfilling this forward contract: (1) produce the 100 MWh energy from its own units at their marginal cost of $20/MWh or (2) buy this energy from the short-term market at the prevailing market-clearing price. The supplier will receive $2,500 from the buyer of the contract for the 100 MWh sold, regardless of how it is supplied. This means that the supplier maximizes the profits it earns from this fixed-price forward contract sale by minimizing the cost of supplying the 100 MWh of energy.

To ensure that the least-cost "make versus buy" decision for this 100 MWh is made, the supplier should offer 100 MWh in the short-term market at its marginal cost of $20/MWh. This offer price for 100 MWh ensures that if it is cheaper to produce the energy from its generation units—the market price is at or above $20/MWh—the supplier's offer to produce the energy will be accepted in the short-term market. If it is cheaper to purchase the energy from the short-term market—the market price is below $20/MW—the supplier's offer will not be accepted and the supplier will purchase the 100 MWh from the short-term market at a price below $20/MWh.

This example demonstrates that the SFPFC approach to long-term RA makes it expected profit-maximizing for each seller to minimize the cost of supplying the quantity of energy sold in this forward contract each hour of the delivery period. By the logic of the above example, each supplier will find it in its unilateral interest to submit an offer price into the short-term market equal to its marginal cost for its hourly SFPFC quantity of energy, to make the efficient "make versus buy" decision for fulfilling this obligation.

The incentives for supplier offer behavior in a short-term wholesale electricity market created by a fixed-price forward contract obligation are analyzed in Wolak (2000). Consider the case of a single hour in the short-term market. Let QS equal the amount of energy produced and sold in the short-term market by the supplier, PS be the short-term wholesale price, PC be the price of SFPFC energy, and QC be the quantity of SFPFCs sold by the supplier for this hour. The supplier's variable profit for the hour is:

$$
\begin{aligned}
\text{Profit} &= PS \times QS - C(QS) - (PS - PC) \times QC \\
&= PS \times (QS - QC) + PC \times QC - C(QS)
\end{aligned}
\tag{1}
$$

where $C(QS)$ is variable cost of producing QS. The first term in the first expression in equation (1) shows the supplier's variable profits from selling QS MWh at PS in the short-term market. The second term is the net payment to the seller of QC SFPFC contracts at price PC. The second expression in the above equation demonstrates that a supplier only has an incentive to raise the short-term price if it sells more energy in the short-term market, QS, than its fixed-price forward contract obligation, QC. This expression also demonstrates that the supplier wants the lowest possible price when it sells less energy in the short-term market than its fixed-price forward contract obligation.

Under the SFPFC mechanism, each supplier knows that the sum of the values of the hourly SFPFC obligations across all suppliers is equal the system demand. This means that each supplier of SFPFCs knows that its competitors have substantial fixed-price forward contract obligations for that hour. This implies that all suppliers know that they have limited opportunities to raise the price they receive for short-term market sales beyond their hourly SFPFC quantity.

As discussed below, a supplier's fixed-price forward quantity for an hour under the SFPFC mechanism increases with the value of hourly system demand. Therefore, the supplier that owns 150 MW of capacity in the above example has a strong incentive to submit an offer price close to its marginal cost for the capacity of its generation unit to ensure that its hourly production is higher than the realized value of its SFPFC energy for that hour. Therefore, the SFPFC mechanism not only ensures that system demand is met every hour of the year but also provides strong incentives for this to occur at the lowest possible short-term price.

A. SFPFC Approach to RA

This long-term RA mechanism requires all electricity retailers to hold SFPFCs for energy for fractions of realized system demand at various horizons to delivery. For example, retailers in total must hold SFPFCs that cover 100% of realized system demand in the current year, 95% of realized system demand 1 year in advance of delivery, 90% 2 years in advance of delivery, 87% 3 years in advance of delivery, and 85% 4 years in advance of delivery. The fractions of system demand and number of years in advance that the SFPFCs must be purchased are parameters set by the regulator to ensure long-term RA. The SFPFCs would clear against the quantity-weighted average of the hourly locational prices at all load withdrawal locations in the short-term wholesale market.

SFPFCs are shaped to the hourly system demand within the delivery period of the contract. Figure 14 contains a sample pattern of system demand for a four-hour delivery horizon. The total demand for the four hours is 1,000 MWh, and the four hourly demands are 100, 200, 400, and 300 MWh. Therefore, Firm 1 that sells 300 MWh of SFPFC energy has the hourly system demand-shaped forward contract obligations of 30 MWh in hour 1, 60 MWh in hour 2, 120 MWh in hour 3, and 90 MWh in hour 4. The hourly forward contract obligations for Firm 2 that sold 200 MWh SFPFC energy and Firm 3 that sold 500 MWh of SFPFC energy are also shown in figure 15. These SFPFC obligations are also allocated across the four hours according to the same four hourly shares of total system demand shown in figure 14. This ensures that the sum of the hourly values of the forward contract obligations for the three suppliers is equal to the hourly value of system demand. Taking the example of hour 3, Firm 1's obligation is 120 MWh, Firm 2's is 80 MWh, and Firm 3's is 200 MWh. These three values sum to 400 MWh, which is equal to the value of system demand in hour 3 shown in figure 14.

These SFPFCs are allocated to retailers based on their share of system demand during the month. Suppose that the four retailers in figure 16 consume 1/10, 2/10, 3/10, and 4/10, respectively, of the total energy consumed during the compliance month for SFPFCs. This means that Retailer 1 is allocated 100 MWh of the 1,000 MWh SFPFC obligations

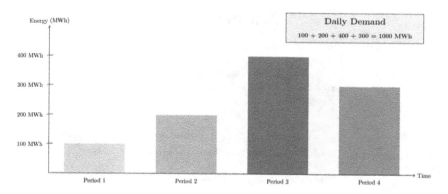

Fig. 14. Hourly system demands. Color version available as an online enhancement.

for the four hours, Retailer 2 is allocated 200 MWh, Retailer 3 is allocated 300 MWh, and Retailer 4 is allocated 400 MWh. The obligations of each retailer are then allocated to the individual hours using the same hourly system demand shares used to allocate the SFPFC energy sales of suppliers

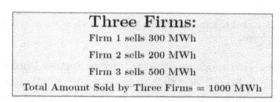

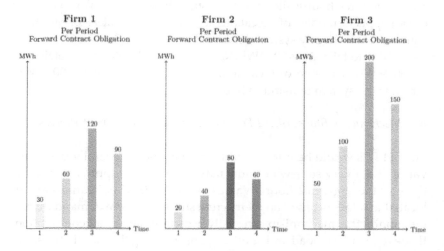

Fig. 15. Hourly forward contract quantities for three suppliers. Color version available as an online enhancement.

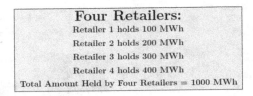

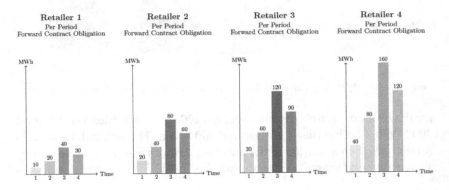

Fig. 16. Hourly forward contract quantities for four retailers. Color version available as an online enhancement.

to the four hours. This allocation process implies Retailer 1 holds 10 MWh in hour 1, 20 MWh in hour 2, 40 MWh in hour 3, and 30 MWh in hour 4. Repeating this same allocation process for the other three retailers yields the remaining three hourly allocations shown in figure 16. Similar to the case of the suppliers, the sum of allocations across the four retailers for each hour equals the total hourly system demand. For period 3, Retailer 1's holding is 40 MWh, Retailer 2's is 80 MWh, Retailer 3's is 120 MWh, and Retailer 4's is 160 MWh. The sum of these four magnitudes is equal to 400 MWh, which is the system demand in hour 3.

B.   Mechanics of Standardized Forward Contract Procurement Process

The SFPFCs would be purchased through auctions several years in advance of delivery so new entrants may compete to supply this energy. Because the aggregate hourly values of these SFPFC obligations are allocated to retailers based on their actual share of system demand during the month, this mechanism can easily accommodate retail competition. If one retailer loses load and another gains it during the month, the share of the aggregate hourly value of SFPFCs allocated to the first retailer falls and the share allocated to the second retailer rises.

The wholesale market operator would run the auctions with oversight by the regulator. One advantage of the design of the SFPFC products is that a simple auction mechanism can be used to purchase each annual product. A multiround auction could be run where suppliers submit the total amount of annual SFPFC energy they would like to sell for a given delivery period at the price for the current round. Each round of the auction the price would decrease until the amount suppliers are willing to sell at that price is less than or equal to the aggregate amount of SFPFC energy demanded.

The wholesale market operator would also run a clearinghouse to manage the counterparty risk associated with these contracts. All US wholesale market operators currently do this for all participants in their energy and ancillary services markets. In several US markets, the market operator also provides counterparty risk management services for long-term financial transmission rights, which is not significantly different from performing this function for SFPFCs. Both buyers and sellers would be required to post collateral with the wholesale market operator to ensure that each market participant finds it unilaterally profit-maximizing to meet its financial commitments for the SFPFC energy that it has purchased or sold.

SFPFCs auctions would be run on an annual basis for deliveries starting 2, 3, and 4 years in the future. In steady state, auctions for incremental amounts of each annual contract would also be needed so that the aggregate share of demand covered by each annual SFPFC could increase over time. The eventual 100% coverage of demand occurs through a final true-up auction that takes place after the realized values for hourly demand for the delivery period are known.

C. True-Up Auctions and Settlement of SFPFCs

The vast majority of SFPFC contracts will be purchased in advance of delivery. However, because the mechanism requires that the total quantity of SFPFC energy sold during the compliance period equal the realized demand during that same period, after each compliance period there needs to be true-up auctions to buy back unused SFPFC energy or purchase additional SFPFC energy.

These true-up auctions serve the same role as the real-time market in a two-settlement short-term energy market, with two key differences. First, the aggregate demand for additional SFPFC energy is known when suppliers submit their offers into incremental true-up auction or the total amount of SFPFC energy to be purchased by suppliers is known when they submit their bids to the true-up auction. Second, suppliers to the true-up auction know the quantity-weighted average hourly short-term market price during compliance period that all SFPFC energy sold or purchased in the true-up auction will clear against when they submit their bids or offers to these auctions. This implies that a supplier would be unlikely to be willing to sell SFPFC energy at a price less than or equal to this quantity-weighted average short-term price or buy SFPFC energy at a price above this quantity-weighted average short-term price.

It is also important to emphasize that the true-up auctions are very unlikely to trade significant quantities of energy given the relatively small rate of growth of energy demand in California. Table 7, taken from the 2017 and 2019 versions of the California ISO's *Annual Report on Market Issues and Performance*, shows the average load (total annual energy demand divided by the number of hours in the year) and annual peak load in the California ISO control area from 2013 to 2019.

The typical rate of growth of the annual demand for energy is substantially less volatile than the rate of growth in annual peak demand. Moreover, total annual energy demand growth is negative for 2018 and 2019. It is also likely to be negative for 2020 because of COVID-19. The volatility of annual peak demand emphasizes the importance of allocating the SFPFC energy using the actual hourly pattern of demand throughout the quarter rather than a forecast of these magnitudes. This precommitment ensures that during all hours of the year the total shortfall of suppliers producing less than their total SFPFC commitments is equal to the total surplus of suppliers producing more than their total SFPFC commitments

Table 7
Annual System Load in California ISO Control Area 2013–2019

Year	Annual Total Energy (GWh)	Average Load (MW)	% Change	Annual Peak Load (MW)	% Change
2013	231,800	26,461	−1.0	45,097	−3.7
2014	231,610	26,440	−.1	45,090	0
2015	231,495	26,426	0	46,519	3.2
2016	228,794	26,047	−1.4	46,232	−.6
2017	227,749	26,002	0	50,116	8.4
2018	220,458	25,169	−3.2	46,427	−7.4
2019	214,955	24,541	−2.5	44,301	−4.6

Note: ISO = Independent System Operators, GWh = gigawatt-hours, MW = megawatts.

for that hour, which means that final consumers have no net exposure to short-term prices.

The most straightforward approach to running the quarterly SFPFC auctions would be to run them as 12 independent auctions, one for each future quarter at least 3 years in the future. However, to facilitate a 3-year future revenue stream that could finance investment in new generation capacity, the 12 quarterly auctions could be run simultaneously so that a potential new entrant could sell prespecified quantities of SFPFC energy in all 12 auctions or nothing at all. For example, the new entrant could submit offers to sell the same amount of energy in all auctions.

The appendix contains several examples using the four-period model to illustrate how the true-up auctions would work. These examples demonstrate that the SFPFC obligation of a supplier provides a strong financial incentive to offer in at least as much energy at its marginal cost as it expects will be its final SFPFC allocation for that hour of the compliance period. If the realized value of the total system demand for the compliance period is higher than expected and the supplier sells SFPFC energy in the true-up auction, its final SFPFC allocation for each hour of compliance period will be higher than its initial SFPFC allocation.

Failure to account for the possibility of selling energy in the true-up auction can result in the supplier purchasing energy from the short-term market at a price that is substantially higher than the marginal cost of the generation capacity that the supplier does not offer into the short-term market. In this sense, the SFPFC obligation provides a supplier with a must-offer obligation for at least its final allocation of the SFPFC energy after the true-up auction for that hour of the compliance period, because the SFPFC mechanism requires the supplier to purchase any shortfall in output from its generation resources relative to this hourly SFPFC allocation at the hourly short-term price.

D. Incentives for Behavior by Intermittent Renewable and Controllable Resources

Because all suppliers know that all energy consumed every hour of the year is covered by a SFPFC in the current year and into the future, there is a strong incentive for suppliers to find the least-cost mix of intermittent and controllable resources to serve these hourly demands. To the extent that there is concern that the generation resources available or likely to be available in the future to meet demand are insufficient, features of the existing capacity-based RA mechanism can be retained until system operators have sufficient confidence in this mechanism leading to a reliable supply of energy. The firm capacity values from the existing capacity-based long-term RA approach can be used to limit the amount of SFPFC energy a supplier can sell.

The firm capacity value multiplied by number of hours in the year would be the maximum amount of SFPFC energy that the unit owner could sell in any given year. Therefore, a controllable thermal generation unit owner could sell significantly more SFPFC energy than it expects to produce annually, and an intermittent renewable resource owner could sell significantly less SFPFC energy than it expects to produce annually. This upper bound on the amount of SFPFC energy any generation unit could sell enforces cross-hedging between controllable in-state generation units and intermittent renewable resources. This mechanism uses the firm capacity construct to limit forward market sales of energy by individual resource owners to ensure that it is physically feasible to serve demand during all hours of the year.

Cross-hedging between a controllable resource and an intermittent resource implies that in most years, the controllable resource owner would be producing energy in a small number of hours of the year but earning the difference between the price at which it sold the energy in the SFPFC auction and the hourly short-term market price times the hourly value of its SFPFC energy obligation for all the hours that it does not produce energy. Intermittent renewables owners would typically produce more than their SFPFC obligation in energy and sell any energy produced beyond this quantity at the short-term price. In years with low renewable output near their SFPRC obligations, controllable resource owners would produce close to the hourly value of their SFPFC energy obligation, thus making average short-term prices significantly higher. However, aggregate retail demand would be shielded from these high short-term prices because of their SFPFC holdings.

E.   *Assessment of the SFPFC Approach to Long-Term RA*

This mechanism has several advantages relative to a capacity-based approach. There is no regulator-mandated aggregate capacity requirement. Generation unit owners are allowed to decide both the total MW and the mix of technologies to meet their SFPFC energy obligations. There is also no prohibition on generation unit owners or retailers engaging in other hedging arrangements outside of this mechanism. Specifically, a retailer could enter into a bilateral contract for energy with a generation unit owner or other retailer to manage the short-term price and quantity risk associated with the difference between their actual hourly load shape and the hourly values of their retail load obligation.

This mechanism provides a nudge to market participants to develop a liquid market for these bilateral contract arrangements at horizons to delivery similar to the SFPFC products. Instead of starting from the baseline of no fixed-price forward contract coverage of system demand by retailers, this mechanism starts with 100% coverage of system demand, which retailers can unwind at their own risk.

This baseline level of SFPFC coverage of final demand is a more prudent approach to long-term RA in a region such as California where the vast majority of customers purchase their electricity according to a fixed retail price or price schedule that does not vary with real-time system conditions. A baseline 100% SFPFC coverage of final demand provides the retailer with wholesale price certainty for virtually all its wholesale energy purchases (except for the small true-up uncertainty described above), which significantly limits the financial risk retailers face from selling retail electricity at a fixed price and purchasing this energy from a short-term wholesale market with increasingly volatile wholesale prices.

An additional benefit of this mechanism is that the retail market regulator, in this case the CPUC, can use the purchase prices of SFPFCs to set the wholesale price implicit in the regulated retail price over the time horizon that the forward contract clears. This would provide retailers with a strong incentive to reduce their average wholesale energy procurement costs below this price through bilateral hedging arrangements, storage investments, or demand response efforts.

There are several reasons why this mechanism should be a more cost-effective approach to long-term RA than a capacity-based mechanism in a zero marginal cost intermittent future. First, the sale of SFPFC energy starting delivery 2 or more years in the future provides a revenue stream that will significantly increase investor confidence in recovering the cost of any investment in new generation capacity.

Second, because retailers are protected from high short-term prices by total hourly SFPFC holdings equaling actual system demand, the offer cap on the short-term market can be raised to increase the incentive for all suppliers to produce as much energy as possible during stressed system conditions. Third, the possibility of higher short-term price spikes can finance investments in storage and load-shifting technologies and encourage active participation of final demand in the wholesale market, further enhancing system reliability in a market with significant intermittent renewable resources.

If SFPFC energy is sold for delivery in 4 years based on a proposed generation unit, the regulator should require construction of the new unit to begin within a prespecified number of months after the signing date of the contract or require posting of a substantially larger amount of collateral in the clearinghouse with the market operator. Otherwise, the amount of SFPFC energy that this proposed unit sold would be automatically liquidated in a subsequent SFPFC auction and a financial penalty would be imposed on the developer. Other completion milestones would have to be met at future dates to ensure the unit is able to provide the amount of firm energy that it committed to provide in the SFPFC contract sold. If any of these milestones were not met, the contract would be liquidated.

F. Empirical Evidence on the Performance of the SFPFC Mechanism

Although the SFPFC mechanism in the form described above does not exist in any currently operating electricity supply industry, the long-term RA mechanisms in Chile and Peru create the same set of incentives for supplier behavior as the SFPFC mechanism by assigning system-wide short-term price and quantity risk during all hours of the year to suppliers. Both Chile and Peru operate a supplier-only, cost-based short-term wholesale electricity market. The system operator employs regulated variable cost estimates for each generation unit and an opportunity cost of water for hydroelectric generation units to dispatch generation units to meet demands throughout each country. All consumers or their retailers are required to purchase full-requirements contracts from suppliers to meet their retail load obligations. Suppliers financially settle imbalances between the amount of energy they produce and the amount of energy their customers consume under these full-requirements contracts. Suppliers that produce more energy than their customers consume receive payments from the suppliers that produce less energy than their customers consume.[19]

To see the equivalence of the incentives created for supplier behavior under the market designs in Chile and Peru and the SFPFC mechanism, let QR_i equal the consumption of customers served by the supplier i and PR_i the quantity-weighted average price paid for full-requirements contracts by customers served by supplier i. Let system demand equal QD, which is also equal to $\Sigma_{i=1}^{N} QR_i$, the sum of the consumption of all customers served by the N suppliers. The variable profit of supplier i is equal to

$$\text{Profit}_i = PS \times QS - C(QS) - (PS - PR_i) \times QR_i$$
$$= PS \times (QS - QR_i) + PR_i \times QR_i - C(QS),$$

(2)

which is identical to equation (1) presented earlier by setting QR_i equal to QC and PR_i equal to PC. Moreover, because $QD = \Sigma_{i=1}^{N} QR_i$; all short-term price and quantity risk is borne jointly by the N suppliers that have sold full-requirements contracts.

The long-term RA mechanisms in Chile and Peru have delivered a reliable supply of electricity for at least the past 15 years in each country in the face of significant hydroelectric energy supply uncertainty and an increasing share of the energy consumed coming from intermittent wind and solar generation units. This outcome has been achieved in two countries with average annual load growth rates that are three to four times that in regions in the United States with formal wholesale electricity markets. Consequently, the experience of Chile and Peru provides a strong argument in favor of the SFPFC mechanism for regions of the United States with significant intermittent renewable energy goals.

VI. Final Comments

Wholesale market design is a process of continuous learning, adaptation, and, hopefully, improvement. As the analyses of Sections II and III have shown, a capacity-based long-term RA mechanism designed for an industry based on dispatchable thermal generation units is poorly suited to an industry with a significant share of energy coming from intermittent renewable generation capacity. These analyses demonstrate that future supply shortfalls similar to those that occurred in California during August 2020 and in Texas during February 2021 are likely in regions with significant intermittent renewable generation capacity without a change in the paradigm for ensuring long-term RA.

These analyses demonstrate that the major system reliability challenge with a significant amount of renewable generation capacity changes, from having sufficient generation capacity to meet annual system demand peaks to the ability to meet the hourly net demands (system demand less intermittent renewable output) for energy throughout the year. Particularly in an electricity supply industry with a summer annual peak demand and significant installed solar generation capacity, meeting daily system demand peaks is relatively straightforward because demand peaks when there is significant solar energy production. The new focus on meeting net demand peaks implies a system-wide focus on energy adequacy where intermittent renewable resources have a financial incentive to hedge their short-term and production quantity risk with dispatchable generation resources to cover these net demand peaks.

The standardized energy contracting approach to long-term RA described in this paper delivers this outcome by allowing dispatchable resources to sell significantly more energy in these standardized forward contracts than they expect to produce to provide the revenue necessary to keep sufficient amounts of this generation capacity available to meet these hourly net demands throughout the year, even though these thermal units operate at smaller annual average capacity factors. Intermittent renewable resources are allowed to sell significantly less energy in these standardized forward contracts than they expect to produce annually to ensure that sufficient dispatchable generation capacity will be available to meet the intermittent net demand peaks throughout the year. The experience of Chile and Peru over the past 15 years, each of which has a market design that creates the same set of incentives for supplier behavior as the SFPFC mechanism, provides encouraging empirical evidence in favor of its adoption in regions with significant intermittent renewable energy goals.

Appendix

I. Examples of Positive and Negative True-Up Auction Outcomes

A compliance auction would be run far in advance of the compliance period to purchase 1,000 MWh of energy for the four time periods shown in figure 14. Suppose this auction cleared at a price of $60/MWh. Figure 15 shows the quantities sold in the auction for the three suppliers and their hourly SFPFC obligations, assuming the pattern of aggregate demand in figure 15 is realized for the four time periods. Figure 16 shows the hourly SFPFC holdings of the four retailers for the four time periods. The total demand across the four periods for each retailer is shown at the top of figure 16.

Now suppose that the realized demand for the compliance period turns out to be 10% higher in each of the four periods. The new demands for the four periods are shown in figure A1. This implies the need for an ex post true-up auction for 100 MWh. Because demand is 10% higher in each of the four periods, the shares that allocate this additional

100 MWh across four time periods to the four retailers are the same as those used to allocate the original 1,000 MWh across the four time periods. The incremental allocations to each of the four retailers are shown in figure A2 and the total realized demands for the four periods for each retailer are shown at the top of the graph. The period-level obligations for the incremental SFPFC energy purchased in the true-up auctions depend on which suppliers sell this energy. If each firm sells 10% more SFPFC energy in the true-up auction and system demand increases by 10% in each of the four periods, the period-level allocations of the additional SFPFC energy for each supplier are shown in figure A3. In this example, we assume that the true-up auction cleared at $70/MWh and the demand-weighted average short-term price for the four periods is $55/MWh.

In addition to the variable profits they would earn from selling the energy they produce from their own generation units in the short-term market, the three suppliers would receive the following difference payments to settle their SFPFC contract positions:

Firm 1 = ($60 − $55)300 + ($70 − $55)30
Firm 2 = ($60 − $55)200 + ($70 − $55)20
Firm 3 = ($60 − $55)500 + ($70 − $55)50.

Besides the variable profits they would earn from purchasing energy from the short-term market and selling to their retail customers at the retail price, the four retailers would pay the following difference payments:

Retailer 1 = ($60 − $55)1,000(110/1,100) + ($70 − $55)(110/1,100)100
Retailer 2 = ($60 − $55)1,000(220/1,100) + ($70 − $55)(220/1,100)100
Retailer 3 = ($60 − $55)1,000(330/1,100) + ($70 − $55)(330/1,100)100
Retailer 4 = ($60 − $55)1,000(440/1,100) + ($70 − $55)(440/1,100)100.

Both the original and true-up aggregate SFPFC purchases are allocated to individual retailers based on their actual share of total demand served during the four demand periods.

If this 100 MWh total demand increase is instead shared equally between periods 1 and 2, period 1 demand would now be 150 MWh and the period 2 demand would now be 250 MWh. Demand in periods 3 and 4 are unchanged from those in figure 14. In the final settlement, 150 MWh of the SFPFCs would be allocated to retailers in period 1, 250 MWh in period 2, 400 MWh in period 3, and 300 MWh in period 4. Suppose that Retailer 1 consumed the entire additional 100 MWh of energy during the compliance period. Retailer 1 would now be assigned 2/11 = (200/1,100) of the above period-level values of SFPFCs as opposed to the values shown in figure 16. Retailer 2, 3, and 4 would be also be assigned 2/11, 3/11, and 4/11, respectively, because their demand totals for the four periods did not change.

Suppose that the entire 100 MWh true-up auction quantity was all sold by Firm 1 at a price of \$65/MWh and as a result of a different pattern of demands throughout the four periods, the demand-weighted average short-term price is \$50/MWh. Now, in addition to the variable profits they would earn from selling energy in the short-term market produced by their generation units, the three suppliers would receive the following difference payments to settle their SFPFC contract positions:

Firm 1 = (\$60 − \$50)300 + (\$65 − \$50)100
Firm 2 = (\$60 − \$50)200
Firm 3 = (\$60 − \$50)500.

Besides the variable profits they would earn from purchasing energy from the short-term market to sell to their customers at the retail price, the four retailers would pay for the following difference payments:

Retailer 1 = (\$60 − \$50)(1,000)(2/11) + (\$65 − \$50)100(2/11)
Retailer 2 = (\$60 − \$50)(1,000)(2/11) + (\$65 − \$50)100(2/11)
Retailer 3 = (\$60 − \$50)(1,000)(3/11) + (\$65 − \$50)100(3/11)
Retailer 4 = (\$60 − \$50)(1,000)(4/11) + (\$65 − \$50)100(4/11).

Again, both the original and true-up aggregate SFPFC purchases are allocated to individual retailers based on their actual share of total demand served during the four demand periods.

What price clears the true-up auction depends on the extent of competition among suppliers to provide this additional energy. Clearly, suppliers are extremely unlikely to offer to supply this energy below the demand-weighted average short-term price over the compliance period because their overall profits would decline. However, if there are a substantial number of suppliers willing to sell this additional SFPFC energy, the price is unlikely to be significantly above the demand-weighted average short-term price.

It is important to note that the lower the demand-weighted average short-term price, the larger are the difference payments that suppliers receive. This is another way of demonstrating that all suppliers have an incentive to minimize the cost of meeting their SFPFC obligations by offering to supply this energy at their marginal cost of production in the short-term market.

The true-up auction for excess SFPFC energy operates in an analogous manner. Suppose that demand is 10% lower in every period as shown in figure A4. Suppose each firm buys back 10% of its SFPFC quantity in the true-up auction. This yields the period-level SFPFC quantities for each supplier in figure A5. If all retailers reduce their consumption in each of the four periods by 10%, their hourly SFPFC allocations and their total demands for the four periods are those shown in figure A6. Suppose that the demand-weighted average short-term price is $45/MWh and true-up auction clears at $40/MWh.

In addition to the variable profits they would earn from selling energy produced by their generation units in the short-term market, the three suppliers would now receive the following difference payments to settle their SFPFC contract positions:

Firm 1 = ($60 − $45)300 − ($40 − $45)30
Firm 2 = ($60 − $45)200 − ($40 − $45)20
Firm 3 = ($60 − $45)500 − ($40 − $45)50.

Besides the variable profits they would earn from purchasing energy from the short-term market to sell to at the retail price to their customers, the four retailers would pay the following difference payments:

Retailer 1 = ($60 − $45)(90/900)1,000 − ($40 − $45)(90/900)100
Retailer 2 = ($60 − $45)(180/900)1,000 − ($40 − $45)(180/900)100
Retailer 3 = ($60 − $45)(270/900)1,000 − ($40 − $45)(270/900)100
Retailer 4 = ($60 − $45)(360/900)1,000 − ($40 − $45)(360/900)100.

Once again, the price that clears the true-up auction depends on the extent of competition among suppliers to purchase the excess energy. Clearly, suppliers are extremely unlikely to bid a price for this energy above the demand-weighted average short-term price over the compliance period. However, if there are a substantial number of suppliers willing to buy this excess SFPFC energy, the auction price is unlikely to be significantly below the demand-weighted average short-term price.

Now suppose that the entire 100 MWh true-up auction quantity was purchased by Firm 1 at a price of $35/MWh and this 100 MWh reduction in demand across the four periods came entirely from period 3 and only from Retailer 3. Suppose that as a result of a different pattern of demand throughout the day, the realized demand-weighted average short-term price is $40/MWh. This implies the following realized system load shares for the four periods: 1/9, 2/9, 3/9, and 3/9. The total realized demands for each retailer are now 100, 200, 200, and 400, so portions of both aggregate SFPFC purchases are allocated to retailers using the following shares: 1/9, 2/9, 2/9, and 4/9.

Now, in addition to the variable profits they would earn from selling the energy produced by their generation units in the short-term market, the three suppliers would receive the following difference payments to settle their SFPFC contract positions:

Firm 1 = ($60 − $40)300 − ($35 − $40)100
Firm 2 = ($60 − $40)200
Firm 3 = ($60 − $40)500.

Besides the variable profits they would earn from purchasing energy from the short-term market to sell to their retail customers, the four retailers would pay for the following difference payments:

Retailer 1 = ($60 − $40)(1,000)(100/900) − ($35 − $40)100(100/900)
Retailer 2 = ($60 − $40)(1,000)(200/900) − ($35 − $40)100(200/900)
Retailer 3 = ($60 − $40)(1,000)(200/900) − ($35 − $40)100(200/900)
Retailer 4 = ($60 − $40)(1,000)(400/900) − ($35 − $40)100(400/900).

The original and true-up aggregate SFPFC purchases are allocated to individual retailers based on their actual share of total demand served during the four demand periods. More details on the SFPFC mechanism and examples of true-up auctions are given in California Public Utilities Commission (2021).

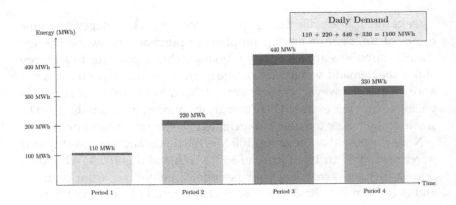

Fig. A1. Hourly system demands (10% higher). Color version available as an online enhancement.

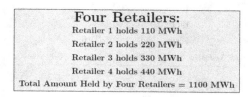

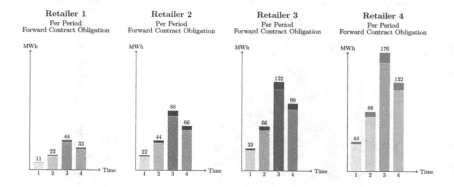

Fig. A2. Hourly forward contract quantities for four retailers (10% higher). Color version available as an online enhancement.

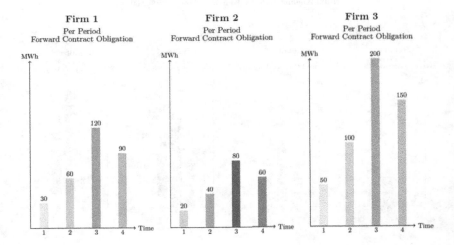

Fig. A3. Hourly forward contract quantities for three suppliers (10% higher). Color version available as an online enhancement.

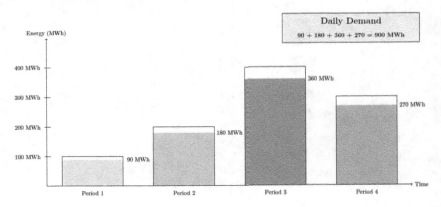

Fig. A4. Hourly system demands (10% lower). Color version available as an online enhancement.

216

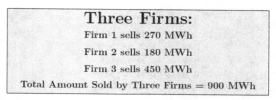

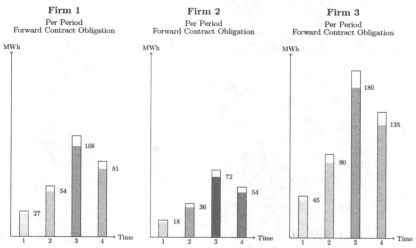

Fig. A5. Hourly forward contract quantities for three suppliers (10% lower). Color version available as an online enhancement.

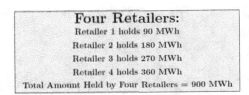

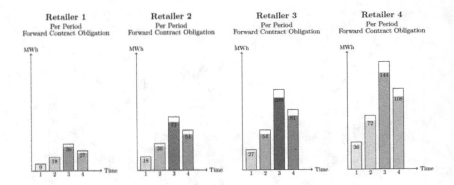

Fig. A6. Hourly forward contract quantities for four retailers (10% lower). Color version available as an online enhancement.

Endnotes

Author email address: Wolak (wolak@zia.stanford.edu). For acknowledgments, sources of research support, and disclosure of the author's material financial relationships, if any, please see https://www.nber.org/books-and-chapters/environmental-and-energy-policy-and -economy-volume-3/long-term-resource-adequacy-wholesale-electricity-markets-significant -intermittent-renewables.
   1. McRae and Wolak (2019) demonstrate the difficulty of ensuring that supply equals demand in the hydroelectric-dominated electricity supply industry in Colombia because of El Niño weather events. Wolak (2003) argues that a key causal factor in the California electricity crisis of 2000–01 was the low levels of hydroelectric energy available in the Pacific Northwest, which typically supplies a substantial amount of electricity to California each year. Wolak (2009) demonstrates that the two supply shortfall periods in 2001 and 2003 in the New Zealand wholesale electricity market were also due in large part to low water availability.
   2. See http://www.ercot.com/content/wcm/key_documents_lists/225373/Urgent_Board _of_Directors_Meeting_2-24-2021.pdf.
   3. The number of generation units available is a binomial random variable with probability $p = .9$ and with number of trials N = the number of generation units. The probability of meeting the demand peak is the probability the available capacity is greater than or equal to the peak demand.
   4. The annual average hourly capacity factor for a generation technology first computes the total production by that technology during each hour of the year divided the total of installed capacity of that technology during that hour. It then computes the annual average of these hourly values over all hours of the year.

5. For a map of all North American Interconnections, see https://www.eia.gov/electricity/data/eia411/images/nerc_old.jpg.

6. Wood, Wollenberg, and Sheblé (2013) provide an accessible introduction to Kirchoff's laws and transmission and distribution grid operation.

7. The monthly firm capacity figures for 2020 are listed in the file NetQualifying CapacityList-2020.xls, available at http://www.caiso.com/planning/Pages/Reliability Requirements/Default.aspx.

8. There are limited direct current interconnections with neighboring states that sell limited amounts of electricity to ERCOT or export energy from ERCOT.

9. See https://data.census.gov/cedsci/table?q=ACSDT1Y2019.B25040.

10. See http://www.ercot.com/content/wcm/key_documents_lists/225373/Urgent _Board_of_Directors_Meeting_2-24-2021.pdf.

11. See https://www.bloomberg.com/news/articles/2021-02-15/texas-power-retailers -in-face-of-freeze-please-leave-us.

12. Ibid.

13. See https://www.houstonchronicle.com/politics/texas/article/Simple-paperwork -blunder-Texans-cold-winter-storm-16032163.php.

14. See https://www.spglobal.com/platts/en/market-insights/blogs/electric-power /041521-texas-electricity-market-february-freeze-power-outages.

15. See https://www.eia.gov/todayinenergy/detail.php?id=46896.

16. See https://www.houstonchronicle.com/politics/texas/article/Simple-paperwork -blunder-Texans-cold-winter-storm-16032163.php.

17. See https://www.texasmonthly.com/news-politics/texas-blackouts-natural-gas.

18. CV = (Standard Deviation)/(Mean).

19. See Section 3.2 of Wolak (2021) for more details on this settlement mechanism.

References

California Public Utilities Commission. 2021. "Addendum to Staff Draft Straw Proposal for Consideration in Track 3B.2 of Proceeding R.19-11-009." February 26. https://docs.cpuc.ca.gov/PublishedDocs/Efile/G000/M372/K082 /372082582.PDF.

Carden, Kevin, Alex Krasny Dombrowsky, and Chase Winkler. 2020. "2020 Joint IOU ELCC Study, Report 1." https://www.astrape.com/2020-joint-ca -iou-elcc-study-report-1.

Doss-Gollin, James, David J. Farnham, Upmanu Lall, and Vijay Modi. 2021. "How Unprecedented Was the February 2021 Texas Cold Snap?" *Environmental Research Letters* 16 (6): 064056.

Garver, Leonard L. 1966. "Effective Load Carrying Capability of Generating Units." *IEEE Transactions on Power Apparatus and Systems* 8:910–19.

Kahn, Edward P. 2004. "Effective Load Carrying Capability of Wind Generation: Initial Results with Public Data." *Electricity Journal* 17 (10): 85–95.

McRae, Shaun D., and Frank A. Wolak. 2016. "Diagnosing the Causes of the Recent El Niño Event and Recommendations for Reform." http://web.stanford .edu/group/fwolak/cgi-bin/sites/default/files/diagnosing-el-nino _mcrae_wolak.pdf.

———. 2019. "Market Power and Incentive-Based Capacity Payment Mechanisms." http://web.stanford.edu/group/fwolak/cgi-bin/sites/default /files/2019-03-mcrae-wolak-capacity.pdf.

Wolak, Frank A. 2000. "An Empirical Analysis of the Impact of Hedge Contracts on Bidding Behavior in a Competitive Electricity Market." *International Economic Journal* 14 (2): 1–39.

————. 2003. "Diagnosing the California Electricity Crisis." *Electricity Journal* 16 (7): 11–37.

————. 2009. "An Assessment of the Performance of the New Zealand Wholesale Electricity Market." Report for the New Zealand Commerce Commission. http://web.stanford.edu/group/fwolak/cgi-bin/sites/default/files/new_zealand_report_redacted.pdf.

————. 2013. "Economic and Political Constraints on the Demand-Side of Electricity Industry Restructuring Processes." *Review of Economics and Institutions* 4 (1): 42.

————. 2016. "Level versus Variability Trade-offs in Wind and Solar Generation Investments: The Case of California." *Energy Journal* 37 (Bollino-Madlener Special Issue).

————. 2021. "Final Report on Thematic Line 2: Transformation of the Peruvian Wholesale Electricity Market." Report for the Ministry of Mines and Energy of Peru. http://web.stanford.edu/group/fwolak/cgi-bin/sites/default/files/report_wolak_June_2021_draft_0.pdf.

Wood, Allen J., Bruce F. Wollenberg, and Gerald B. Sheblé. 2013. *Power Generation, Operation, and Control.* Hoboken, NJ: Wiley.

Business Cycles and Environmental Policy: A Primer

Barbara Annicchiarico, *University of Rome Tor Vergata,* Italy

Stefano Carattini, *Georgia State University,* United States of America

Carolyn Fischer, *The World Bank,* United States of America, *Vrije Universiteit Amsterdam,* The Netherlands, *and University of Ottawa,* Canada

Garth Heutel, *Georgia State University and NBER,* United States of America

Executive Summary

We study the relationship between business cycles and the design and effects of environmental policies, particularly those with economy-wide significance like climate policies. First, we provide a brief review of the literature related to this topic, from initial explorations using real business-cycle models to New Keynesian extensions, open-economy variations, and issues of monetary policy and financial regulations. Next, we provide a list of the main findings that emerge from this literature that are potentially most relevant to policy makers, including the impacts of policy on volatility and how to design policy to adjust to cycles. Finally, we propose several important remaining research questions.

JEL Codes: Q58, E32

Keywords: fluctuations, climate change, real business cycles, dynamic stochastic general equilibrium, carbon tax, cap-and-trade

I. Introduction

Environmental economists have long strived to identify the "optimal" level of environmental regulation for many pollutants, including, in recent decades, greenhouse gases. This optimal balance between the economy and the environment is usually defined based on efficiency, considering both the marginal benefits and marginal costs of regulation. Optimal

Environmental and Energy Policy and the Economy, volume 3, 2022.

pollution pricing has been one of the main activities of environmental economics as a field, an area where economists have been especially influential in shaping public policy (Hahn 1989; Fourcade, Ollion, and Algan 2015).

Importantly, the costs and benefits of environmental regulation, as well as their distribution, may vary over the course of business cycles. Pollution is highly procyclical and more volatile than gross domestic product (GDP; Doda 2014). For example, the United States generated 11% less greenhouse gas emissions between 2007 and 2013, largely due to the Great Recession (Feng et al. 2015). Recent evidence from the COVID-19 pandemic is even more striking, given the exceptional circumstances of its related recession. Daily global carbon dioxide (CO_2) emissions had already decreased on average by 17% by April 2020 since the beginning of the COVID-19 pandemic (Le Quéré et al. 2020), due to the responses by governments, individuals, and firms, which all contributed to limit economic activity following the outbreak. Overall, global CO_2 emissions decreased by about 7% from 2019 to 2020 (Le Quéré et al. 2021). Because pollution varies with the business cycle, it seems reasonable to conclude that pollution policy ought to adapt to the business cycle as well, following fluctuations in marginal costs and benefits.

Some real-world environmental policies do have automatic adjustment mechanisms that business cycles may trigger. The European Union Emissions Trading System (EU ETS) has created a Market Stability Reserve to insulate the system from allowance supply imbalances linked to business-cycle shocks (Perino et al. 2021). California and Quebec have auction reserve prices, and the Regional Greenhouse Gas Initiative has adopted an emissions containment reserve with price-triggered quantity adjustments. However, most real-world environmental policies—whether market-based policies such as taxes or cap-and-trade, or command-and-control policies—do not explicitly respond to business cycles and instead maintain a constant stringency over cycles. Several reasons may explain this phenomenon.

First, business-cycle adaptations may be seen as of second-order importance in environmental policy, whereas getting the stringency right on average is considered of first-order importance. Environmental policies may be on average too lenient, and fixing this may be seen as more important than making sure policies adjust to business cycles. When policies are too lenient, the economic rationale for adjusting their stringency to the business cycle may be weaker.[1] Many carbon tax proposals, for example, are designed with embedded tax escalators, which may allow them to reach, after several years, a level of stringency that is compatible with the goal of maintaining global temperatures within +1.5–2°C with respect to preindustrial levels (see Stiglitz et al. 2017; IMF 2019). In the meantime, tax rates remain below efficient levels, thus weakening the rationale for business-cycle adjustments. Cap-and-trade programs also struggle with excessive leniency, at least initially. Lacking full information about the costs of regulation, and concerned about price volatility, governments tend to err on the side of avoiding potential high-cost outcomes, and as a result consistently set caps too leniently (Burtraw and Keyes 2018).[2] The fact that allowance prices react endogenously to the business cycle can in principle be a benefit of cap-and-trade schemes.[3] However, evidence suggests that prices in CO_2 trading systems are likely to overreact, because the range of uncertainty over energy demand (and thus baseline emissions) tends to be much larger the range of feasible abatement opportunities, leading to large price swings or trading at administratively set boundaries (Borenstein et al. 2019). Information limitations and political biases can thus pose challenges to ensuring that the average level of stringency is appropriate, much less efficiently adapting to cycles.

A second reason why environmental policy does not adapt to business cycles is a political economy concern: the rationale could be abused by regulators, leading to a persistent weakening of environmental policy. One example is the decisions made by the Trump administration during the COVID-19 recession. By March 2020, the Environmental Protection Agency decided to exempt facilities that release toxic chemicals from reporting their emissions to the Toxic Release Inventory (TRI), which led to an increase in pollution around TRI facilities (Persico and Johnson 2021). Although the decision was motivated mostly by the inability of facilities to meet TRI requirements due to the direct effects of the COVID-19 pandemic, additional rollbacks referred explicitly to the recessionary forces generated by the pandemic.[4] These additional rollbacks often reduced stringency to virtually zero, which is hard to justify as a business-cycle adjustment. A case in point is the regulation of methane, where the federal administration in August 2020 eliminated requirements for oil and gas companies to monitor and repair methane leaks from pipelines, storage facilities, and wells. These requirements, known as Oil and Natural Gas New Source Performance Standards, were recently reinstated by the Biden administration.

A final reason is simply that the literature studying this issue is so recent that it has not yet been able to address the most pressing questions or has not yet been properly communicated to policy makers. The literature on business cycles and environmental policy effectively started just about a decade ago with Fischer and Springborn (2011) and is thus relatively recent.[5] The research has not yet addressed all dimensions of the problem nor all questions that policy makers may have about the implications of tying environmental policy to the business cycle, including distributional effects.

Our goal in this paper is threefold. First, we review the literature on environmental policy and the business cycle, with the goal of summarizing and conveying in a palatable way the economic rationale for business-cycle adjustments to environmental policy, as well as the effects of policy on economic volatility. In this respect, our paper updates early synthesis papers, including Fischer and Heutel (2013). Second, we present an assessment of the main results from this literature that are most relevant for policy makers today. This includes how different types of policy can lead to different volatilities of outcomes, and how policy makers can adapt environmental policy to cycles, ideally ex ante, tying their hands to limit the risk of business-cycle adjustments being abused. Third, we identify areas for future research that have currently been underexplored, with the goal of filling the current knowledge gaps that may contribute to limiting the adoption of business-cycle adjustments in environmental policy. Our general focus is on the climate externality, due to its importance in the current policy landscape, although many of our insights may also carry important implications for other environmental issues. We discuss the importance of considering other pollutants as well, particularly given the fact that greenhouse gases are long-lived stock pollutants, whereas other pollutants such as particulate matter are flow pollutants for which cyclical fluctuations in emissions likely have a larger effect on damages.

We present four main sets of policy-relevant findings from the literature, described in detail in Section IV. First, we discuss how different policies can influence the volatility of outcomes over the business cycle, even when those policies themselves do not vary over the cycle. A main finding here is that policy type matters—a quantity-based instrument such as cap-and-trade leads to overall less volatility, whereas a price-based policy such as a carbon tax leads to more volatility. Second, policy can be designed to vary over the business cycle and these adjustments affect the economy and welfare. Both the dynamically efficient carbon tax rate and the dynamically efficient carbon cap are procyclical—increasing during expansions and decreasing during recessions. However, the magnitude of the welfare advantages of these dynamically efficient policies over static policies remains unclear. Third, policy implications vary depending on the source of the business cycle; that is, the type of shock triggering the business-cycle fluctuation. Almost all of the modeling literature consider aggregate productivity shocks, although some empirical literature suggests that other shocks may contribute more to emissions fluctuations. Productivity shocks may also be sector specific. When productivity shocks are specific to energy-intensive polluting sectors, a tax may have a welfare advantage over a cap, though yielding higher volatility. Fourth and finally, we discuss how environmental policy interacts with other policies or other distortions over the business cycle. Other policies, including monetary policy, and other distortions, including labor market frictions, can affect the efficient cyclicality of policy or its effects on volatility.

The remainder of this paper is organized as follows. Section II describes the basics of the environmental dynamic stochastic general equilibrium (E-DSGE) model, the main toolbox to study business cycles in macroeconomics and their relationship to the environment. Section III very briefly summarizes the most important extensions to the basic E-DSGE models, and the companion working paper provides a more thorough literature review (see Annicchiarico et al. 2021). Section IV summarizes what we see as the main findings of the literature most relevant to policy makers. Section V discusses the most promising and most urgent avenues for future research.

II.   Description of Basic E-DSGE Model

In this section, we describe the basic DSGE model used in the literature examining environmental policy and business cycles. DSGE models have been frequently used in the literature for decades to study business cycles (Christiano, Eichenbaum, and Trabandt 2018). Models that extend the basic DSGE model to include some aspects of the environment have been called environmental DSGE, or E-DSGE, models (Khan et al. 2019). The workhorse model is based on the real business cycle (RBC) model, where business cycles are fueled by random autocorrelated productivity shocks (Rebelo 2005). Fischer and Springborn (2011), Heutel (2012), and Angelopoulos, Economides, and Philippopoulos (2013) are three early papers that modify the standard RBC model by including pollution and pollution policy. Briefly, the model consists of an aggregate representative agent choosing consumption, labor, and investment to maximize total discounted utility. Capital evolves dynamically based on investment. Pollution arises from production and can negatively affect productivity or utility, but the agent's choices can affect the level of pollution. Given a series of exogenous shocks to productivity, the model can be used to find the efficient level of investment and pollution that maximizes total discounted utility. The model can also analyze pollution policies, such as pollution taxes or cap-and-trade.

We first describe a centralized model, where a representative agent acts the same as a social planner would act. The representative agent chooses consumption c_t, investment i_t, and leisure l_t in each period t to maximize expected discounted lifetime utility. The single-period utility function is $U_t(c_t, l_t)$. The resource constraint is $c_t + i_t = y_t$, where y_t is the level of output or production. A capital stock evolves according to $k_{t+1} = i_t + (1 - \delta)k_t$. Time is normalized to one each period and allocated between labor (n_t) and leisure: $l_t + n_t = 1$. Production is based on the labor and capital inputs along with a productivity shock: $y_t = a_t f(k_t, n_t)$. The productivity shock a_t is exogenous and evolves according to an autoregressive process.

So far, the model described is the standard RBC model. At this point, the model can be modified to include pollution and pollution policy, and there is more than one way to do so. As in Fischer and Springborn (2011), and as is commonly done in computable general equilibrium models, one would modify the production function to also include a polluting input m_t, so that output is $y_t = a_t f(k_t, n_t, m_t)$. The polluting input is costly, so the resource constraint becomes $c_t + i_t + m_t = y_t$. The polluting input is a choice variable and so can be changed in response to economic conditions or policies (described below). An alternative way of modeling pollution, following Heutel (2012) based on the representation in the Dynamic Integrated Climate-Economy (DICE) model (see Nordhaus 1993, 2017), is to let pollution emissions e_t be a byproduct of production that can be reduced through abatement spending z_t. Emissions are $e_t = g(z_t)h(y_t)$, where the increasing function h maps how output creates emissions, holding abatement z_t fixed, and the decreasing function g maps how abatement spending reduces emissions, holding output y_t fixed. The resource constraint under this specification of pollution is $c_t + i_t + z_t = y_t$.

The relationship between emissions in one period e_t and the total stock of pollution x_t can be given by a stock evolution equation. For example, in Heutel (2012), the pollution stock evolves according to $x_{t+1} = \eta x_t + e_t + e_t^{exog}$, where η is a pollution depreciation rate and e_t^{exog} is the exogenous level of emissions from other economies (e.g., for a global pollutant such as carbon dioxide, this represents emissions from other countries). Another way of incorporating the stock of pollution is done in

Angelopoulos et al. (2013), where the stock variable Q_t represents environmental quality (a good) rather than the pollution stock (a bad). The evolution of environmental quality is $Q_{t+1} = (1 - \delta^q)\underline{Q} + \delta^q Q_t - e_t + \nu z_t$, where $\underline{Q}$ is environmental quality without any pollution and δ^q is a pollution persistence parameter. Emissions e_t negatively affects environmental quality, and abatement spending z_t positively affects environmental quality measured by the parameter ν.

We next describe how damages from pollution can be incorporated into the model. There are two places where pollution damages can enter: Pollution can either negatively affect utility directly, or it can indirectly affect utility by negatively affecting output or productivity. Under the first specification, following Angelopoulos et al. (2013), we can modify the utility function to include the level of environmental quality Q_t: $U_t(c_t, l_t, Q_t)$. Under the second specification, following Heutel (2012), we can modify the production function to include the level of the pollution stock x_t: $y_t = (1 - d(x_t))a_t f(k_t, n_t)$, where d is a damage function that relates the level of the pollution stock to a reduction in output. Several integrated assessment models of climate change, including the DICE model (Nordhaus 1993, 2017, 2018), model carbon pollution as affecting output rather than utility directly.

The centralized model is now complete, and the model can be solved as a social planner's problem, where the damages from pollution are incorporated into the decision-making process. A social planner trades off the benefits of reducing emissions (reducing pollution damages) with its costs (abatement costs). The solution represents the first-best response of all economic variables to exogenous productivity shocks. Solutions can be presented as impulse response functions, which show how all of the variables optimally respond to a one-unit innovation in the productivity shock. Or, solutions can be presented as simulations of business cycles, in which an exogenous series of productivity shocks are drawn and the economy is allowed to optimally respond. Figures 1 and 2 present results from the first-best dynamic policy simulations, based on the model in Heutel (2012), showing impulse response functions and business-cycle simulations, respectively.[6] The model used here is identical to that used in Heutel (2012), though the calibration is updated based on Gibson and Heutel (2020).[7]

Figure 1 shows impulse response functions for the productivity shock (after a one-time innovation in period 0) along with three variables related to the environment: single-period emissions e_t, the pollution stock x_t, and abatement spending z_t. The continuous line shows that the productivity

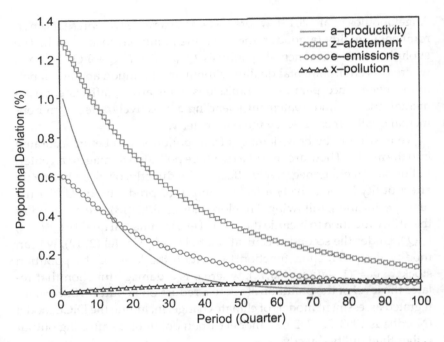

Fig. 1. Impulse response functions—centralized efficient model. Color version available as an online enhancement.

Notes: The productivity shock a increases exogenously in period 0, and all other variables respond endogenously. The y-axis units are the percentage deviation from each variable's steady-state value. The simulations are from the E-DSGE model in Heutel (2012) with updated calibration as described in the text.

shock value decays exogenously at a constant rate. In response to that productivity increase, emissions are higher than their steady-state value. During an economic boom, when output increases (not shown in fig. 1), emissions also are allowed to increase. However, figure 1 also shows that abatement spending increases above its steady-state value. Although emissions are increasing during the boom, they are not increasing by as much as they otherwise would if it were not for the efficient response of the economy in increasing abatement spending. The optimal cyclicality of emissions is thus procyclical but less so than they would be absent the dynamically optimal policy.

Figure 2 shows business-cycle simulations for the centralized model without policy, drawn from an arbitrary draw of productivity shocks. Capital is procyclical but less volatile and somewhat lagged from output due to its stock nature. Emissions are strongly procyclical, though not quite as variable as output is. The pollution stock has such a slow decay

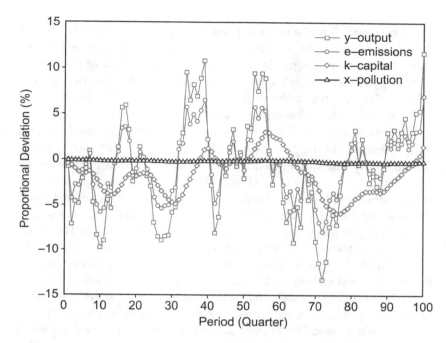

Fig. 2. Business-cycle simulation—centralized efficient model. Color version available as an online enhancement.

Notes: Productivity shocks (not graphed here) are exogenously generated, and all other variables respond endogenously. The y-axis units are the percentage deviation from each variable's steady-state value. The simulations are from the E-DSGE model in Heutel (2012) with updated calibration as described in the text.

rate that these business-cycle fluctuations have very limited impact on its value (pollution here is calibrated to carbon dioxide, a stock pollutant that remains in the atmosphere for decades).

Next, we turn to a decentralized model, in which a representative firm maximizes profits and a representative consumer maximizes utility. By assuming that the firm ignores the effect that its pollution has on either productivity or utility, the decentralized model features an externality, so that the decentralized solution will generally not be first best. Either the consumer or the firm can be subject to an environmental policy; for example, a tax on emissions.

The model can also be used to analyze the effect of these policies on various economic outcomes. Fischer and Springborn (2011) analyze the effect of three environmental policies: an emissions tax, an emissions cap, and an intensity standard that fixes the ratio of emissions to output. They generate business-cycle simulations and show how various economic variables respond to the draw of productivity shocks under each of the three policies. We replicate these simulations here in figure 3. In response to an exogenous draw of productivity shocks (identical to the draw in fig. 2), figure 3 plots the response of emissions (panel A) and output (panel B) under each of the three policies: the intensity standard (IT), the emissions cap (Cap), and the emissions tax (Tax).

The three policies are all calibrated to yield the efficient first-best level in steady state, but the policy values do not adjust to the business cycle. Consequently, the three policies yield different cyclical properties. Of course, because the cap is fixed over time, it results in emissions fixed at their steady-state level, whereas the tax and intensity standard result in emissions that vary over the business cycle. Output is slightly less volatile under the cap policy than under the other two policies. This demonstrates that the intensity standard is more accommodating of business cycles due to its flexibility—by restricting emissions per unit output rather than total emissions, it includes a built-in cyclical adaptation.

The decentralized model can also be used to solve for the efficient level of the policy variables that internalizes the pollution externality and reaches the theoretical first best. Such an exercise is performed in Heutel (2012), which includes a specification of external damages from pollution affecting productivity, though unlike Fischer and Springborn (2011) it does not include a labor decision or an intensity standard policy. Results from business-cycle simulations of efficient policy are presented here in figure 4. For the same draw of shocks simulated in figures 2 and 3, figure 4 shows the efficient response of both a tax policy and an emissions cap. Here, the policy values endogenously respond to the draw of the shocks and the changing economy and thus are not fixed over time as in figure 3. Figure 4 shows that both the emissions cap and the emissions tax are procyclical. However, that means the cyclicality of the stringency of each policy is different. During an expansion, the efficient emissions tax increases, which is an increase in stringency, and the efficient emissions cap also increases, which is a decrease in stringency. As also can be seen from figure 4, the efficient emissions tax is more procyclical than the efficient emissions cap.

III.   Extensions to the Basic Model

In the more technical working paper (Annicchiarico et al. 2021), we provide an extensive literature review of the state of the E-DSGE literature. Here, we briefly summarize the four broad areas where extensions have

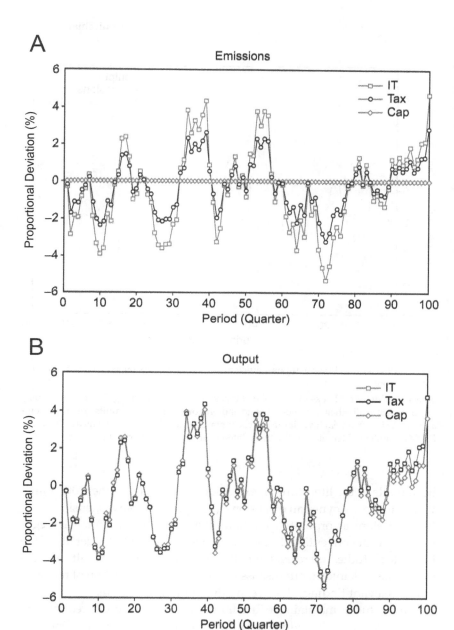

Fig. 3. Business-cycle simulation—effects of policies set ex ante. Color version available as an online enhancement.

Notes: Productivity shocks (not graphed here, identical to those in fig. 2) are exogenously generated, and all other variables respond endogenously. The top panel plots emissions, and the bottom panel plots output, both in percentage deviation from each variable's steady-state value. IT, Cap, and Tax denote the intensity standard, the emissions cap, and the emissions tax, respectively.

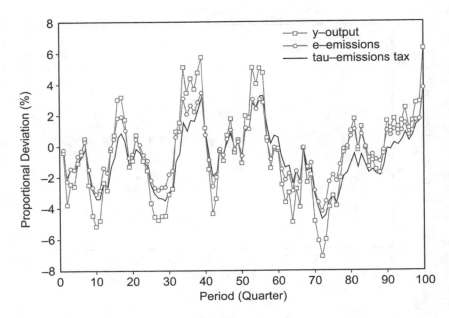

Fig. 4. Business-cycle simulations—efficient policy. Color version available as an online enhancement.

Notes: Productivity shocks (not graphed here, identical to those in fig. 2) are exogenously generated, and all other variables respond endogenously. The y-axis units are the percentage deviation from each variable's steady-state value. The simulations are from the E-DSGE model in Heutel (2012) with updated calibration as described in the text.

been made in the literature: (i) extensions that maintain the RBC framework, (ii) New Keynesian extensions, (iii) open-economy extensions, and (iv) extensions incorporating credit market imperfections, financial regulation, and unconventional monetary policy. Although the details of the individual studies are relegated to the working paper, the results of these extensions will inform our discussion in the following section of the most policy-relevant findings that we identified in the literature.

Several studies maintain the RBC framework of cycles produced through autocorrelated productivity shocks but add more complications. One such study (Dissou and Karnizova 2016) develops a multisector economy, where shocks can be sector specific, including shocks arising to emissions-intensive industries such as the fossil fuel sector. Other papers consider different types of productivity shocks, including anticipated versus unanticipated shocks and investment-specific shocks (Khan et al. 2019), or frictions arising from other sources such as the labor market (Gibson and Heutel 2020). These variations influence the interactions between business cycle and emissions volatility.

The second set of extensions includes New Keynesian (NK) elements. The heart of the NK framework includes imperfect competition, nominal rigidities, and nonneutral monetary policy. For instance, Annicchiarico and Di Dio (2015) modify the E-DSGE model to include imperfect price adjustments and an interest-rate rule governing monetary policy. They explore how the optimal design of the carbon tax (including its cyclicality) depends on the degree of price stickiness and on monetary policy. Several other extensions in this vein explore related issues under alternative modeling assumptions. For example, Economides and Xepapadeas (2018) study the challenges climate change poses to monetary policy and the potential inflationary effects of carbon pricing, which are among the main concerns for central banks (NGFS 2021).

The third variant of the literature uses open-economy versions of E-DSGE models to look at cross-country pollution and policy spillovers and international environmental agreements. Several of these papers also incorporate some elements of the NK approach, including nominal rigidities and imperfect competition. For example, Annicchiarico and Diluiso (2019) develop a two-country model to explore how real and monetary policy shocks propagate across borders, and how this propagation is influenced by environmental regulation.

Finally, the fourth set of extensions considers credit market imperfections, financial regulation, and unconventional monetary policy. This strand of the literature is motivated by the concerns that climate-related risks may represent a threat to financial and macroeconomic stability. A debate exists about whether and to what extent financial regulators can or should address climate change; for example, by creating new tools like green-biased regulations to encourage the transition to a low-carbon economy. A related concern is that of the transition risk that arises from an abrupt implementation of ambitious climate policy in an economy where leveraged banks have a large stake in affected industries and assets like those related to fossil fuels and other carbon-intensive industries. In this case, climate policy could create stranded assets, which may trigger financial instability risks. Several recent studies explore these and other related issues. Two concurrent studies in this literature are by Diluiso et al. (2020) and Carattini, Heutel, and Melkadze (2021), which combine a multisector E-DSGE model with a model of financial frictions and study how unconventional monetary policy such as green quantitative easing (in Diluiso et al. 2020) or green-biased capital requirements (in

Carattini et al. 2021) can stabilize the economy in response to a potential crisis brought about by asset stranding in the context of a gradual (in Diluiso et al. 2020) or abrupt (in Carattini et al. 2021) implementation of ambitious climate policy.

IV.   Policy-Relevant Findings from the Literature

In this section, we provide a brief overview of the main findings from the literature that are most relevant to policy makers, who may seek either to design policies to accommodate business cycles or to assess the impacts of business cycles on policy effectiveness or pollution. The first two subsections describe positive findings from the literature about the effect of policy on economic volatility and the design of policy over the business cycle. The last two subsections discuss caveats to these findings, pointing out that the source of fluctuations matters and that other macroeconomic market failures or distortions interact with environmental policy.

A.   Policy Effects on Volatility

Emissions are a byproduct of production and are thus naturally procyclical. Empirical evidence suggests that emissions are even more volatile than GDP, indicating they arise from sectors more vulnerable to business-cycle variations (Doda 2014). The flip side of this relationship is that policies to control emissions will also influence the response of other macroeconomic factors to exogenous shocks.

A cap on emissions has a built-in dampening effect on the business cycle. A positive productivity shock will expand output and demand for emissions, but the cap will require further efforts to limit polluting inputs or abate emissions, manifesting in an increase in the emissions price. With a negative productivity shock, the cap becomes less constraining; emissions prices fall with demand, and less abatement effort is required in a downturn. Because one means of reducing emissions is reducing output, less of this output-related abatement is needed in a downturn. As a result, an emissions cap limits volatility of other macroeconomic variables. This effect becomes even more pronounced when prices are more difficult to adjust, because these rigidities tend to exacerbate business cycles (Annicchiarico and Di Dio 2015). However, the stabilizing properties of a cap are mitigated when wages are sticky, because the effects of uncertainty on employment are greater (Jaimes 2020). In contrast, the procyclical response of emissions prices under cap-and-trade system could exacerbate inflation volatility, so monetary policy interactions matter too (Annicchiarico and Di Dio 2017).

An emissions tax, by contrast, fixes the price of emissions and allows the quantity of emissions to respond. Investment and production decisions take the emissions price into account, but a positive productivity shock will cause output and emissions to expand. A tax does little to deter this response to the business cycle, and may even exacerbate volatility by making investment more sensitive to productivity shocks (Fischer and Springborn 2011). A carbon tax is also likely to allow greater transmission of business cycles across borders (Annicchiarico and Diluiso 2019).

An emissions intensity standard—fixing emissions per unit of output—offers a road in between a tax or a cap. A positive productivity shock increases demand for emissions, but an increase in output also loosens the emissions constraint, which is set per unit of output. As a result, the emissions price rises, but to a lesser extent than with a fixed cap. The output-based allocation of emission allowances implicit in intensity targets also provides a general incentive boost to output, leading to higher levels of investment and output than a cap or tax. However, in terms of volatility, an intensity target does little to change how the macroeconomy responds to business cycles, compared with no policy (Fischer and Springborn 2011).

The above comparisons are largely based on stark policy choices. In practice, many emissions trading systems adopt provisions with banking and borrowing that will allow emissions price responses to macroeconomic shocks to be spread over time (e.g., Kollenberg and Taschini 2019). Recognizing that the economy is composed of many sectors with different emissions intensities, the influence of climate policy on macroeconomic volatility may depend on the source of business-cycle variation. For example, shocks related to the energy sector are more likely to interact with climate policies than other productivity shocks (Dissou and Karnizova 2016).

Besides the pollution policies discussed above, macroprudential financial regulations, designed to align environmental and financial stability objectives, are also shown to influence the transmission of the business cycle. Green-biased regulations may bring down the volatility of business-cycle fluctuations, while favoring green investments and reducing the exposure of financial intermediaries to assets at risk of stranding (Punzi 2019; Benmir and Roman 2020; Diluiso et al. 2020; Carattini et al. 2021).

B.   Dynamically Optimal Policies and Welfare

Allowing policy variables to vary along with the business cycle gives more flexibility for the policy to address market imperfections and improve welfare. Some policies, such as unemployment insurance, are clearly designed so that their intensity or stringency responds to business cycles. For an environmental policy such as a pollution tax or cap-and-trade system, the goal would be to design it so that the stringency of the policy (the tax rate, or the level of the cap) can vary in ways that keep emissions prices better aligned with marginal environmental damages over the business cycle. However, in practice, for adaptive policies to do more good than harm relative to fixed policies, not only must the adjustments be well targeted but the efficiency advantages from the policy's variance over the cycle must also outweigh any costs that might be incurred by allowing it to vary. These costs could include administrative costs of the cyclical adjustments, costs arising from households' or firms' uncertainties about policy values, increased trading frictions or transaction costs, or even higher political economy barriers to implementation. We return below to the question of how policy makers can introduce simple rules requiring limited information to mimic "optimal" cyclical adjustments.

Designing a policy such as a tax so that its values in each period efficiently respond to business-cycle conditions is often called the Ramsey problem (Chari, Christiano, and Kehoe 1994). Heutel (2012) solves the Ramsey problem for both an emissions tax and cap-and-trade system, calibrated to the US economy and carbon dioxide emissions. As we showed in figure 4 (using an updated calibration of that earlier model), both the Ramsey-optimal carbon tax and the Ramsey-optimal carbon emissions cap are procyclical, increasing during expansions and decreasing during recessions. This implies that a carbon tax becomes more stringent during expansions and less stringent during recessions, whereas a cap-and-trade system becomes less stringent during expansions and more stringent during recessions.[8] This pattern may provide a political economy advantage for taxes over cap-and-trade, given that tax relief can be communicated to the public during recessions, rather than a cap adjustment that would increase prices. However, under this calibration the Ramsey-optimal carbon tax is more volatile than the Ramsey-optimal cap, which may be a disadvantage of it.[9]

To consider specifically how to design policy to adjust to the business cycle, Heutel (2012) provides something close to "rules-of-thumb" based on GDP. Ideally, as mentioned in our introductory paragraphs, business-cycle adjustments should be a policy feature that is introduced from the start and operates according to a clear and transparent rule. Rules-based adjustments would allow timely responses, avoiding the delay of passing new legislation or promulgating amendments to regulations. They also would tie the hands of policy makers and avoid arbitrary decisions once a shock materializes. If the regulator can set the policy stringency as a function of lagged GDP (or its deviation from trend), then what is the function mapping GDP into the efficient policy? Heutel (2012) finds that the efficient carbon tax rate increases by about 142% of the deviation of output; for example, if output is 10% higher than trend in a particular quarter, then the efficient carbon tax rate is 14.2% higher than trend in the following quarter. For the efficient emissions cap, the response is 66% of the deviation of output; if output is 10% higher than trend in a particular quarter, then the efficient carbon cap is 6.6% higher than trend in the following quarter.[10] In addition to or instead of GDP, regulators may use leading indicators to forecast shocks. In the United States, for instance, prominent leading indicators are the Purchasing Managers Index and the Consumer Confidence Index.[11]

How important are the business-cycle adjustments for welfare? Lintunen and Vilmi (2013) compare the Ramsey-optimal emissions tax with a constant tax (they do not consider cap-and-trade) and find slight differences in emissions but negligible overall economic effects. Heutel (2012) notes that the welfare comparison can depend on the shock values (see following subsection). Both papers are calibrated to greenhouse gas pollutants for which the accumulated stock matters rather than the flow of emissions in any period. For flow pollutants, business-cycle policy adjustments may have larger welfare impacts than for stock pollutants, as we discuss in Subsection V.D. Likewise, the question of whether a tax or a cap is more efficient in response to business cycles can also depend on shock values, and the answer may differ for stock versus flow pollutants.

C. Source of Shocks

Most of the papers that we have reviewed here use an RBC model, where cycles are fueled by exogenous shocks to aggregate productivity. Whether or not productivity shocks are in fact a predominant driver of real-world business cycles is a question up for debate in the broader macroeconomic literature.[12] More specifically, two recent papers investigate the source of emissions fluctuations over the business cycle, and both find that other types of shocks besides productivity shocks—such as shocks to energy efficiency, specific technologies, or nonenvironmental policies—are important drivers.

Khan et al. (2019) empirically study the drivers of emissions variation in the United States, including monetary and government spending shocks as additional sources of uncertainty. They consider six different shocks—anticipated and unanticipated neutral technology (TFP) shocks, anticipated and unanticipated investment-specific technology shocks, government spending policy shocks, and monetary policy shocks—and find empirically that the largest impact on pollution among these shocks comes from the anticipated investment-specific technology shock. Jo and Karnizova (2021) provide a similar analysis, including shocks to energy efficiency that can cause a negative correlation between output and emissions. Jo and Karnizova (2021) identify shocks that can cause emissions and output to be negatively rather than positively correlated with each other, and they find that these types of shocks explain almost half of the overall volatility of emissions. They argue that shocks to energy efficiency are the primary example of these negative-correlation shocks. Because other types of shocks may have different implications for the relationship between business cycles and emissions and, as Jo and Karnizova (2021) suggest, some shocks cause emissions and output to move in opposite directions, then it is likely that the optimal response of policy to these shocks is different than the optimal response to productivity shocks. Unfortunately, as of today, the literature has little to say about how policy can respond to these types of shocks, so more research is needed to shed light on this question.

In the context of E-DSGE models, some initial indication of the importance of the source of shocks is given by Dissou and Karnizova (2016), who study sector-specific productivity shocks. Their main finding is that under productivity shocks localized to energy sectors, a carbon tax outperforms a cap in welfare terms, although it leads to higher volatility of macroeconomic aggregates. However, for shocks to sectors other than energy-intensive sectors, a tax and a cap (even in the absence of intertemporal considerations such as banking) have statistically equivalent welfare implications. This result indicates that including flexibility mechanisms may be more important for quantity-based policies, especially when energy sector volatility is a primary issue.

D.   *Interaction with Other Policies or Distortions*

Policies targeting pollutants that are widespread throughout the economy, such as carbon dioxide emissions, are likely to give rise to equally pervasive effects on macroeconomic responses to other policies and market distortions. Carbon prices and regulations influence a range of household and producer behavior, which may have nontrivial implications for the frequency and severity of business cycles.

Climate change is not the only policy issue of macroeconomic importance. Policy makers must grapple with market power and barriers to competition, frictions in labor markets that result in excess unemployment, regulations or behavioral practices that impede the adjustment of prices and wages, and financial market imperfections that may elevate the cost of borrowing and limit the amount of credit. The literature has pointed out that simultaneously addressing environmental issues and other market failures is particularly challenging in the presence of different sources of uncertainty. From this perspective, the literature on environmental policy and business cycles has drawn attention toward the interactions between environmental regulations and other policies, especially those aimed at stabilizing the economy over the business cycle, such as monetary policy, financial regulations, and labor market policies.

The underlying monetary policy affects optimal environmental policy design in response to exogenous shocks. Depending on the degree to which monetary policy reacts to the level of economic activity and stabilizes the economy, the optimal carbon price may be more or less procyclical, relative to what one would expect without monetary accommodation (see Annicchiarico and Di Dio 2015, 2017). The interaction also goes both ways: the stronger the negative environmental externality, the less accommodative—and so the more stringent—the optimal monetary policy should be to avoid excess expansion and emissions. In addition, an ambitious greening policy may produce large fluctuations in consumer prices. In this sense, unanticipated and abrupt climate actions may potentially represent a challenge for monetary stability (e.g., Economides and Xepapadeas 2018; Carattini et al. 2021).

Some unconventional monetary policies aim at changing the composition of central banks' balance sheets toward green assets. Early studies on the effects of such green-biased quantitative easing programs point to a very limited scope of these policies in greening the economy, as well as little difference in their effectiveness in reviving the economy following an adverse shock as compared with market-neutral quantitative easing programs (see Benmir and Roman 2020; Diluiso et al. 2020; and Ferrari and Nispi Landi 2020). However, emerging analyses of the effects of the introduction of nonneutral financial regulatory schemes, such as green-supporting and/or brown-penalizing regulations (see

D'Orazio and Popoyan 2019), suggest that by inducing a portfolio real-location of financial intermediaries toward green investments, these schemes encourage the greening process and reduce the exposure of banks to climate-sensitive assets, mitigating the financial effects of stranded assets (see Punzi 2019; Benmir and Roman 2020; Diluiso et al. 2020; Carattini et al. 2021).

Finally, labor market frictions—such as the costs of searching for employment, relocating for a job, or finding suitable employees—also affect environmental policy over the business cycle. Such frictions are often represented as congestion problems: Adding an unemployed worker to the pool of job seekers reduces everyone else's probability of finding a job, but raises the probability for hiring firms of finding a good match. Similarly, more job vacancies make it harder for firms but easier for unemployed workers to find a match. Depending on how these balance out, the level of employment may be inefficiently high (too many vacancies) or low (too many job seekers). Economic efficiency then requires combining a pollution policy (e.g., carbon tax) with a labor market policy (e.g., a tax or subsidy on job creation), so as to jointly address the environmental externality and labor market imperfections. However, when the labor market instrument is unavailable, the optimal design of the emission tax is more challenging: The optimal carbon tax will be less or more pro-cyclical depending on whether the market delivers an inefficiently high or low employment level. Gibson and Heutel (2020) find in their preferred calibration that the procyclicality of the efficient carbon tax is only half as high once labor market frictions are accounted for. The existence of labor frictions and unemployment would then provide a further rationale, based on equity as well as efficiency, for designing a state-contingent environmental policy.

V.   Remaining Questions

A number of important questions related to environmental policies and business cycles remain to be addressed. In this section, we categorize some promising directions for future research.

A.   Heterogeneous Agents and Distribution of Impacts

Over the recent decades, building on the work of Hopenhayn (1992) and Aiyagari (1994), DSGE models have gone beyond the representative firm and household assumptions to incorporate micro-level heterogeneity.

This incorporation has broadened the range of problems that can be studied in business-cycle analysis. The attention is no longer on the study of aggregate dynamics, but rather on the analysis of the evolution of the distribution of heterogeneous agents in response to aggregate and/or idiosyncratic shocks.[13]

On the production side, firms can differ in terms of size, efficiency, products, production processes, access to credit, and innovation ability. The entry and exit of heterogeneous firms shape the aggregate fluctuations in economic activity and the associated creation and destruction of jobs. Firms can also differ in their abatement capacity, can be more or less polluting, or can differ in their innovation in clean technologies. In this context, aggregate dynamics and the performance of pollution policies will also be influenced by composition effects, due to the reallocation of market shares among heterogeneous firms. The underlying environmental regulation is likely to affect firm dynamics and eventually aggregate productivity, GDP, and employment. In contrast, the changing composition of the production structure in response to shocks may affect policy effectiveness and optimal design.

Households, meanwhile, can differ in terms of age, wealth, skills, income, occupation, portfolio composition, access to credit, and expectations. All these dimensions matter for many of households' economic decisions and can be relevant for the propagation mechanisms of shocks and for the impact of policies falling in various domains. Incorporating heterogeneous households in an environmental business-cycle model may open up, for instance, questions about the impact of pollution policies on inequality and on wealth reallocation.

The literature to date has largely avoided issues of equity, but existing results have important implications for the two main observations that follow. First, the models demonstrate that efficient emissions are less procyclical than they would be in laissez-faire. The efficient level of climate policy's stringency (e.g., the carbon tax rate) is lower in recessions than in expansions. This conclusion, however, neglects the distributional implications of policy, including carbon tax revenues. Redistributing revenues in a lump-sum way, as "carbon dividends," would be progressive (Cronin, Fullerton, and Sexton 2018). The federal carbon tax of Canada, for instance, makes about 70% of Canadians financially better off, disproportionately improving the livelihood of low-income households (PBO 2019). It is not obvious, then, how reducing a carbon tax in times of recession, and thus the size of carbon dividends to households, would affect equity, especially when accounting for the fact that utility from dividends may decrease with income, so that a disproportionate impact on low-income households would disproportionally affect overall utility, even assuming a homogeneous effect of the recession on households. Such a research question could be addressed by introducing heterogeneous households (for instance, to reflect income distribution) and several ways of redistributing tax revenues or revenues from auctioning permits. Such ways may also include the possibility of shifting part of the dividends over time (i.e., from good times to bad times), although this solution would also need to be defined ex ante to avoid any arbitrariness and ensure that citizens' trust in the government is not eroded.

Second, the efficient level of regulation, which accounts for the business cycle, implies both lower emissions and lower employment than the unregulated equilibrium (Gibson and Heutel 2020). If labor market frictions imply that vacancies are too high, then the environmental policy creates an additional efficiency benefit by reducing the labor market distortion. However, accounting for distributional effects on who is employed and who is not in a recession may lead to different policy implications, in particular if low-income households, which derive a higher utility from their salaries, would be more affected by layoffs driven by recessionary forces. The standard framework could thus be extended to include distributional effects in job creation and destruction, as well as interactions with other policies, including policies aimed at fostering economic recovery (e.g., stimulus packages) or redirecting the economy toward cleaner production modes (e.g., Green New Deal). Also in this case, part of the revenues could be banked during good times to fund Green New Deals in bad times, with the abovementioned condition about embedding such mechanism in the design of the policy since the outset to avoid arbitrariness still applying.

B.   Interaction between Environmental and Other Public Policies

Environmental policies are not the only ones that respond to market changes over the business cycle. Many topics related to the interaction between environmental and other policies remain either unexplored or still in early stages. Prime targets for further research on environmental policy interactions are fiscal policy, trade policy, monetary policy, and financial regulation.

Fiscal policy leads that list because tax policies and government spending tend to be countercyclical themselves (at least at the federal level in the United States). Furthermore, environmental priorities are increasingly being incorporated into fiscal responses. At present, many postpandemic recovery plans around the world include green stimulus packages to both restart the economy and favor transition to a cleaner and more sustainable path, including the Recovery Plan for Europe, the American Rescue Plan, and the proposed American Jobs Plan. Such fiscal responses are likely to influence the optimal adjustment of stringency of carbon pricing regulations, for example. These issues could be addressed by modeling the public sector in more detail, accounting for the composition of public spending (capital spending and current spending) and for different tax instruments.[14]

Trade policy can be intertwined with climate policy, with important business-cycle implications. The most obvious example is represented by carbon border adjustments, which are currently receiving serious consideration from the European Commission in the context of the Green Deal, at least for trialing in selected sectors covered by the EU ETS. Besides the direct effects that the introduction of such a policy may have on border prices and trade flows, one may expect it to have an influence on the international propagation of the business cycle. The study of this issue requires the use of fully fledged open-economy models in which countries are interlinked with each other and where the different steps of the production process are located across different countries. Furthermore, the fact that different countries may be on different points of the business cycle may or may not justify deviations from an equal carbon price for domestic and foreign production. The same logic would apply to a global carbon tax or system of harmonized carbon taxes, which have both attracted substantial attention in recent times by scholars (Hoel 1992; Thalmann 2013; Weitzman 2014; Nordhaus 2015; Cramton et al. 2017; Stiglitz et al. 2017; Weitzman 2017; Carattini, Kallbekken, and Orlov 2019; IMF 2019) and policy makers, with for instance the International Monetary Fund pushing for a minimum carbon price among large emitters covering about 80% of global greenhouse gas emissions. In this case, the reference price (and escalator) may include some room for idiosyncratic business-cycle adjustments, so that countries can adjust to the business cycle without leaving a carbon pricing coalition. Of course, it is also important in this case that the business-cycle argument is not abused by domestic or foreign vested interests.

Regarding the implications for monetary policy, future research should address the challenges posed by physical and transition risks to different monetary policy regimes and study how different carbon pricing policies are likely to affect inflation dynamics. Central banks and financial regulatory authorities are increasingly interested in climate-related issues (e.g.,

Carney 2015; Vermeulen et al. 2018; Rudebusch 2021). The debate revolves around the need to enrich their mandate by opening the door to climate challenges in the conduct of monetary policy and in the design of the financial regulatory framework (see Campiglio et al. 2018; D'Orazio and Popoyan 2019). Hence, future research should also explore more in depth the possibility of incorporating climate objectives in the mandate of central banks. This would mainly imply giving up market neutrality in asset buying and would enlarge the area of activity of central banks and their tools.

Concerning financial regulation, the literature on climate-related financial system risks is still nascent; further studies could contribute to move the frontier further and shed additional light on how to design a macroprudential regulatory framework able to favor green investments, reduce climate-related financial risk, and possibly also preserve financial stability. Numerous green macroprudential tools have been proposed (e.g., brown-penalizing and green-supporting capital requirements, green-biased liquidity regulation, and differentiated reserves requirements), calling for further research investigating their potential ability to align environmental and financial objectives.

C. Suboptimal Policy Stringency and Nonpricing Policies

The E-DSGE literature tends to assume that environmental policy's stringency can be set to balance marginal costs and benefits in its steady state, from which it should fluctuate "optimally" in response to productivity shocks. As discussed in the introduction to this paper, important constraints can prevent environmental policies from reaching their optimal level, much less adjusting with the business cycle.

In the case of climate change in particular, although economists have yet to agree on the optimal level of carbon pricing—for instance, exactly how high the social cost of carbon is—a general consensus has formed that it should be well above current levels (Howard and Sylvan 2015). Carbon pricing remains the favorite policy tool of economists to tackle climate change (see, e.g., Goulder and Parry 2008; Aldy et al. 2010; Baranzini et al. 2017; Stiglitz et al. 2017). In the decade since 2010, when it covered about 5% of global greenhouse gas emissions, carbon pricing has expanded rapidly and currently covers about 22.5% of global greenhouse gas emissions; however, only for a few schemes do they exceed $50 per ton of CO_2 (World Bank 2020).

Hence, an important question that the literature has arguably yet to tackle is whether, or to what extent, environmental policies that are set at a "suboptimally" low level of stringency should also adjust to the business cycle. In this context, three possible scenarios merit investigation: (1) a scenario in which the policy does not adjust to the business cycle, (2) a scenario in which the policy does adjust to the business cycle, and (3) a scenario in which the policy adjusts upward during economic booms but does not adjust downward during recessions. Furthermore, the uncertainty surrounding climate damages may call for more price certainty than would otherwise be the case. Business-cycle adjustments may also be embedded in a price trajectory that accounts for learning as in Bayesian models (Kelly and Kolstad 1999; Kelly and Tan 2015).

Additional attention should be paid to the design of environmental policies—particularly banking and borrowing provisions in cap-and-trade systems—and how they respond to business cycles. Pizer and Prest (2020) show in a micro model that when governments optimally adjust policies to shocks, quantity regulation with intertemporal allowance trading can have advantages over price regulation, due to the intertemporal transmission of expectations into prices. Lintunen and Kuusela (2018) incorporate such expectations into a business-cycle model, with a regulator that sets the periodic cap so that the number of banked allowances together with the new ones equals the desired cap level. Expected future permit prices create an effective floor for current prices, allowing the regulator room to increase the emission cap when needed to avoid the risk of undesirably high prices. The result of active allowance supply management is less volatile permit prices and less buildup of banked allowances in a downturn than without banking.

Pizer and Prest (2020) caution that if governments set policy inefficiently or firms imperfectly anticipate policy changes, taxes have advantages again. In this respect, Aldy and Armitage (2020) study how cap-and-trade systems lead to price uncertainty, because shocks can affect how a given cap is priced. When the investment in pollution abatement is irreversible, excessive volatility in the allowance prices can increase the effective cost of achieving a given mitigation target. In contrast, this price uncertainty can also have a dampening effect on irreversible investments in new capital goods. These issues should be explored in macro models. More generally, most of the literature to date has made stark policy comparisons between taxes and caps, but in practice many design features—such as free allocation, alternative compliance options, and international linking, as well as certain built-in adjustment mechanisms such as price floors, safety valves, and quantity-based triggers—are increasingly included and may have macroeconomic implications.

Another aspect of suboptimal policy design recognizes that a great number of environmental policies do not price carbon explicitly or even implicitly. Clean energy standards or market share mandates for renewable generation, biofuels, or zero-emission vehicles are common tools in transition policy portfolios. Although they may impose an implicit tax on sources that do not qualify as clean, they do not distinguish among the carbon intensity of nonqualifying sources. Similarly, mandatory phaseouts of coal-fired generation or internal combustion engine vehicles do not differentiate among the carbon profiles of nonprohibited sources. However, these types of target-based approaches do impose constraints on the economy, and the shadow values of those constraints will respond to business cycles. The Green New Deal proposal framework in the United States (H.R. 109, 116th Cong.), for instance, does not even mention carbon pricing. Incorporating nonpricing mechanisms—and especially multiple and overlapping ones—into macroeconomic models is challenging, but a worthy area for future research. Finally, the issue of enforcement or imperfect monitoring may be importantly related to business cycles. For example, as state revenues fluctuate, the resources devoted to enforcement may also fluctuate, and how optimal policy or optimal enforcement responds to those fluctuations remains to be explored. That is, it is possible that the cyclicality of enforcement affects the cyclicality of emissions, beyond what is usually considered in analyses of optimal tax rates or caps.

D. Non-GHG Pollutants

Most of the literature has focused on climate policy rather than policies for other environmental issues and pollutants. This view is understandable, because the broader environmental policy literature is increasingly focused on climate change and greenhouse gases (GHG). Hence, the focus of our paper is also mostly on climate change.

However, the relationship between business cycles and environmental policy may be equally or more important for non-GHG pollutants. Most GHGs, for instance carbon dioxide, are long-lived stock pollutants that stay in the atmosphere for decades. Business-cycle-level fluctuations in emissions have little effect on the aggregate stock of atmospheric carbon, which is what affects climate change. This can be seen in figure 2—over the business cycle the pollution stock (x) stays nearly constant though quarterly emissions (e) vary considerably. For this reason, the marginal benefits of climate mitigation stay relatively stable.

Many other pollutants are primarily flow pollutants, remaining in the environment and affecting the economy only for a short period. For these pollutants, business-cycle fluctuations in emissions can have serious effects on their damages. For example, ozone damages can vary considerably even over the course of a single day (Adler and Severnini 2020). As we discussed in Subsection IV.B., this may mean that the welfare benefit of policies that dynamically adjust to business cycles is higher for non-greenhouse-gas policy, because the cyclical adjustments in the policy values are able to respond to the cyclicality of damages. E-DSGE models solving for optimal policy or evaluating the effects of policy over the business cycle should study flow pollutants such as ozone or sulfur dioxide. Furthermore, even for analyses of climate policy, the cobenefits of reduced emissions of flow pollutants represent a substantial fraction of the social cost of carbon (Parry, Veung, and Heine 2015), meaning that incorporation of these benefits in business-cycle models is crucial. Finally, regulation of pollutants other than greenhouse gases may be more likely to be closer to what economists tend to consider the appropriate level of stringency (e.g., Shapiro and Walker 2020).

However, it is not certain that business-cycle considerations are always more important for non-GHG flow pollutants than for GHG stock pollutants. Because a stock pollutant accumulates, the effect on damages of a cyclical increase in emissions (from a business-cycle expansionary period) will last longer, as will the effect from a cyclical decrease in emissions. If policy fails to account for these cycles, then this variation in damages will extend over a longer period than it would under flow pollutants. It is thus an open empirical question as to whether or not cycles are more important in policy design for stock and flow pollutants, and so studying this question is crucial.

VI. Conclusion

To explore the relationship between business cycles and environmental policy, we have reviewed the growing literature using dynamic stochastic general equilibrium (DSGE) models to study the effects of policy over business cycles and the response of optimal policy to cyclical fluctuations. The majority of this literature focused on price-based climate policies, including carbon taxes and cap-and-trade, with additional economic features such as NK price rigidities. We highlight several important findings from this literature that are most relevant to policy makers, who may seek to craft policy to respond to business cycles. We also offer suggestions for important policy-relevant questions that remain unanswered, to guide the future of the literature.

Endnotes

Author email addresses: Annicchiarico (barbara.annicchiarico@uniroma2.it), Carattini (scarattini@gsu.edu), Fischer (fischer@rff.org), Heutel (gheutel@gsu.edu). This paper is prepared for the NBER's *Environmental and Energy Policy and the Economy* conference and publication. We thank the volume's editors, Tatyana Deryugina, Matthew Kotchen, and James Stock, as well as Spencer Banzhaf, Baran Doda, and Roberton Williams for very useful comments. We also thank Kukhee Han for valuable research assistance. For acknowledgments, sources of research support, and disclosure of the authors' material financial relationships, if any, please see https://www.nber.org/books-and-chapters/environmental-and-energy-policy-and-economy-volume-3/business-cycles-and-environmental-policy-primer.

1. Environmental policies may be too lenient for several reasons. First, due to uncertainties arising from difficulties in estimating costs and benefits properly (e.g., Pindyck 2013), leading standard economic analysis such as integrated assessment models (e.g., Nordhaus 1993) to provide estimates of optimal stringency that may be the source of important debates (e.g., Stern 2007; Pindyck 2013; Stern and Stiglitz 2021). Second, due to a consistent tendency of policy makers to overweight or overestimate costs versus benefits (Harrington, Morgenstern, and Nelson 2000). Third, due to similar information asymmetries between experts and citizens, leading them to overestimate drawbacks and underestimate benefits of market-based instruments for environmental policy (Carattini, Carvalho, and Fankhauser 2018; Dal Bó, Dal Bó, and Eyster 2018). Finally, economic efficiency or other economics-based optimization criteria may not be the primary consideration in policy design.

2. An example is the European Union Emissions Trading System (EU ETS), in which allowance prices collapsed early on and remained persistently low for nearly a decade (EC 2012). Although such low price outcomes were largely due to an overallocation of permits (Martin et al. 2014), the Great Recession also contributed to depress prices (Koch et al. 2014).

3. Some commentators, however, do not seem to have been able or willing to disentangle the two elements, overallocation of permits and effect of the business cycle, in their critique of the EU ETS. Fortunately, in a cap-and-trade system, the appropriate response to either price-depressing element is to tighten the cap, which recent reforms have done (see Hepburn et al. 2016), but it remains far from clear whether the accompanying reforms are sufficient to address future shocks (Fischer et al. 2020).

4. With the executive order "Accelerating the Nation's Economic Recovery From the COVID-19 Emergency by Expediting Infrastructure Investments and Other Activities" of June 2020, the Trump administration instructed agencies to waive long-standing environmental laws given that "Unnecessary regulatory delays will deny our citizens opportunities for jobs and economic security, keeping millions of Americans out of work and hindering our economic recovery from the national emergency."

5. Of course, there is a much larger and older literature on business cycles more generally, which is beyond this scope of this paper to discuss.

6. These graphs update figs. 4 and 5 in Heutel (2012). This model (like the model in Angelopoulos et al. 2013 but unlike the model in Fischer and Springborn 2011) omits labor and leisure.

7. This updated calibration is based both on the most recently available version of the DICE model's damage function, and emissions elasticity estimated from monthly emissions and GDP data through 2019. See details in Gibson and Heutel (2020).

8. The efficient carbon tax is procyclical despite the fact that the pollution stock is almost entirely unchanged over the business cycle. This is because damages from pollution (calibrated from DICE) are expressed as a fraction of gross output. Over the business cycle, that fraction does not change much because the pollution stock does not change much, but gross output changes, and so therefore the marginal damages from pollution change, justifying the procyclical efficient tax.

9. Gibson and Heutel (2020) and Carattini et al. (2021) also solve for Ramsey-efficient carbon taxes in response to RBC shocks, with other market failures in their DSGE models.

10. Karp and Traeger (2021) consider a similar exercise, where the cap in a cap-and-trade scheme can endogenously adjust to macroeconomic and technology shocks, though not in a DSGE context.

11. Additional indicators that may be relevant for this exercise and could be examined in future research include jobless claims and unemployment rates, yield curves—for instance for the 10-year Treasury bond—or stock market returns. It is an open normative question whether environmental policy should be tied to GDP, rather than jobs or the unemployment rate of the most disadvantaged members of society.

12. For example, see Christiano, Eichenbaum, and Vigfusson (2003), Galí and Rabanal (2004), and Angeletos, Collard, and Dellas (2020).

13. See, e.g., Heathcote, Storesletten, and Violante (2009), Clementi and Palazzo (2016), and Kaplan, Moll, and Violante (2018).

14. As an example, the design of the optimal dynamic carbon tax should be made in conjunction with other preexisting tax instruments, as recently shown by Barrage (2020).

References

Adler, David, and Edson R. Severnini. 2020. "Timing Matters: Shifting Economic Activity and Intra-Day Variation in Ambient Ozone Concentrations." Discussion Paper no. 13428, IZA Institute of Labor Economics, Bonn.

Aiyagari, S. Rao. 1994. "Uninsured Idiosyncratic Risk and Aggregate Saving." *Quarterly Journal of Economics* 109 (3): 659–84.

Aldy, Joseph E., and Sarah Armitage. 2020. "The Cost-effectiveness Implications of Carbon Price Certainty." *AEA Papers and Proceedings* 110:113–18.

Aldy, Joseph E., Alan J. Krupnick, Richard G. Newell, Ian W. H. Parry, and William A. Pizer. 2010. "Designing Climate Mitigation Policy." *Journal of Economic Literature* 48 (4): 903–34.

Angeletos, George-Marios, Fabrice Collard, and Harris Dellas. 2020. "Business-Cycle Anatomy." *American Economic Review* 110 (10): 3030–70.

Angelopoulos, Konstantinos, George Economides, and Apostolis Philippopoulos. 2013. "First-and Second-best Allocations Under Economic and Environmental Uncertainty." *International Tax and Public Finance* 20 (3): 360–80.

Annicchiarico, Barbara, Stefano Carattini, Carolyn Fischer, and Garth Heutel. 2021. "Business Cycles and Environmental Policy: Literature Review and Policy Implications." Working paper, NBER, Cambridge, MA.

Annicchiarico, Barbara, and Fabio Di Dio. 2015. "Environmental Policy and Macroeconomic Dynamics in a New Keynesian Model." *Journal of Environmental Economics and Management* 69:1–21.

———. 2017. "GHG Emissions Control and Monetary Policy." *Environmental and Resource Economics* 67 (4): 823–51.

Annicchiarico, Barbara, and Francesca Diluiso. 2019. "International Transmission of the Business Cycle and Environmental Policy." *Resource and Energy Economics* 58:101112.

Baranzini, Andrea, Jeroen C. J. M. van den Bergh, Stefano Carattini, Richard B. Howarth, Emilio Padilla, and Jordi Roca. 2017. "Carbon Pricing in Climate Policy: Seven Reasons, Complementary Instruments, and Political Economy Considerations." *Wiley Interdisciplinary Reviews: Climate Change* 8 (4): e462.

Barrage, Lint. 2020. "Optimal Dynamic Carbon Taxes in a Climate-Economy Model with Distortionary Fiscal Policy." *Review of Economic Studies* 87 (1): 1–39.

Benmir, Ghassane, and Josselin Roman. 2020. "Policy Interactions and the Transition to Clean Technology." Working Paper no. 368, Grantham Research Institute on Climate Change and the Environment, London.

Borenstein, Severin, James Bushnell, Frank A. Wolak, and Matthew Zaragoza-Watkins. 2019. "Expecting the Unexpected: Emissions Uncertainty and Environmental Market Design." *American Economic Review* 109 (11): 3953–77.

Burtraw, D., and A. Keyes. 2018. "Recognizing Gravity as a Strong Force in Atmosphere Emissions Markets." *Agriculture and Resource Economics Review* 47 (2): 201–19.

Campiglio, Emanuele, Yannis Dafermos, Pierre Monnin, Josh Ryan-Collins, Guido Schotten, and Misa Tanaka. 2018. "Climate Change Challenges for Central Banks and Financial Regulators." *Nature Climate Change* 8 (6): 462–68.

Carattini, Stefano, Maria Carvalho, and Sam Fankhauser. 2018. "Overcoming Public Resistance to Carbon Taxes." *Wiley Interdisciplinary Reviews: Climate Change* 9 (5): e531.

Carattini, Stefano, Garth Heutel, and Givi Melkadze. 2021. "Climate Policy, Financial Frictions, and Transition Risk." Working Paper no. 28525, NBER, Cambridge, MA.

Carattini, Stefano, Steffen Kallbekken, and Anton Orlov. 2019. "How to Win Public Support for a Global Carbon Tax." *Nature* 565:289–91.

Carney, Mark. 2015. "Breaking the Tragedy of the Horizon—Climate Change and Financial Stability." Speech, Bank of England, London.

Chari, Varadarajan V., Lawrence J. Christiano, and Patrick J. Kehoe. 1994. "Optimal Fiscal Policy in a Business Cycle Model." *Journal of Political Economy* 102 (4): 617–52.

Christiano, Lawrence J., Martin Eichenbaum, and Robert Vigfusson. 2003. "What Happens after a Technology Shock?" Working Paper no. 9819, NBER, Cambridge, MA.

Christiano, Lawrence J., Martin S. Eichenbaum, and Mathias Trabandt. 2018. "On DSGE Models." *Journal of Economic Perspectives* 32 (3): 113–40.

Clementi, Gian Luca, and Berardino Palazzo. 2016. "Entry, Exit, Firm Dynamics, and Aggregate Fluctuations." *American Economic Journal: Macroeconomics* 8 (3): 1–41.

Cramton, Peter, David J. C. MacKay, Axel Ockenfels, and Steven Stoft, eds. 2017. *Global Carbon Pricing: The Path to Climate Cooperation.* Cambridge, MA: MIT Press.

Cronin, Julie Anne, Don Fullerton, and Steven Sexton. 2018. "Vertical and Horizontal Redistributions from a Carbon Tax and Rebate." *Journal of the Association of Environmental and Resource Economists* 6 (S1): S169–208.

Dal Bó, Ernesto, Pedro Dal Bó, and Erik Eyster. 2018. "The Demand for Bad Policy When Voters Underappreciate Equilibrium Effects." *Review of Economic Studies* 85 (2): 964–98.

Diluiso, Francesca, Barbara Annicchiarico, Matthias Kalkuhl, and Jan Christoph Minx. 2020. "Climate Actions and Stranded Assets: The Role of Financial Regulation and Monetary Policy." Working Paper no. 8486, CESifo Group, Munich.

Dissou, Yazid, and Lilia Karnizova. 2016. "Emissions Cap or Emissions Tax? A Multi-sector Business Cycle Analysis." *Journal of Environmental Economics and Management* 79:169–88.

Doda, Baran. 2014. "Evidence on Business Cycles and CO_2 Emissions." *Journal of Macroeconomics* 40:214–27.

D'Orazio, Paola, and Lilit Popoyan. 2019. "Fostering Green Investments and Tackling Climate-Related Financial Risks: Which Role for Macroprudential Policies?" *Ecological Economics* 160:25–37.

EC (European Commission). 2012. "The State of the European Carbon Market in 2012." COM (2012) 652, final report from the EC to the European Parliament and the Council, Brussels.

Economides, George, and Anastasios Xepapadeas. 2018. "Monetary Policy Under Climate Change." Working Paper no. 247, Bank of Greece, Athens.

Feng, Kuishuang, Steven J. Davis, Laixiang Sun, and Klaus Hubacek. 2015. "Drivers of the US CO_2 Emissions 1997–2013." *Nature Communications* 6 (1): 7714.

Ferrari, Alessandro, and Valerio Nispi Landi. 2020. "Whatever It Takes to Save the Planet? Central Banks and Unconventional Green Policy." Working Paper no. 2500, European Central Bank, Frankfurt.

Fischer, Carolyn, and Garth Heutel. 2013. "Environmental Macroeconomics: Environmental Policy, Business Cycles, and Directed Technical Change." *Annual Review of Resource Economics* 5:197–210.

Fischer, C., L. Reins, D. Burtraw, D. Langlet, A. Lofgren, M. Mehling, S. Weishaar, L. Zetterberg, H. van Asselt, and K. Kulovesi. 2020. "The Legal and Economic Case for an Auction Reserve Price in the EU Emissions Trading System." *Columbia Journal of European Law* 26 (1): 1–35.

Fischer, Carolyn, and Michael Springborn. 2011. "Emissions Targets and the Real Business Cycle: Intensity Targets versus Caps or Taxes." *Journal of Environmental Economics and Management* 62 (3): 352–66.

Fourcade, Marion, Etienne Ollion, and Yann Algan. 2015. "The Superiority of Economists." *Journal of Economic Perspectives* 29 (1): 89–114.

Galí, Jordi, and Pau Rabanal. 2004. "Technology Shocks and Aggregate Fluctuations: How Well Does the Real Business Cycle Model Fit Postwar US Data?" *NBER Macroeconomics Annual* 19:225–88.

Gibson, John, and Garth Heutel. 2020. "Pollution and Labor Market Search Externalities Over the Business Cycle." Working Paper no. 27445, NBER, Cambridge, MA.

Goulder, Lawrence H., and Ian W. H. Parry. 2008. "Instrument Choice in Environmental Policy." *Review of Environmental Economics and Policy* 2 (2): 152–74.

Hahn, Robert W. 1989. "Economic Prescriptions for Environmental Problems: How the Patient Followed the Doctor's Orders." *Journal of Economic Perspectives* 3 (2): 95–114.

Harrington, Winston, Richard D. Morgenstern, and Peter Nelson. 2000. "On the Accuracy of Regulatory Cost Estimates." *Journal of Policy Analysis and Management* 19 (2): 297–322.

Heathcote, Jonathan, Kjetil Storesletten, and Giovanni L. Violante. 2009. "Quantitative Macroeconomics with Heterogeneous Households." *Annual Review of Economics* 1 (1): 319–54.

Hepburn, Cameron, Karsten Neuhoff, William Acworth, Dallas Burtraw, and Frank Jotzo. 2016. "The Economics of the EU ETS Market Stability Reserve." *Journal of Environmental Economics and Management* 80:1–5.

Heutel, Garth. 2012. "How Should Environmental Policy Respond to Business Cycles? Optimal Policy Under Persistent Productivity Shocks." *Review of Economic Dynamics* 15 (2): 244–64.

Hoel, Michael. 1992. "Carbon Taxes: An International Tax or Harmonized Domestic Taxes?" *European Economic Review* 36 (2–3): 400–6.

Hopenhayn, Hugo A. 1992. "Entry, Exit, and Firm Dynamics in Long Run Equilibrium." *Econometrica* 60 (5): 1127–50.

Howard, Peter H., and Derek Sylvan. 2015. "The Economic Climate: Establishing Consensus on the Economics of Climate Change." Paper presented at the

2015 AAEA and WAEA Joint Annual Meeting, San Francisco, CA, July 26–28.

IMF (International Monetary Fund). 2019. *Fiscal Monitor: How to Mitigate Climate Change*. Washington, DC: IMF.

Jaimes, Richard. 2020. "The Dynamic Effects of Environmental and Fiscal Policy Shocks." Manuscript, University of Tilburg.

Jo, Soojin, and Lilia Karnizova. 2021. "Energy Efficiency and CO_2 Emission Fluctuations." Working paper, Bank of Canada, Ottawa.

Kaplan, Greg, Benjamin Moll, and Giovanni L. Violante. 2018. "Monetary Policy According to HANK." *American Economic Review* 108 (3): 697–743.

Karp, Larry, and Christian Traeger. 2021. "Smart Caps." Discussion Paper no. 15941, Centre for Economic Policy Research, London.

Kelly, David L., and Charles D. Kolstad. 1999. "Bayesian Learning, Growth, and Pollution." *Journal of Economic Dynamics and Control* 23 (4): 491–518.

Kelly, David L., and Zhuo Tan. 2015. "Learning and Climate Feedbacks: Optimal Climate Insurance and Fat Tails." *Journal of Environmental Economics and Management* 72:98–122.

Khan, Hashmat, Konstantinos Metaxoglou, Christopher R. Knittel, and Maya Papineau. 2019. "Carbon Emissions and Business Cycles." *Journal of Macroeconomics* 60:1–19.

Koch, Nicolas, Sabine Fuss, Godefroy Grosjean, Ottmar Edenhofer. 2014. "Causes of the EU ETS Price Drop: Recession, CDM, Renewable Policies or a Bit of Everything?—New Evidence." *Energy Policy* 73:676–85.

Kollenberg, Sascha, and Luca Taschini. 2019. "Dynamic Supply Adjustment and Banking under Uncertainty in an Emission Trading Scheme: The Market Stability Reserve." *European Economic Review* 118:213–26.

Le Quéré, Corinne, Robert B. Jackson, Matthew W. Jones, Adam J. P. Smith, Sam Abernethy, Robbie M. Andrew, Anthony J. De-Gol, et al. 2020. "Temporary Reduction in Daily Global CO_2 Emissions during the COVID-19 Forced Confinement." *Nature Climate Change* 10 (7): 647–53.

Le Quéré, Corinne, Glen P. Peters, Pierre Friedlingstein, Robbie M. Andrew, Josep G. Canadell, Steven J. Davis, Robert B. Jackson, and Matthew W. Jones. 2021. "Fossil CO_2 Emissions in the Post-COVID-19 Era." *Nature Climate Change* 11 (3): 197–99.

Lintunen, Jussi, and Olli-Pekka Kuusela. 2018. "Business Cycles and Emission Trading with Banking." *European Economic Review* 101:397–417.

Lintunen, Jussi, and Lauri Vilmi. 2013. "On Optimal Emission Control—Taxes, Substitution and Business Cycles." Research Discussion Paper no. 24, Bank of Finland, Helsinki.

Martin, Ralf, Mirabelle Muûls, Laure B. de Preux, and Ulrich J. Wagner. 2014. "Industry Compensation under Relocation Risk: A Firm-Level Analysis of the EU Emissions Trading Scheme." *American Economic Review* 104 (8): 2482–508.

NGFS (Network for Greening the Financial System). 2021. "Adapting Central Bank Operations to a Hotter World—Reviewing Some Options." Technical document, NGFS, Paris.

Nordhaus, William. 1993. "Optimal Greenhouse-Gas Reductions and Tax Policy in the 'Dice' Model." *American Economic Review* 83 (2): 313–17.

———. 2015. "Climate Clubs: Overcoming Free-Riding in International Climate Policy." *American Economic Review* 105 (4): 1339–70.

———. 2017. "Revisiting the Social Cost of Carbon." *Proceedings of the National Academy of Sciences* 114 (7): 1518–23.

————. 2018. "Evolution of Modeling of the Economics of Global Warming: Changes in the DICE Model, 1992–2017." *Climatic Change* 148 (4): 623–40.

Parry, Ian, Chandara Veung, and Dirk Heine. 2015. "How Much Carbon Pricing Is in Countries' Own Interests? The Critical Role of Co-Benefits." *Climate Change Economics* 6 (4): 1550019.

PBO (Office of the Parliamentary Budget Officer). 2019. "Fiscal and Distributional Analysis of the Federal Carbon Pricing System." Report, PBO, Ottawa.

Perino, Grischa, Michael Pahle, Fabian Pause, Simon Quemin, Hannah Scheuing, and Maximilian Willner. 2021. "EU ETS Stability Mechanism Needs New Design." Policy Brief 2021-1, Chaire Économie du Climat, Paris.

Persico, Claudia L., and Kathryn R. Johnson. 2021. "The Effects of Increased Pollution on COVID-19 Cases and Deaths." *Journal of Environmental Economics and Management* 107 (C): 102431.

Pindyck, Robert S. 2013. "Climate Change Policy: What Do the Models Tell Us?" *Journal of Economic Literature* 51 (3): 860–72.

Pizer, William A., and Brian C. Prest. 2020. "Prices versus Quantities with Policy Updating." *Journal of the Association of Environmental and Resource Economists* 7 (3): 483–518.

Punzi, Maria T. 2019. "Role of Bank Lending in Financing Green Projects: A Dynamic Stochastic General Equilibrium Approach." In *Handbook of Green Finance: Energy Security and Sustainable Development*, ed. J. Sachs, W. T. Woo, N. Yoshino, and F. Taghizadeh-Hesary. Singapore: Springer.

Rebelo, Sergio. 2005. "Real Business Cycle Models: Past, Present and Future." *Scandinavian Journal of Economics* 107 (2): 217–38.

Rudebusch, Glenn D. 2021. "Climate Change Is a Source of Financial Risk." Economic Letter, Federal Reserve Bank of San Francisco.

Shapiro, Joseph S., and Reed Walker. 2020. "Is Air Pollution Regulation Too Stringent?" Working paper, NBER, Cambridge, MA.

Stern, Nicholas. 2007. *The Economics of Climate Change: The Stern Review*. New York: Cambridge University Press.

Stern, Nicholas, and Joseph E. Stiglitz. 2021. "The Social Cost of Carbon, Risk, Distribution, Market Failures: An Alternative Approach." Working Paper no. 28472, NBER, Cambridge MA.

Stiglitz, Joseph E., Nicholas Stern, Maosheng Duan, Ottmar Edenhofer, Gaël Giraud, Geoffrey Heal, Emilio Lèbre la Rovere, et al. 2017. "Report of the High-Level Commission on Carbon Prices." Carbon Pricing Leadership Coalition, Washington, DC.

Thalmann, Philippe. 2013. "Global Environmental Taxes." In *Handbook of Research on Environmental Taxation*, ed. Janet E. Milne and Mikael Skou Andersen. Northampton, MA: Edward Elgar.

Vermeulen, Robert, Edo Schets, Melanie Lohuis, Barbara Kolbl, David-Jan Jansen, and Willem Heeringa. 2018. "An Energy Transition Risk Stress Test for the Financial System of the Netherlands." DNB Occasional Studies, Netherlands Central Bank, Amsterdam.

Weitzman, Martin L. 2014. "Can Negotiating a Uniform Carbon Price Help to Internalize the Global Warming Externality?" *Journal of the Association of Environmental and Resource Economists* 1 (1/2): 29–49.

————. 2017. "Voting on Prices vs. Voting on Quantities in a World Climate Assembly." *Research in Economics* 71 (2): 199–211.

World Bank. 2020. "State and Trends of Carbon Pricing—2020." Serial publication, World Bank, Washington, DC.